Leading Health Care Transformation

A Primer for Clinical Leaders

Maulik Joshi, DrPH ✦ Natalie Erb, MPH
Sonia Zhang, MPH ✦ Rishi Sikka, MD

Foreword by
Jonathan B. Perlin, MD, PhD, MSHA, FACP, FACMI

CRC Press
Taylor & Francis Group
Boca Raton London New York

CRC Press is an imprint of the
Taylor & Francis Group, an **informa** business
A PRODUCTIVITY PRESS BOOK

CRC Press
Taylor & Francis Group
6000 Broken Sound Parkway NW, Suite 300
Boca Raton, FL 33487-2742

Printed on acid-free paper
Version Date: 20150609

International Standard Book Number-13: 978-1-4987-0018-4 (Hardback)

Library of Congress Cataloging-in-Publication Data

Joshi, Maulik, author.
   Leading Health Care transformation : a primer for clinical leaders / Maulik Joshi, Rishi Sikka, Natalie Erb, and Sonia Zhang.
     p. ; cm.
   Includes bibliographical references and index.
   ISBN 978-1-4987-0018-4 (hardcover : alk. paper)
   I. Sikka, Rishi, author. II. Erb, Natalie, author. III. Zhang, Sonia, author. IV. Title.
   [DNLM: 1. Health Facility Administration--methods--United States. 2. Quality Improvement--organization & administration--United States. 3. Health Care Reform--organization & administration--United States. 4. Leadership--United States. 5. Physician's Role--United States. WX 153]

RA393
362.1--dc23   2015002259

Visit the Taylor & Francis Web site at
http://www.taylorandfrancis.com

and the CRC Press Web site at
http://www.crcpress.com

Contents

Foreword

Effective transformational leaders must be able to both interpret the environment and act effectively to foster constructive change resulting in desirable outcomes. This general challenge is amplified substantially in health care. First, the outcomes ultimately affect health and human life. Second, technologies, organizational structures, relationships with patients, sources of care, and governmental requirements are changing rapidly. Finally, there is an unprecedented demand for greater transparency and accountability in both clinical performance and delivery of value. Fortunately, there are some constants. The Institute for Healthcare Improvement enunciated a set of durable goals that simultaneously encapsulate the aspirations for better health care, as well as the challenges all health care leaders face. There is, likely, no class of health care leaders more on-point for realizing the "Triple Aim" than clinical leaders, nor is there any group with more categorical potential for influencing the experience of care, the promise of health, and the cost of health care services. However, reflecting the challenge for society and clinical leaders, most clinical education has focused more strongly on *care* than on the two other dimensions of the Triple Aim, *health* and *value*.

Health care providers, ranging from small clinics and critical access hospitals to large systems and clinically integrated organizations, are depending on transformational clinical leadership to safely navigate the turbulent waters of accelerated change. In the process, some organizations are facing an existential crisis, while others are using the turbulence to redefine their mission, their approach to serving community needs, and their working relationship with non-traditional service providers in addressing health, care and value. Never has there been a time that required more alignment between the clinical and operating agendas.

Clinical leaders with the ability to unify quality and cost agendas add extraordinary value in solving for the simultaneous improvement of clinical and operating outcomes. That's what this book is about. It provides practical guidance for clinical—and non-clinical—leaders to better understand the context of demands outside of their organization and the operating pressures within, for framing challenges for productive intervention, and for developing skills to overcome inertia or even outright resistance to change.

Leading Health Care Transformation provides a handbook of essential tools for defining transformational opportunities, leading high-functioning teams, being a good team player, and using evidence, measurement and narrative for effectively communicating and fostering a change agenda. The book is punctuated by salient case studies that offer valuable insight into deploying change tools in real-world situations, illustrating not only technique, but the context of their application. In that regard, this is really much more than a "primer"; it offers both expert knowledge, as well as the wisdom borne of colleagues' experience and lessons learned.

This book should also provide a source of optimism and courage for health leaders seeking to use turbulence to accelerate change. Through the tools and lessons, it offers an affirming message that improving care, reliability, safety, and culture is not only possible, and the final chapter, "Compendium of Action Steps," is a playbook for applying transformational strategies.

Paraphrasing George Bernard Shaw, perhaps no one has spoken more eloquently about transformational possibility than Robert Kennedy. He said, "There are those that look at things the way they are, and ask why? I dream of things that never were, and ask why not?" As health care leaders, it is our continuous responsibility to ask "why not?" In equal measure, it is our privilege and obligation to answer that question with informed and practical actions that improve the care we deliver, the health of those we serve, and the value we produce.

Jonathan B. Perlin, MD, PhD, MSHA, FACP, FACMI
President, Clinical Services and Chief Medical Officer
HCA – Hospital Corporation of America

Clinical Professor of Medicine and Biomedical Informatics, Vanderbilt University
Adjunct Professor of Health Administration, Virginia Commonwealth University

Chair, American Hospital Association

Acknowledgments

Many thanks to Marie Cleary-Fishman and Ken Anderson for their contributions in reviewing and editing this work and to Kathy Durrant for her administrative support and assistance in review throughout the process.

About the Authors

Maulik S. Joshi, DrPH, is associate executive vice president of the American Hospital Association, Clinical Leadership and Health Improvement and president of the Health Research & Educational Trust. HRET conducts applied research in critical areas of the health care system and leads Hospitals in Pursuit of Excellence, AHA's strategy to accelerate performance improvement. In 2014, HRET was awarded the Illinois Performance Excellence Silver Award. Dr. Joshi also oversees AHA's Institute for Diversity in Health Management and the Association for Community Health Improvement.

Previously, Dr. Joshi served as senior advisor at the Agency for Healthcare Research and Quality; president and CEO of the Delmarva Foundation, recipient of the 2005 U.S. Senate Productivity Award, which is based on the Malcolm Baldrige Award; vice president at the Institute for Healthcare Improvement; senior director of quality for the University of Pennsylvania Health System; and executive vice president for The HMO Group.

Dr. Joshi earned a doctorate in public health and a master's degree in health services administration from the University of Michigan and a bachelor of science degree in mathematics from Lafayette College. Dr. Joshi is editor-in-chief for the *Journal for Healthcare Quality.* He also co-edited *The Healthcare Quality Book: Vision, Strategy and Tools* (Health Administration Press, third edition published in 2014), and authored *Healthcare Transformation: A Guide for the Hospital Board Member* (CRC Press and AHA Press, published in 2009).

Dr. Joshi also serves on the Board of Trustees for the Anne Arundel Health System, the Board Quality and Patient Safety Committee for Mercy Health System, the Health Outcomes Committee for Advocate Health Care, and is Treasurer of the Board of Trustees for the Center for Advancing Health.

Natalie Erb, MPH, is a program manager at the Health Research & Educational Trust where she contributes to creating and editing HRET educational materials including guides and articles on strategies for quality improvement in health care. At HRET, Natalie also facilitates large-scale national improvement projects and staffs a membership group for professionals in quality and patient safety, the Symposium for Leaders in Healthcare Quality. Natalie previously worked at the

University of Michigan School of Public Health on an evaluation of the Physician Group Incentive Program, a Blue Cross Blue Shield of Michigan pay-for-performance program. She has published articles related to that evaluation and on mechanisms in pay-for-performance programs.

Natalie earned a master's degree in public health from the University of Michigan School of Public Health.

Sonia Zhang, MPH, is the current administrative fellow at the Health Research & Educational Trust. Her responsibilities include providing programmatic support to the HRET Hospital Engagement Network and writing for Hospitals in Pursuit of Excellence. Previously, Sonia worked at the University of Arizona College of Public Health on the implementation and evaluation of Pima County Communities Putting Prevention to Work, a program funded by the Centers for Disease Control and Prevention.

Sonia earned a master's degree in health management and policy from the University of Michigan School of Public Health.

Rishi Sikka, MD, is a senior vice president of clinical transformation at Advocate Health Care. He has system-level responsibility for clinical operations—including pharmacy, critical care, quality, safety, clinical effectiveness, and business intelligence/"big data." He also serves on the board of Advocate Physician Partners, a clinically integrated network with 4,000 physicians serving over 600,000 attributable lives. He continues to practice emergency medicine and is a clinical associate professor in the Department of Emergency Medicine at the University of Illinois-Chicago School of Medicine.

Dr. Sikka's career has spanned a variety of leadership roles in fields including media, technology start-ups, hospital administration, managed care and big data. His time included roles at Advocate Christ Medical Center, Oak Lawn, Illinois; Boston Medical Center, Boston, Massachusetts; Medco Health Solutions, Franklin Lakes, New Jersey; Health Benchmarks, Woodland Hills, California (acquired by IMS); Praxeon, Cambridge, Massachusetts (a Boston health technology start-up); Prudential Health Care, Atlanta, Georgia; and KTTC-NBC, Rochester, Minnesota.

Dr. Sikka earned his medical degree from Mayo Medical School, Rochester, Minnesota. His internship in internal medicine was completed at St. Vincent's Hospital, New York, New York and his residency in emergency medicine at Boston Medical Center, Boston, Massachusetts. He earned his bachelor of science degree in economics from the Wharton School at the University of Pennsylvania, Philadelphia, Pennsylvania.

Chapter 1

The Health Care Landscape

Introduction

In March 2010, President Barack Obama signed the Affordable Care Act into law, expanding health insurance coverage to millions of previously uninsured Americans. In addition to coverage expansions, the ACA also includes numerous provisions that promote a shift toward value-based reimbursement, the creation of new models of care (e.g., patient-centered medical homes and accountable care organizations), and funding to test new strategies to improve quality, reduce costs, and improve the patient experience of care. The reforms in the ACA accelerate the pace of transformation, but even absent government-mandated reform, the many forces outlined in this chapter will compel the inevitable transformation of the U.S. health care system.

First Curve to Second Curve

The health care industry is transitioning from a "first curve" business model, one based on volume, to a "second curve" business model based on value (Figure 1.1). This shift is driven by many factors and is most notably due to the high, growing, and unsustainable cost of health care. As payment incentives shift to reward value, health care organizations must change their business models to deliver second curve outcomes: high-quality, low-cost, patient-centered care.

Organizations that do not adapt to a new second-curve business model will not make the leap from the first curve. This was evident in the movie-rental business where Blockbuster thrived in a first-curve transaction-based business model (where

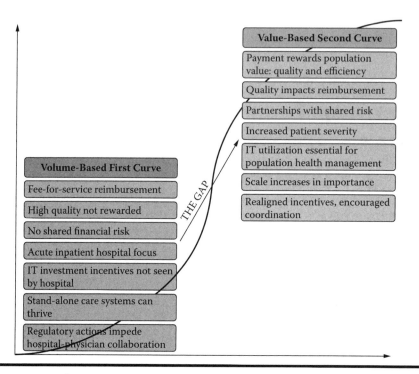

Figure 1.1 First curve to second curve transition. (American Hospital Association. 2011. Committee on Performance Improvement, Jeanette Clough, Chairperson. Hospitals and Care Systems of the Future. Chicago: American Hospital Association, September 2011, adapted from Ian Morrison.)

more stores and supply of movies maximized revenues), but did not succeed in a second-curve business model (where bricks and mortar did not matter and having a "capitated" model like Netflix led to financial success).

As the system shifts from the first curve to the second curve, the biggest challenge for health care leaders is navigating "life in the gap," the period of transition between the two operational models. Organizations that transition to the second curve ahead of the payers in their market may experience reductions in revenue in the short term. Alternatively, those organizations that do not prepare for the second curve will find they are unable to transition quickly enough once payers inevitably begin to reward providers based on quality and cost.

In 2011, the American Hospital Association Committee on Performance Improvement (AHA CPI) identified a set of core competencies and must-do strategies for hospitals to transition from the first curve to the second curve business model. Figure 1.2 lists those 10 must-do strategies, emphasizing the first four as the most important.

The AHA CPI also identified seven core competencies for organizations to develop to survive and thrive in the era of value-based health care (Figure 1.3).

Must-Do Strategies
1. Align hospitals, physicians and other clinical providers across the continuum of care.
2. Utilize evidence-based practices to improve quality and patient safety.
3. Improve efficiency through productivity and financial management.
4. Develop integrated information systems.
5. Join and grow integrated provider networks and care systems.
6. Educate and engage employees and physicians to create leaders.
7. Strengthen finances to facilitate reinvestment and innovation.
8. Partner with payers.
9. Advance an organization through scenario-based strategic, financial and operational planning.
10. Seek population health improvement through pursuit of the Triple Aim.

Figure 1.2 Must-do strategies. (American Hospital Association. 2011. Committee on Performance Improvement, Jeanette Clough, Chairperson. Hospitals and Care Systems of the Future. Chicago: American Hospital Association, September 2011.)

Core Competencies
1. Design and implement patient-centered, integrated care.
2. Create accountable governance and leadership.
3. Strategic planning in an unstable environment.
4. Internal and external collaboration.
5. Financial stewardship and enterprise risk management.
6. Engagement of full employee potential.
7. Collection and utilization of electronic data for performance improvement.

Figure 1.3 Core competencies. (American Hospital Association. 2011. Committee on Performance Improvement, Jeanette Clough, Chairperson. Hospitals and Care Systems of the Future. Chicago: American Hospital Association, September 2011.)

Leading Transformation

There is certainly lots of talk directed at reform, but why do organizations need to change? This chapter provides an overview of the key factors driving transformation including:

- High and increasing cost of care
- Shifting demographics of patients and workforce
- Transition to value-based reimbursement
- Variable quality and patient safety outcomes and persistent disparities in care
- Expansion of coverage and access to care
- Advances in health information technology

■ Shift from defined benefit to defined contribution health plans and the rise of consumerism in health care

These are turbulent and exciting times, and the health care industry is in need of diverse leaders who can effectively navigate the rapid and often disruptive changes underway in hospitals and health systems. While the delivery system is changing, the face of leadership is also changing. As physicians and health systems become aligned, organizations are adopting hybrid leadership models that include both clinical and administrative leaders. In all new models of alignment, physicians and other clinicians are taking on leadership roles and are faced with the many challenges presented by health care transformation.

The chapter concludes with six leadership competencies to successfully lead health care transformation:

1. Effectively communicate the imperative for and steps to achieve health care transformation
2. Understand the relationship between cost and quality in practice and how to drive value
3. Build, deploy, and lead improvement teams across all dimensions of care
4. Lead effective and coordinated multidisciplinary care teams
5. Leverage data to improve clinical and organizational practice
6. Realize the role of patient as consumer

Key Factors Driving Transformation

High Cost of Care

The U.S. spends far more on health care than any other country and yet does not consistently deliver superior quality or achieve better outcomes when compared to less expensive heath care systems. In 2012, the U.S. spent $2.8 trillion on health care, which accounted for 17.2% of gross domestic product, equating to per capita spending of $8,915. Predictions for 2014 estimate health care spending will reach 18.3% of GDP or $9,697 per capita (CMS 2012).

In addition to contributing to a large portion of GDP, numerous studies have demonstrated that U.S. health care spending drastically exceeds that of other countries, both per capita and as a percentage of GDP. A 2012 study by the Commonwealth Fund compared U.S. spending to that of 13 other industrialized countries* and found that comparison countries spent between one-third and two-thirds as much as the U.S. This study and others have controlled for differences in

---

* Comparison countries include Australia, Canada, Denmark, France, Germany, Japan, the Netherlands, New Zealand, Norway, Sweden, Switzerland, and the United Kingdom.

national income, an older population, and both supply and utilization of hospitals and doctors (Squires 2012).

The high cost of health care has important implications. For individuals, the high cost of care can pose a significant financial burden, particularly for those without insurance. For employers providing health insurance coverage, the high and increasing cost of care adds significantly to the cost of business. As a result, employers are beginning to shift costs to employees through new benefit design (i.e., high deductible health plans) or dropping employee-sponsored coverage (Kaiser 2013). At the state and federal levels, the cost of public insurance programs, including Medicare and Medicaid, contributes significantly to state and federal budget challenges and crowd out other spending, notably on education, transportation, and other government priorities (NASBO 2013).

Since 2009, health care spending has slowed (Hartman 2013). This slowing has been attributed to the overall impact of the Great Recession including slowed growth in GDP and declines in insurance coverage due to increased unemployment. Without insurance, many individuals may cut back on health care services, particularly elective procedures. Continued slowing growth past the end of the recession, however, has led analysts to attribute the slow in spending to payment reform and structural changes in the U.S. health care system, including those initiated by the Affordable Care Act (Executive Office 2013).

Despite the recent slowdown in spending, growth in U.S. health care costs continues to outpace GDP growth and represents a significantly larger portion of U.S. spending and GDP as compared with other industrialized nations.

Shifting Demographics: Patients and Workforce

Impending demographic shifts will significantly impact the demand for care, both the amount and type (i.e., acute vs. long term). How the U.S. health care system adapts to this shift in demand will be a challenge for providers and patients in the coming decades. For the next 20 years, about 3 million members of the baby boom generation will enter retirement age each year. The U.S. Census Bureau estimates that by 2029, 71 million Americans will be 65 or older, a 73% increase from 2011. This will result in a massive shift in insurance coverage from commercial plans to Medicare. The solvency of Medicare is already a highly charged political issue, and this will further aggravate an already financially strapped program.

The aging population will also impact the type of care delivered. Over a quarter of those over age 65 are living with multiple chronic conditions (Ward 2010). Providers and health care organizations must develop new models to effectively care for patients with chronic conditions, including coordinating services across the continuum of care and ensuring effective care transitions from one provider to another.

In addition to growth in demand for care, the demographic shift will also exacerbate existing clinician shortages. The IOM estimates the largest shortfall in direct care workers will be among home health and personal care aides (IOM 2008). Additionally, health care organizations must grapple with the consequences of management and leadership retiring at a faster rate than perhaps ever before.

Transition to Value-Based Reimbursement

Historically, the U.S. health care system has been financed primarily through fee-for-service reimbursement. Hospitals and physicians were paid for the number of services, tests, and procedures provided, regardless of the value of those services. The fee-for-service reimbursement structure provides perverse incentives for care providers and is a key driver of the high, unsustainable cost of health care in the U.S. (The Miller Center 2014). To incentivize hospitals and clinicians to provide high quality care, which may actually include fewer tests and procedures, the reimbursement structure must change to reward the desired behaviors. In an attempt to both contain costs and improve quality, private and public insurance programs alike are implementing "value-based payment," a methodology that rewards quality through incentives and transparency (Keckley 2011).

Generally, payment reform initiatives including bundled payments, value-based purchasing, pay-for-performance, capitation, and others attempt to align incentives to provide care that is necessary, appropriate, timely, and cost-effective. Such initiatives have been underway for years, albeit in pilot or relatively small-scale efforts. The Affordable Care Act accelerates the implementation of value-based payment programs through applying VBP to the Medicare and Medicaid reimbursement structure and through providing funding to support research in the private sector related to VBP (Kaiser Family Foundation 2013). In January 2015, the Centers for Medicare and Medicaid announced that by the end of 2018 50 percent of Medicare payments will be tied to quality or value through alternative payment models such as accountable care organizations or bundled payment arrangements (Keckley 2015). Recent analyses estimate that VBP reform will reduce Medicare spending by nearly $214 billion over the next 10 years (Keckley 2011). In response, providers must find new ways to deliver high-quality care in a cost-efficient way.

The transition from volume to value is a key driver of rapid transformation. Those who do not transform quickly enough to produce value through more efficient care processes will no longer flourish. Value-based purchasing models aim to incent and reward safe, high-quality, patient-centered care. To reward such behavior, hospitals and payers must have systems that accurately measure and track such indicators. Successful value-based purchasing programs are contingent on identifying, tracking, and tying payment to those quality and patient satisfaction indicators that produce the most value for the health care system. As such, the ability to use data and measurement to drive decision-making will be a key competency for leaders in the transition from volume- to value-based payment.

Variable Quality Outcomes

Despite spending significantly more on health care than any other industrialized nation, the U.S. health care system's quality outcomes lag behind those of many other industrialized counties. Some organizations and systems within the U.S. provide some of the highest quality care in the world. As a whole, however, compared to other OECD countries, quality of care in the U.S. is more highly variable and not notably superior to other far less expensive systems. For example, the U.S. asthma mortality rate among those age 5 to 39 is 0.4 per 100,000 population, second highest among OEC countries and significantly larger than the OECD median of 0.09. Indicators of in-hospital mortality show the U.S. performing slightly better than the median for acute myocardial infarction and ischemic stroke, and slightly worse than the median for hemorrhagic stroke. Additionally, the U.S. infant mortality rate of 5.4 ranks 34th in the world, and is more than twice that of Singapore, Japan, and Iceland (World Bank, 2014). Particularly given the expense of the U.S. health care system, the underperformance on numerous quality indicators continues to be a challenge for providers and patients alike.

In addition to variation in quality, there is also great variation in the cost of care across the U.S. Furthermore, this variation in cost frequently does not correlate with quality, generating concerns and questions around the efficiency and effectiveness of the system as a whole. Numerous studies have documented widespread and significant variations in the cost of care (Ellis 2012). Similarly, there is a large body of literature documenting variation in treatments, procedures, and surgeries given a particular diagnosis (Weinstein 2004). Identifying and explaining variation in cost and quality of care helps to identify irregularity and incompatibility as well as opportunities for innovation and improvement (Wheeler 2000).

Along with regional and small area variation in cost and quality, the U.S. also experiences significant disparities in care across racial, ethnic, and other demographic indicators. In 2002, the Institute of Medicine defined health care disparities as "racial or ethnic differences in the quality of health care that are not due to access-related factors or clinical needs, preferences and appropriateness of the intervention." Disparities in both health care and health outcomes are well documented. Examples include:

- The infant mortality rate for non-Hispanic black babies is greater than twice that of non-Hispanic white babies (12.8 vs. 5.5).
- Vietnamese-American women have a cervical cancer rate nearly five times the rate for Caucasian-Americans.
- Lower household income is directly related to an increased risk in chronic conditions in children.
- Rural Americans are more likely to have chronic illnesses such as high blood pressure, heart disease, and diabetes (Smedley 2003).

Not only is there a moral imperative to eliminate disparities, there are also financial and efficiency incentives, as disparities impact quality and cost of care as well. Racial and ethnic minorities are more likely to experience medical errors, adverse outcomes, longer lengths of stay, and readmission and are also less likely to receive evidence-based care for certain conditions (HRET 2013). A recent analysis by the Kaiser Family Foundation suggests that 30% of direct medical costs for African-Americans, Hispanics, and Asian-Americans are excess costs due to health inequities (Kaiser 2012). Identifying the causes of both variation and disparities in care and, more importantly, identifying solutions to address these inequities, are keystones of twenty-first century medicine.

Expansion of Coverage under the Affordable Care Act

In 2010, President Obama signed the Affordable Care Act (ACA) into law, marking the largest expansion of health insurance coverage in the U.S. since the creation of Medicare and Medicaid in 1965. The ACA expands coverage through two key mechanisms: (1) providing states the option to expand Medicaid to all individuals under 138% of the federal poverty line and (2) supporting the creation and implementation of federal- or state-based health insurance exchanges. As of February 2015, 28 states and the District of Columbia are currently implementing an expansion of Medicaid, 14 states are implementing state-based marketplaces, 10 states are implementing partnership marketplaces, and 27 states are implementing federally facilitated marketplaces (Kaiser 2015). In addition to these two major expansions, the individual and employer mandates drive expansions of coverage. Finally, the ACA allows children to stay on their parents' health insurance until age 26. The combined effect of these coverage expansions has been a drop in the rate of uninsured from a high of 18.0% in 2013 to 13.4% in April 2014 (Gallup 2014). This translates to an estimated 20 million Americans who gained coverage through expansions initiated by the Affordable Care Act by 2014 (Blumenthal 2014).

While the coverage expansions increase access to care for millions of Americans, this large influx of users presents challenges for the health care delivery system. The U.S. is currently experiencing a shortage of primary care physicians, particularly for adults. Recent estimates suggest that the gap will exceed 52,000 physicians by 2025 and that growing demand—including from aging baby boomers, insurance expansions, and increases in the number of individuals living with diabetes and obesity—will continue to accelerate the demand for primary care physicians (NRMP 2014). Traditionally, solutions to the primary care physician shortage have focused on educating more physicians. More recent policy recommendations focus on changing care delivery models to empower other personnel to practice at the top of their licenses; enable non-licensed health personnel to function as panel managers and health coaches to address preventive and chronic care needs; increase capacity for patient self-care and utilize technology to add capacity (Bodenheimer 2013). Regardless of the policy changes implemented, the imperative remains the same—adding more than 20 million new lives to the current health care system will require significant transformation in the way care is delivered, coordinated, and financed.

In addition to the large influx of patients, the coverage expansions in the Affordable Care Act also have a significant financial impact for the delivery system. As more individuals now have insurance, either through public or private exchange plans or through Medicaid, hospitals will see their uncompensated care and need for charity care decrease. Fewer patients will be responsible for self-pay, increasing the likelihood that the delivery system will receive payment of some form. Additionally, as noted below, many of the newly insured have defined contribution plans, one form of which is a high-deductible health plan. These plans require patients to pay for a greater percentage of their care up to a given deductible, shifting the cost burden to consumers. Compared with more traditional insurance, these plans require the delivery system to have a more active role in collecting co-pays and other payments from patients directly. Overall, the expansion of health insurance coverage has many financial impacts on the delivery system including new revenue streams, and thus far has had a largely positive impact on the delivery system.

Advances in Health Information Technology

Another ongoing and potentially disruptive driver of transformation is the implementation of health information technology. The Health Information and Technology for Economic and Clinical Health Act (HITECH Act), enacted through the American Recovery and Reinvestment Act of 2009, invests $25.9 billion to promote and expand the adoption of health information technology and create a nationwide network of electronic health records (EHR). In 2013, 78% of office-based physicians reported having some type of EHR system while 48% reported having a basic EHR system. This represents a doubling from the adoption rate in 2009 (Keckley 2011).

Though EHR implementation is accelerating, the touted benefits of HIT (e.g., cost-saving efficiencies, sophisticated analytics, and modeling capabilities) are in many instances still unrealized (Kellermann 2013). Challenges remain concerning integrating new technology into existing workflows, data extraction for analysis and quality improvement, efficacy of technologies, and continued resistance to adoption. Technologies such as electronic prescribing, computerized decision support, computerized physician order entry, and health information exchanges hold potential to reduce inefficiencies and produce cost savings; however, leaders will continue to face challenges over the next decade in the adoption and implementation of these technologies.

In addition to these more traditional technologies, there are numerous disruptive technologies affecting the health care system as well. Telehealth, the use of electronic information and telecommunications technologies to support long-distance clinical care, is changing the way patients can access care. Specifically, as telehealth becomes more effective and widespread, it is beginning to challenge the way health care is delivered in small and rural communities.

Another disruptive technology is the rise of mobile health and the concept of the "quantified self." Mobile health includes phone and tablet applications and other personal devices that are enabling consumers to track their diet, exercise, and sleep patterns and are also enabling consumers to track their own biometrics and in many cases self-diagnose and treat minor illnesses or injuries. The combination of rapid expansion of technology along with a movement toward greater consumer engagement in health care creates exciting opportunities in this space. As with any disruptive technology, there are risks and opportunities. Managing and capitalizing on the rise of mobile health technologies is an important role for clinical leaders in the twenty-first century.

Shift from Defined Benefit to Defined Contribution Health Plans

Another factor that is having a significant impact on patients and their decisions to seek care is the shift in insurance from defined benefit to defined contribution health plans. This shift has been driven largely by the reforms implemented under the Affordable Care Act, specifically the public and private insurance exchanges. Across all health plans, however, as health care costs increase insurers are finding new ways to design plans that shift costs to consumers. This shift to defined contribution plans has increased consumers' financial responsibility for care, thus making them more cost conscious. This in turn has driven the rise of consumerism and retail in health care. As consumers have more "skin in the game" financially, they are increasingly looking for the best value for what they pay. Faced with these new financial incentives, consumers are becoming more engaged in the process of seeking care and are driving the delivery system to demonstrate value.

The Role of a Clinical Leader

The collective impact of these forces is rapidly driving the U.S. health care system to be financially unsustainable and increasingly difficult for patients and consumers to navigate. For the U.S. to continue to provide affordable, high-quality care, nothing short of complete transformation is required. Leadership will be required at all levels, but especially from clinicians stepping into new leadership roles across the continuum of care. Here are six key competencies for clinical leaders to successfully lead health care transformation.

1. **Effectively communicate the imperative for health care transformation and the steps to achieve change.** The forces driving transformation are many, varied, and complex. Leaders must be able to effectively communicate to staff, leadership, governance, and their communities the imperative for transformation. They must be effective in translating how national drivers have a local impact and how changes and decisions, often very difficult ones, relate to a larger context driving change.

2. **Understand the relationship between cost and quality in practice and how to drive value.** The health care system of the future will be based on value—a combination of cost and quality. Clinical leaders must be proficient in measuring and managing costs and quality and understanding the relationship between the two to drive value. It is no longer an option for clinicians or patients to ignore costs. Costs must become a part of a larger conversation on how to create the most high-quality, value-driven health care system.

3. **Build, deploy, and lead improvement teams across all dimensions of care.** The ability to build teams and implement improvement cycles is a critical element of success. Clinical leaders, however, must also be able to teach those skills to others and build organizations focused around continuous improvement in all dimensions of care—quality, efficiency, and financial. Clinical leaders must be proficient in the systems and tools of quality improvement and create a culture of continuous improvement, safety, and accountability.

4. **Build and lead effective multidisciplinary teams.** Siloed care is a way of the past. The health care organization of the future will deliver care through multidisciplinary teams. Leaders must enable practitioners to practice at the top of their license and build a culture of transparency and open communication. Teams must be able to communicate effectively internally and with external organizations and partners, particularly about care transitions.

5. **Leverage data to improve clinical and organizational practice.** Health care is becoming a data-driven industry. Leaders must track and understand data related to quality, cost, efficiency, patient experience, and more. Effective clinical leaders will use data to drive decision-making and to create a culture of transparency and continuous improvement.

6. **Realizing the role of patient as consumer.** Delivery systems are increasingly recognizing the potential of patients and families as engaged and active participants in care. In addition to improving patient satisfaction and experience, patient and family engagement initiatives have been linked to high quality, lower cost, and improved outcomes in care. Beyond patient and family engagement in care delivery, however, clinical leaders in the twenty-first century must be able to innovate new ways to capitalize on the transition of patients to consumers. As consumerism increases in health care and patients face more incentives and opportunities to engage in health behaviors or in seeking care, delivery systems have a role in optimizing those interactions in order to achieve the best outcomes.

Conclusion

Leaders in the U.S. health care system face difficult challenges in the twenty-first century. The combination of the above-identified key forces results in the imperative to undertake no less than a complete transformation of the U.S. health care system. Health care facilities that collaborate across the continuum of care need strong and innovative leaders to develop and implement initiatives to control costs, improve quality, and transform the patient experience.

References

American Hospital Association. 2011 Committee on performance Improvement, Jeanette Clough, Chairperson. Hospitals and Care Systems of the Future. Chicago: American Hospital Association, September 2011.

Barr, Paul. 2014. The Boomer Challenge. Hospitals and Health Networks. http://www.hhn-mag.com/display/HHN-news-article.dhtml?dcrPath=/templatedata/HF_Common/NewsArticle/data/HHN/Magazine/2014/Jan/cover-story-baby-boomers.

Blumenthal, David, and Sara R. Collins. 2014. Health Care Coverage Under the Affordable Care Act—a Progress Report. *New England Journal of Medicine* 371(3): 275–281.

Bodenheimer, Thomas S., and Mark D. Smith. 2013. Primary Care: Proposed Solutions to the Physician Shortage without Training More Physicians. *Health Affairs* 32(11): 1881–1886.

Centers for Medicare and Medicaid Services. National Health Expenditure Projections 2012–2022: Forecast Summary. 2012. http://www.cms.gov/Research-Statistics-Data-and-Systems/Statistics-Trends-and-Reports/NationalHealthExpendData/downloads/proj2012.pdf.

Claxton Gary, Matthew Rae, Nirmita Panchal et al. 2013. Employer Health Benefits 2013 Annual Survey. Menlo Park, CA: Kaiser Family Foundation, and Chicago, IL: Health Research and Educational Trust.

Davis, K., K. Stremikis, D. Squires, and C. Schoen. 2014. Mirror, Mirror on the Wall: How the Performance of the U.S. Health Care System Compares Internationally—2014 Update. The Commonwealth Fund.

Disparities in Health and Health Care: Five Key Questions and Answers. The Henry J. Kaiser Family Foundation. 2012. http://kaiserfamilyfoundation.files.wordpress.com/2012/11/8396-disparities-in-health-and-health-care-five-key-questions-and-answers.pdf.

Ellis, Philip, Lewis G. Sandy, Aaron J. Larson, and Simon L. Stevens. 2012. Wide Variation in Episode Costs within a Commercially Insured Population Highlights Potential to Improve the Efficiency of Care. *Health Affairs* 31(9): 2084–2093.

Executive Office of the President of the United States. 2013. Trends in Health Care Cost Growth and the Role of the Affordable Care Act. http://www.whitehouse.gov/sites/default/files/docs/healthcostreport_final_noembargo_v2.pdf.

Hartman, Micah, Anne B. Martin, Joseph Benson, and Aaron Catlin. 2013. National Health Spending in 2011: Overall Growth Remains Low, but Some Payers and Services Show Signs of Acceleration. *Health Affairs* 32(1): 87–99.

Health Disparities: The Basics. American Public Health Association. 2008. http://ajph. aphapublications.org/doi/abs/10.2105/AJPH.2010.300062.

Health Expenditure, Total (% of GDP), The World Bank, http://data.worldbank.org/indi-cator/SH.XPD.TOTL.ZS.

Himmelstein, David U., Deborah Thorne, Elizabeth Warren, and Steffie Woolhandler. 2009. Medical Bankruptcy in the United States, 2007: Results of a National Study. *The American Journal of Medicine* 122(8): 741–746.

Institute of Medicine. *Retooling for an Aging America: Building the Health Care Workforce.* Washington, DC: The National Academies Press, 2008.

Kaiser Family Foundation. 2013. Assessing the Effects of the Economy on the Recent Slowdown in Health Spending. http://kff.org/health-costs/issue-brief/assessing-the-effects-of-the-economy-on-the-recent-slowdown-in-health-spending-2/.

Kaiser Family Foundation. Summary of the Affordable Care Act. 2013. http://kff.org/health-reform/fact-sheet/summary-of-the-affordable-care-act/.

Kaiser Family Foundation and Health Research and Educational Trust. *Employer Health Benefits: 2013 Summary of Findings.* http://kaiserfamilyfoundation.files.wordpress.com/2013/08/8466-employer-health-benefits-2013_summary-of-findings2.pdf.

Keckley, P. 2015. HHS doubles down on shift from volume to value. H&HN Daily. February 2, 2015.

Keckley, P., S. Coughlin, and S. Gupta. 2011. Value-Based Purchasing: A Strategic Overview for Health Care Industry Stakeholders. Deloitte Center for Health Solutions. http://www.deloitte.com/assets/Dcom-UnitedStates/Local%20Assets/Documents/Health%20Reform%20Issues%20Briefs/US_CHS_ValueBasedPurchasing_031811.pdf.

Kellermann, Arthur L., and Spencer S. Jones. 2013. What Will It Take to Achieve the As-Yet-Unfulfilled Promises of Health Information Technology. *Health Affairs* 32(1): 63–68.

Miller, David C., Cathryn Gust, Justin B. Dimick, Nancy Birkmeyer, Jonathan Skinner, and John D. Birkmeyer. 2011. Large Variations in Medicare Payments for Surgery Highlight Savings Potential from Bundled Payment Programs. *Health Affairs* 30(11): 2107–2115.

Reschovsky, James D., Arkadipta Ghosh, Kate A. Stewart, and Deborah J. Chollet. 2012. Durable Medical Requirement and Home Health among the Largest Contributors to Area Variations in Use of Medicare Services. *Health Affairs* 31(5): 956–964.

Rising above the Noise: Making the Case for Equity in Care. 2013. Health Research & Educational Trust. http://www.hpoe.org/resources/hpoehretaha-guides/1459.

Smedley, Brian D., Adrienne Y. Stith, and Alan R. Nelson. 2003. Unequal Treatment: Confronting Racial and Ethnic Disparities in Health Care. Institute of Medicine, Committee on Understanding and Eliminating Racial and Ethnic Disparities in Health Care. 1–781.

Squires, David A. 2012. Explaining High Health Care Spending in the United States: An International Comparison of Supply, Utilization, Prices, and Quality. Issue brief (Commonwealth Fund) 10: 1–14.

State Decisions on Health Insurance Marketplaces and the Medicaid Expansion. Kaiser Family Foundation. Last modified August 28, 2014. http://kff.org/health-reform/state-indicator/state-decisions-for-creating-health-insurance-exchanges-and-expand-ing-medicaid/.

Summary: NASBO State Expenditure Report. The National Association of State Budget Officers. 2013. http://www.nasbo.org/sites/default/files/State%20Expenditure%20Report-Summary.pdf.

The Facts on Medicare Spending and Financing. 2014. The Henry J. Kaiser Family Foundation. http://kff.org/medicare/fact-sheet/medicare-spending-and-financing-fact-sheet/.

The Match, National Resident Matching Program (NRMP). Accessed August 27, 2014. http://www.nrmp.org/.

The Miller Center. Cracking the Code on Health Care Costs: A Report by the State Health Care Cost Containment Commission. University of Virginia, 2014.

The World Bank. Mortality rate, infant (per 1000 live births). Data.worldbank.org. Accessed October 2014.

U.S. Uninsured Rate Drops to 13.4%. Gallup Well-Being. Last modified October 16, 2014. http://www.gallup.com/poll/168821/uninsured-rate-drops.aspx.

Ward, B.W., and J.S. Schiller. 2013. Prevalence of Multiple Chronic Conditions among U.S. Adults: Estimates from the National Health Interview Survey, 2010. *Prev Chronic Dis.* 10:120203. DOI: http://dx.doi.org/10.5888/pcd10.120203.

Weinstein, James N., Kristen K. Bronner, Tamara Shawver Morgan, and John E. Wennberg. 2004. Trends and Geographic Variations in Major Surgery for Degenerative Diseases of the Hip, Knee, and Spine. *Health Affairs* (Millwood) 23: w81.

Wheeler, D.J. 2000. Understanding Variation. The Key to Managing Chaos.

Chapter 2

Effectively Implementing Quality and Safety Improvement

Recent reforms in health care, including the implementation of the Patient Protection and Affordable Care Act and the Health Information Technology for Economic and Clinical Health Act, are creating strong external incentives to improve quality of care. Reimbursement reform, investment in infrastructure, and advances in health care decision-making technologies are driving health care to become more efficient, effective, and value-driven. During this innovative time in health care, leaders have both the opportunity and imperative to improve care delivery and organizational efficiency in pursuit of providing high-value, patient-centered care.

This chapter provides an overview of the systems and processes that comprise the framework for health care quality improvement initiatives and identifies the core commonalities across those systems and tools. Although this chapter does not include an exhaustive list of performance improvement systems and tools, the most commonly used frameworks are emphasized in order to provide the clinical leader with a basic understanding of how to implement performance improvement activities within health care facilities.

The Evidence

The Model for Improvement

The Model for Improvement, developed by the Associates in Process Improvement, is perhaps the most basic and accessible framework on conducting improvement cycles. This model can be applied both horizontally and vertically throughout the organization and to nearly all improvement opportunities, from efforts to streamline workflows to initiatives to reduce surgical site infections to projects to reduce the number of no-show patients. It introduces three fundamental questions to be addressed by the improvement team: (1) What are we trying to accomplish? (2) How will we know that a change is an improvement? (3) What change can we make that will result in improvement? These questions guide teams to establish measurable and time-specific aims for the project, define the patient population that will be impacted, and establish quantitative measures to monitor progress, and implement evidence-based change concepts (IHI 2014a). Once a team has identified answers to these guiding questions, the next step is to implement PDSA cycles to test changes and watch for improvement.

Developed by Walter A. Shewhart in the 1920s, Plan–Do–Study–Act (PDSA) is a framework for planning and executing performance improvement efforts. PDSA provides the structure for most formally recognized performance improvement models, including Lean and Six Sigma. PDSA, alternatively known as the PDCA cycle (Plan–Do–Check–Act), includes the steps listed in Figure 2.1 (Warren 2014).

The first step in any performance improvement project is to develop the aim statement or goal using the three questions in Model for Improvement. Next, the project lead must recruit participants to join the improvement team (see Chapter 9 for more detail). Given the project's aim, the team then plans a change, observes the results, and acts upon what is learned, conducting a PDSA cycle or small test of change (IHI 2014c). A project may require multiple PDSA cycles to arrive at an effective and sustainable improvement to the system. Once a successful intervention is established, it should be spread across the organization to increase efficiency and effectiveness on a larger scale (IHI 2014a).

PDSA is a very accessible tool for improvement teams at all levels of the organization. Teams or individuals can implement improvement cycles with or without a formal team charter. Organizations that support a culture of continuous improvement should also support PDSA cycles throughout the organization to improve processes and workflow on an ongoing basis.

Lean

Taiichi Ohno, co-founder of the Toyota Production System, originally developed Lean thinking as an improvement methodology applied to manufacturing (Graban

Plan–Do–Study–Act
Plan
✓ Establish a goal.
✓ Ask specific questions and develop hypotheses or predictions.
✓ Plan the logistics of the cycle: what steps will be performed, who will be performing the functions, the timeline of implementation, deadline for completion and location of the work.
Do
✓ Train and educate staff.
✓ Carry out the plan, preferably by starting out with a pilot or small-scale version.
✓ During implementation, document unexpected observations/results and problems.
✓ Initiate data analysis.
Study/Check
✓ Assess and measure the effects of the intervention.
✓ Compare the results of the process changes with your hypotheses/predictions.
✓ Determine the level of achieved success as compared to the goal or objective.
✓ Summarize lessons learned.
✓ Determine what modifications need to be made to improve the process and determine next steps.
Act
✓ Act on lessons learned.
✓ Determine whether the plan can continue with modifications or if a new plan should be developed.
✓ Make changes if needed.
✓ Identify missing components in the process.
✓ Carry out iterative PDSA cycles until the goal or objective is achieved.

Figure 2.1 Plan–Do–Study–Act. (Warren, K. 2014. Quality Improvement: Foundation, Processes, Tools, and Knowledge Transfer Techniques. In The Healthcare Quality Book: Vision, Strategy, and Tools, ed. Maulik S. Joshi et al. (Chicago, IL: Health Administration Press, 2014), 83–107.)

2011). The Lean Enterprise Institute offers the definition: "Lean is a set of concepts, principles and tools used to create and deliver the most value from the customers' perspectives while consuming the fewest resources and fully utilizing the knowledge and skills of the people performing the work" (Graban 2011). After extensive study of the TPS system, it has been distilled into four essential principles, three of which describe work design and one describes the learning process for improvement:

1. **The content, sequence, time frame, and expected outcome of all work will be highly specified.** The more specified each step in a task is, the easier it is to identify discrepancies between the guidelines and actual behaviors. This enables a prompt response for problem solving, by the worker and supervisor, through either process modification or additional worker training.

2. **Every customer-supplier connection must be standardized and direct by having an unambiguous yes-or-no way to send requests and receive responses.** This connection explicitly specifies which people are involved, what goods or services will be provided, the customer's request, and the expected time frame. By assigning direct connections between people, assistance and trouble-shooting can be efficiently provided. Furthermore, accountability is strengthened when each person has a specific responsibility to another person.

3. **The pathway for every product and service must be simple and direct.** Contrary to the conventional method of sending the product or service to the next available person, this pathway requires that it is sent to a specific person. If that person is not available, he or she will have a designated person to take his or her place, and so forth. This pathway also applies to workers' requests for help. This rule effectively tests the hypothesis that every worker in the pathway is needed, and any worker not in the pathway is not needed.

4. **Testing changes to create improvement must be made within the frame-work of the scientific method, under the guidance of a teacher and at the lowest possible organization level.** This rule emphasizes that *how* changes are made is as important as what changes are made. It is not enough to be complacent with an observed improvement when it is made with seemingly random changes. Rather, the scientific method of testing a hypothesis—that is, a proposed change leading to an expected outcome—will explicitly identify the gap between the actual and expected outcome, if there is one. This, in turn, enables workers to make further modifications to their work processes, while deeply questioning assumptions about their work, until they get closer and closer to the expected outcome.

Although the above four principles emphasize rigidly structured steps, the underpinning of TPS is a flexible, highly experimentalist system that promotes learning and problem solving on every level of the organization. This system has shown to be especially effective within an organization that has a nested, modular structure. This means that supervisors can enable workers to make design changes in one section of the organization without disrupting other sections. This is because each organizational section's ability to respond uniquely to its own problems remains intact. Therefore, different approaches to problem solving in distinct sections can concurrently function within one umbrella organization (Spear and Bowen 1999).

The goal of applying this system's four essential principles is to reach an organizational ideal. This ideal explicitly constitutes that the product or service is defect free, can be supplied on demand in the requested version, delivered immediately, produced without any unnecessary materials, labor, or other resources, and is produced in a safe work environment (Spear and Bowen 1999).

Due to the unprecedented effectiveness and success of the Toyota Production System, it has been applied to numerous other companies and industries, such as consumer products, aerospace, and health care, and evolved into the Lean framework.

When applying this framework to health care, the primary question to ask is: How can the health care system deliver the most value to patients and maximize the use of providers' skills and knowledge, all while using the least amount of needed resources? Lean is comprised of a tool set, a management system, a method for continuous improvement, and a philosophy of employee engagement. Lean tools and methods include A3 problem solving, *kanban*, 5S, *kaizen*, error proofing, and visual management (Figure 2.2) (Graban 2011).

However, it is not sufficient to use a single tool or even a combination of tools to achieve the full benefits of Lean. The four principles described above form the backbone of the Lean system and require a substantial investment of time and effort. A common pitfall or shortcut among leaders is to mistake Lean tools as the Lean

Lean Tool	Definition
A3 Report	A piece of paper, typically 11 x 17 inches, that standardizes and simplifies problem solving and follows the PDCA cycle. The report is generally structured by: 1) Background, 2) Current Situation and Problem, 3) Goal, 4) Root Cause Analysis, 5) Action Items/ Implementation Plan, 6) Results, 7) Follow Up.
Kanban	Japanese term meaning "signal," a method for managing inventory.
5S	Method for organizing workplaces to reduce waste time and motion for employees, making problems more readily apparent.
Kaizen	Japanese term meaning "continuous improvement," focused on workplace improvement by employees.
Error Proofing	Method for designing or improving processes so errors are less likely to occur.
Visual Management	Method for making problems visible, providing for fast response and problem solving.

Figure 2.2 Lean Tools. (Graban, Mark. 2011. Overview of Lean for Hospitals. In Lean hospitals: improving quality, patient safety, and employee satisfaction, 17–29. CRC Press.)

system itself (Spear and Bowen 1999). A clinical leader must implement tools that specifically address the unique problems and needs of the health care organization. Furthermore, these tools must be implemented with the appropriate leadership and management mindset, one that guides employees toward understanding why improvement is needed and how Lean methods provide a path towards improvement (Graban 2011).

Lean works to create a shift from the top-down authoritative model, in which leaders issue commands to workers, to one that has leaders actively listening to and asking for employees' opinions, engaging them in solving problems, and training them to drive improvement in their departments (Graban 2011).

In addition to the tools listed previously, Lean efforts focus on reducing waste, or *muda*, from care delivery or employees' workloads in order to improve efficiency (Graban 2011). From the patient's perspective, waste encompasses activities that do not advance diagnosis, treatment, or discharge and include unnecessary waiting time and transport, overproduction, and harmful medical errors (Graban 2011).

Lean thinking reinforces the idea that leaders should form a partnership with employees and nurture the intrinsic motivation to engage in continuous improvement. Employee engagement is maintained, in part, by ensuring that they are not subject to overwork (*muri*) and uneven workloads (*mura*) so as to avoid frustration and burnout (Graban 2011). Therefore, a key difference between the Lean approach and traditional methods of increasing efficiency (e.g., cost cutting through budget reduction, layoffs) is that Lean improvement efforts must always strike a balance between efficiency and eliminating waste, while also respecting and engaging employees (Graban 2011).

Six Sigma

Six Sigma, which denotes 3.4 defects per million, is a system to reduce variation and eliminate defects in key business processes by using statistical tools to analyze process flow and fluctuation. Six Sigma enables managers to predict outcomes of future processes and use statistical tools to understand the elements that influence those projections. The five steps of Six Sigma are outlined in Figure 2.3 (Warren 2014).

Similar to Lean, Six Sigma is commonly utilized by hospitals to improve operational efficiency related to patient safety and quality of care. Examples include initiatives to reduce variance of length of stay within a hospital, reduce wait times for appointments within a transplant center, and eliminate health care-associated infections (iSixSigma 2008). Lean and Six Sigma share similar concepts, allowing them to be blended in order to best address a hospital's mission to provide value for the customer—their patients. Individual training and certification are available for Six Sigma, including designations for yellow belt, green belt, and black belt.

Six Sigma DMAIC Model	
Define	Identify customers and specific key processes and characteristics that are important to them, their problems, current process elements, and associated output conditions.
Measure	Measure and collect data on key characteristics that influence processes. This is the most time consuming step in the DMAIC model.
Analyze	Use statistical tools to analyze the collected data in order to analyze the variation in the process and how to minimize it. This analysis can also identify the root causes of defects or problems and whether the problem is a random event.
Improve	If the problem is not a random event, identify and test possible solutions to observe whether the changes are beneficial and how they affect other variables. Refine or select new changes as judged necessary.
Control	Control planning is required for sustained improvement. Quality control data must be collected in order to monitor processes and verify measurements regularly. This ensures that processes continue to run efficiently with no unexpected changes.

Figure 2.3 Six Sigma: DMAIC. (Warren, K. 2014. Quality Improvement: Foundation, Processes, Tools, and Knowledge Transfer Techniques. In The Healthcare Quality Book: Vision, Strategy, and Tools, ed. Maulik S. Joshi et al. (Chicago, IL: Health Administration Press, 2014), 83–107.

International Standards Organization 9001

The ISO 9001 is a set of quality management criteria that has been implemented in organizations in over 170 countries and can readily be applied to health care organizations (International Standards Organization). Its core components focus on controlled key functions, processes, and protocols as well as audits and measurements of key functions. The ISO 9001 standards are comprised of the following seven principles and recommended actions (ISO Central Secretariat 2012):

1. **Strong customer focus**. Research and understand current and future customer needs and expectations. Ensure that organizational goals are linked to them. Measure customer satisfaction and use results to modify processes as necessary. Balance customer needs with the needs of other stakeholders, including suppliers, employees, and the community.
2. **Motivated high-level leadership.** Leaders provide clarity of purpose and organizational direction. Concurrently, they need to be cognizant of stakeholder needs and maintain a non-punitive work environment in which workers are empowered to fully engage in achieving organizational goals.
3. **Involvement of people.** People, at all levels of the organization, should understand the importance and contribution of their role. They should be equipped to evaluate their performance against personal goals, empowered to accept ownership of problems and constraints in performance, as well as seek

opportunities to improve their competence and knowledge. This is facilitated by the open discussion of problems and sharing of knowledge.

4. **Process approach.** Systematically define necessary activities for the desired outcome. Establish clear roles with distinct responsibilities along with key interfaces of key activities within the organization. Analyze the risks and effects of key activities on customers, suppliers, and employees.

5. **System approach to management.** Understand the interdependencies of processes within the system and integrate these processes to achieve objectives in the most effective and efficient way. Consider resource constraints and organizational capacity prior to performing activities.

6. **Continual improvement.** Use a consistent performance improvement approach across the organization that equips people with relevant training and tools. Establish guiding goals and tracking measures, while consistently recognizing and acknowledging improvements.

7. **Fact-based decision-making.** Act upon data and information that is verified to be sufficiently accurate and reliable, while balancing it with intuition and experience. Make data accessible to stakeholders who need it.

By achieving the ISO 9001 Standards, health care organizations can improve customer satisfaction, employee engagement and accountability, consistency and predictability of results, and their ability to review and challenge decisions. Furthermore, processes will become more efficient and better aligned with organizational strategic objectives, while allowing for flexibility and high responsiveness (International Standards Organization 2008). ISO 9001 certification is increasingly being offered by accreditation bodies such as The Joint Commission, Det Norse Veritas (DNV) Healthcare, which is also known as National Integrated Accreditation for Healthcare Organizations (NIAHO), and Healthcare Facilities Accreditation Program (HFAP) (Lazarus and Chapman 2013).

Lessons Learned

Over the past few decades, emphasis on quality improvement has taken many forms. For many, this has led to a feeling that the industry jumps from one fad to another, never seeming to stick to one philosophy or method to drive improvement. Clinical leaders can glean many lessons from the experiences of the past implementation cycles in order to move forward with a more comprehensive, sustainable approach to improvement.

Form follows function. There are many frameworks, systems, and tools to guide quality improvement efforts, as noted previously. A clinical leader's role is to lead the improvement team to define goals and objectives before selecting the system and tools to use. There is no "one size fits all" approach; improvement teams should abide by the philosophy "form follows function" in selecting a system and tools for improvement (Warren 2014).

Knowledge transfer and spread. Once an intervention proves successful at a unit or department level, organizations should have systems in place to scale and spread the success across the organization. Without systems to effectively transfer insights and knowledge, organizations will experience stagnation, waste, inconsistent performance, and missed opportunities to improve performance (Warren 2014). The Institute for Healthcare Improvement's "A Framework for Spread: From Local Improvements to System-Wide Change" describes the spread of innovation as a "key factor in closing the gap between *best* practice and *common* practice" and identifies the following four questions to address when planning to spread an improvement (Massoud et al. 2006):

- How are decisions about the adoption of improvements made?
- What infrastructure enhancements will assist in achieving the spread aim?
- What transition issues need to be addressed?
- How will spread of practices be transitioned to operational responsibilities?

The Health Research & Educational Trust, an affiliate of the American Hospital Association, has developed a spread assessment tool to identify how readily an initiative will achieve widespread adoption. The tool ranks initiatives across four factors: environmental, innovation, target audience, and organizational, and produces a readiness score that helps predict initiatives that hold the most promise for wide-scale adoption (HRET 2010). Chapter 3 provides additional tools and information on spreading improvement.

Create a culture of safety. Patient safety should be the number one priority and the core of the patient experience. Work processes, culture, and teams must be redesigned in order to cultivate a non-punitive environment in which employees are able to identify and report near misses or errors without fear of punishment. This may require new team communication methods, systems for reporting errors, and safer care processes. Without a culture of safety, it will be difficult to initiate, execute, and sustain improvements.

Process design—human factors and high reliability. Due to the complex nature of the U.S. health care system, improvement work cannot simply focus on staff "working harder." Nearly 80% of medical errors are attributed to system design, not individual incompetence. Therefore, improvement work should focus on redesigning processes and systems, through the methods identified previously, to make it easier for employees to "do the right thing" and harder for them to do the wrong thing. This can be achieved by human factors engineering, the design of facilities, and utilizing equipment and processes that promote safety and safeguard against human fallibility. Examples of human factors design include understanding human limitations and designing jobs with those in mind (e.g., avoiding reliance on memory by providing reminders), using constraints, forcing functions, user-centered design strategies, and simplifying and standardizing procedures when applicable.

Engage leadership, frontline staff, patients, and families. Leadership provides the system-level expectations for improved quality and patient safety. However, a strategy's ultimate success is measured by how effectively it is executed. Excellent strategies often fail due to failure by senior leadership to entrust employees with authority and duty to make day-to-day decisions. As leaders guide direct actions, employees should feel empowered to actively drive those actions.

Patients and families are also powerful drivers of improvement. Patients and families should be engaged at the bedside as partners in care through strategies such as increased patient education and shared decision-making. Additionally, patients and families can contribute to quality and patient safety improvement initiatives through serving in advisory roles, participating in a patient/family advisory council, or sharing their experiences at board meetings to promote the importance of quality and safety.

Rewards and recognition—celebrate the wins. Establishing a culture of safety will take time before the aims are realized and many improvement initiatives are burdensome, disruptive, and time-consuming. Therefore, it is important to acknowledge the efforts of employees and how they contribute to the overall transformation of the organization. Recognizing and rewarding short-term wins, including through feedback and recognition from leadership, is essential in sustaining a high level of urgency, momentum, and optimism among staff.

Case Studies

The following case studies provide examples of organizations that identified an opportunity for improvement, built an improvement team, and executed improvement cycles to achieve the aim.

NCH Healthcare System: Improving Medication Communication with Patients

After surveying patients, NCH Healthcare learned that many did not understand their medication prescriptions and the possible side effects associated with them. Recognizing that this presented a significant risk to patient safety, NCH Healthcare developed an improvement team with the aim to improve its process of communicating medication instructions through standardization.

In 2010, the organization formed a medication communication committee that included staff nurses and pharmacy representatives. They first assessed process measures, which included the consistency of teaching methods across nursing units and the number of medication education materials that were available to nurses. Next, they conducted a small test of change within a nursing unit to standardize communication methods and education. Preliminary outcomes showed an increase in patients' understanding of medications along with higher medication compliance. This provided encouragement to expand the implementation of the improvement. Through feedback gathered from staff, the committee learned that nurses wanted more IT solutions, such as computerized medication teaching cards and the ability to print from the computer. A second improvement cycle was dedicated to exploring and integrating these additional improvements (The Beryl Institute 2010).

Memorial Health System: Hourly Nurse Rounds Reduce Patient Harm and Improve Patient Satisfaction

Memorial Health System was experiencing a high volume of unpredictable call light summons from patients, many of which were non-urgent. This was impacting patient safety on the unit by diverting nurses' attention from other high-priority patients and tasks. To mediate this problem, Memorial Health System implemented hourly nurse rounding.

Hourly rounding was designed to proactively address patient safety through identifying and assessing the 4 Ps: pain, potty, position, and possessions. After implementing hourly rounding, the unit experienced a decrease in falls from 4.52 per 1000 patients in 2010 to 2.4 per 1000 patients in 2011, a greater than 50% decrease in pressure ulcers, and nearly a one-third decrease in call light use. Furthermore, patient satisfaction with nursing improved from the 23rd percentile to the 67th percentile after a year. These latter outcomes were unintended benefits of this intervention and demonstrate the potential of crosscutting interventions to improve care across multiple dimensions.

While this intervention did not require new staff, it did require upfront costs, such as time spent in training. Furthermore, sustained commitment was required of staff because the program could take between 12 to 18 months to become "hardwired" into the nursing workflow (AHRQ 2012). This experience demonstrates the importance of having an executive champion, or someone who is able and willing to support teams as they require resources to drive improvement. This is a key role for a clinical leader.

Action Steps to Lead

As a clinical leader, you will need to lead improvement efforts, support and advise improvement teams, and foster the culture necessary to engender continuous improvement. Here are six action steps to lead:

1. **Become proficient in at least one improvement methodology.** As described previously, there are many methods, systems, and tools for quality improvement. Many organizations make significant investments in Lean or Six Sigma certification and have adopted an organization-wide improvement methodology. If your organization has a designated methodology, become proficient in that method. If not, lead your unit, department, or organization to adopt a methodology to promote continuous improvement.

2. **Create a culture of safety.** Begin by objectively assessing the current climate to identify opportunities for improvement. There are many surveys available to identify and address specific challenges, including the Agency for Healthcare Research and Quality's Patient Safety Culture Survey and the Safety Attitudes Questionnaire. As a leader, you contribute to creating a culture of safety through promoting transparency, accountability, and open communication. One example is encouraging employees to identify when mistakes and near misses occur.

3. **Become data driven.** Improvement opportunities should be identified based on data that show there is a gap related to quality or patient safety. Improvement projects should be developed and executed with a specific, data-driven aim in mind. Measurement and reporting are crucial components to demonstrating the value of an intervention, engaging employees, and facilitating spread. Whenever possible, leadership should present data as evidence to support their decisions.

4. **Empower frontline staff to lead.** Frontline employees, including nurses, physicians, physician therapists, and pharmacists are well-equipped to implement changes and sustain improvement, as they are most familiar with the local environment and can identify problems in their daily work. Frontline employees who are engaged in the change process are more likely to take ownership over it, require less oversight, achieve greater success, and sustain any improvements. In order to effectively empower frontline staff to become involved in the change process, middle managers can model the way, inspire a shared vision, challenge current processes, encourage the heart, and enable staff to act.

5. **Provide resources to support improvement work.** As a clinical leader, you provide the resources—financial, human, and time—that are necessary to support improvement projects. This can include funding for new materials or tools, allocating non-patient care time for improvement work meetings, and advocating on behalf of the teams in senior leadership meetings.

6. **Lead by example.** As a clinical leader, you will be engaged in many projects and teams. You can teach and empower your employees to conduct improvement projects by demonstrating how to lead a quality improvement project. By modeling these skills and behaviors, you will encourage and empower others in the organization to improve quality and safety.

References

A3 Thinking. 2008. Accessed at http://a3thinking.com/faq.html.

AHRQ. 2012. Hourly Nurse Rounds Help to Reduce Falls, Pressure Ulcers, and Call Light Use, and Contribute to Rise in Patient Satisfaction. Accessed from https://innovations.ahrq.gov/profiles/hourly-nurse-rounds-help-reduce-falls-pressure-ulcers-and-call-light-use-and-contribute?id=3204).

Berwick, Donald M., and Andrew D. Hackbarth. 2012. Eliminating waste in U.S. health care. *JAMA* 307(14): 1513–1516.

Blumenthal, David. 2012. Performance improvement in health care—seizing the moment. *New England Journal of Medicine* 366(21): 1953–1955.

Collins, James Charles. 2001. *Good to Great: Why Some Companies Make the Leap... And Others Don't.* New York: Random House.

Graban, Mark. 2011. Overview of Lean for hospitals. In *Lean Hospitals: Improving Quality, Patient Safety, and Employee Satisfaction.* Boca Raton, FL: CRC Press, 17–29.

Griffin, Frances A. 2014. Patient safety and medical errors. In *The Healthcare Quality Book: Vision, Strategy, and Tools*, Maulik S. Joshi et al. (Eds.). Chicago, IL: Health Administration Press, 269.

Health Research & Educational Trust. 2010. HRET Spread Assessment Tool. Accessed at http://www.hret.org/dissemination/projects/hret_spread_assessment_tool.shtml.

Implementation Guide Part I: A How-To Guide for Improvement for the AHA/HRET HEN Partnership for Patients. 2014. American Hospital Association and Health Research & Educational Trust.

Institute for Healthcare Improvement. 2014a. Science of Improvement: How to Improve. http://www.ihi.org/resources/Pages/HowtoImprove/ScienceofImprovementHowtoImprove.aspx.

Institute for Healthcare Improvement. 2014b. Science of Improvement: Selecting Changes. http://www.ihi.org/resources/Pages/HowtoImprove/ScienceofImprovementTestingChanges.aspx.

Institute for Healthcare Improvement. 2014c. Science of Improvement: Testing Changes. http://www.ihi.org/resources/Pages/HowtoImprove/ScienceofImprovementSelectingChanges.aspx.

International Standards Organization. ISO 9000–Quality management. Accessed at http://www.iso.org/iso/iso_9000.

ISO Central Secretariat. 2012. Quality management principles. Accessed at http://www.iso.org/iso/qmp_2012.pdf.

iSixSigma Magazine. Jan/Feb 2008. Healing Healthcare. Accessed from http://www.isixsigma.com/industries/healthcare/5-tips-applying-six-sigma-three-top-hospitals/.

Lazarus, Ian R., and M. Wes Chapman. 2013. ISO-Style Healthcare: Designed to Keep Patients, Practitioners and Management Safe. Becker's Hospital Review. Accessed at http://www.beckershospitalreview.com/hospital-management-administration/iso-style-healthcare-designed-to-keep-patients-practitioners-and-management-safe.html.

Massoud, M.R., G. Nielsen, K. Nolan et al. 2006. A Framework for Spread: From Local Improvements to System-Wide Change. IHI Innovation Series white paper. Cambridge, MA: Institute for Healthcare Improvement. (Available on www.IHI.org.)

MBA, Ade Asefeso MCIPS. Lean Healthcare. AA Global Sourcing Ltd, 2013.

Ransom, S.B., and Ransom, E.R. 2014. Implementing quality as the core organizational strategy. In *The Healthcare Quality Book: Vision, Strategy, and Tools*, Maulik S. Joshi et al. (Eds.). Chicago, IL: Health Administration Press, 393.

Silow-Carroll, Sharon, Tanya Alteras, and Jack A. Meyer. 2007. Hospital quality improvement: Strategies and lessons from U.S. hospitals. Commonwealth Fund.

Six Sigma Online: Aveta Business Institute. 2014. The DMAIC Model in Six Sigma. Accessed at http://www.sixsigmaonline.org/six-sigma-training-certification-information/articles/the-dmaic-model-in-six-sigma.html.

Spear, Steven, and H. Kent Bowen. 1999. Decoding the DNA of the Toyota Production System. *Harvard Business Review.* Accessed at https://hbr.org/1999/09/decoding-the-dna-of-the-toyota-production-system.

The Beryl Institute. 2010. Patient Experience Case Study—NCH Healthcare. Accessed from https://theberylinstitute.site-ym.com/?page=CASE112010.

Toussaint, John S., and Leonard L. Berry. 2013. The promise of Lean in health care. *Mayo Clinic Proceedings* 88(1): 74–82.

Warren, K. 2014. Quality improvement: Foundation, processes, tools, and knowledge transfer techniques. In *The Healthcare Quality Book: Vision, Strategy, and Tools*, Maulik S. Joshi et al. (Eds.). Chicago, IL: Health Administration Press, 83–107.

Chapter 3

Spreading Improvement

Throughout the U.S. health care system there are numerous, ongoing quality improvement initiatives. These initiatives result in improved processes at the unit, department, or even facility level. New knowledge is discovered on a daily basis. However, these local improvements and best practices often remain isolated. Too often, organizations do not have mechanisms in place to effectively transfer knowledge and best practices across and between organizations.

In large, complex organizations, this ongoing challenge is referred to as "spread": the process of ensuring that improvements are made known to everyone, from senior leaders to physicians and frontline caregivers, until they become standard practice across the organization (Bristol and Joshi 2014). This chapter provides insights on how to lead spread initiatives.

Evidence

Spreading an improvement initiative within a hospital or health care system is a complex and multidimensional process, with both technical and cultural factors influencing its success.

Technical factors include those that assure the improvement is worth spreading, such as the amount and quality of clinical evidence associated with improvement. When strong evidence exists for an intervention or treatment, external pressures often drive its implementation, such as required reporting or inclusion in value-based purchasing. Another important technical factor is the relevance of the improvement to the patient population within the given unit or department. A technical factor is the number of change elements. To promote adoption, the number of change elements should be limited and as simple as possible.

Cultural factors are equally as important as technical factors in successfully promoting spread. In addition to awareness and a sense of urgency, there should be a sense of ownership for the improvement by those that are directly involved in the processes and systems associated with it. Support by organizational leadership as well as unit or department leadership is a foundational component for all improvement efforts. There must be effective communication between the improvement team and those accountable for executing the processes or systems under scrutiny. Lastly, there must be accountability for not only the design of systems, but also the behavioral choices to obtain and sustain the improvement. Once teams are involved in successful improvement efforts, the cultural components serve as a platform for other successful improvement interventions.

In the late 1990s, a team at the Institute for Healthcare Improvement was charged with the aim to "develop, test and implement a system for accelerating improvement by spreading change ideas between and within organizations." The result was the well-known and often-cited "Framework for Spread" (Massoud et al. 2006). In 2006, IHI expounded upon this framework in a white paper that has become the basis for toolkits developed by numerous researchers, government agencies including the Agency for Healthcare Research and Quality and many health care delivery organizations. The three key components of the IHI framework are preparing for spread; establishing an aim for spread; and developing, executing, and refining a spread plan.

Preparing for Spread

Despite the promising results of a new initiative, history has demonstrated that even the best innovations rarely spread organically. Accordingly, hospital leaders must devote significant resources and commitment to supporting the dissemination of "best practices" to ensure they become common practices.

A first step in preparing for spread is to assess organizational readiness, including identifying potential barriers and facilitators of spread. The Health Research & Educational Trust, an affiliate of the American Hospital Association, has developed a spread assessment tool to assess the feasibility and likelihood of widespread adoption for a given initiative. This assessment tool evaluates the initiative across four factors: environmental factors, the degree of innovation, factors related to the target audience, and organizational factors. Figure 3.1 displays the four domains and accompanying questions to assess an initiative. The assessment tool subsequently produces a spread readiness score that helps to identify initiatives with the most organizational compatibility and promise for wide-scale adoption. Insights derived from the spread assessment tool may also inform the development of the spread plan (HRET 2010).

In addition to using the HRET Spread Assessment Tool, clinical leaders should consider whether the initiative aligns with broader strategic priorities including state or national requirements for reimbursement, reporting, or performance-based incentives. If so, the organization may have greater incentives to incorporate the

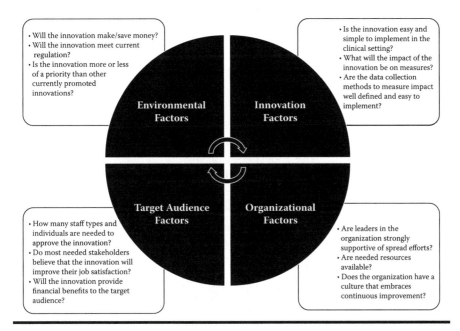

Figure 3.1   HRET spread assessment tool. (Health Research & Educational Trust, 2013.)

innovation as a strategic priority and commit resources to its spread (Erb, Joshi, and Perlin 2015).

Clinical leaders play a pivotal role in initiating a spread plan and actively facilitating its implementation (Massoud et al. 2006). First, leaders can effectively "set the agenda" by communicating that the improvement is a key strategic initiative. In some cases, it may be useful to communicae the initiative's alignment with existing incentive programs (Rogers 2010). This communication can take place in leadership and staff meetings and information can be provided on the organization's website and in publications. Leaders should also emphasize the importance of committing not only funding but also staff time to support the initiative's spread. Since this staff time will most likely be in addition to the staff's regular duties, communicating this up front will facilitate transparency (Massoud et al. 2006).

Establishing an Aim for Spread

The next step for spread is to establish an aim. The aim is essentially the "who, what, and where" of spread. The following should be addressed in order to clarify the purpose of spread efforts:

■ Target population
■ Specific desired goals

- Specific improvement processes/protocols that will be undertaken by the target population
- Quantifiable and measurable targets for spread
- Time frame of spread effort

Developing a Spread Plan

Once the aim is established, the organization must create a plan to address "how" spread will be achieved. The leadership team should develop a logical plan based on their knowledge of the organization's infrastructure and decision-making processes. For example, for nested organizations, in which one unit is directly related to other units within the centralized organizational structure, successive waves of spread among organizational units is often most effective.

Leadership should also consider whether decisions are made in a centralized, top-down manner or if decisions are largely based on consensus. This will affect the timeline of the initiative and reasonable expectations for spread efforts. Furthermore, teams should attempt to anticipate challenges and barriers in transitioning to a new system. For example, lack of staff knowledge on how to use an electronic health record would hinder progress in providing customized electronic reports during patient handoffs between nurses (IHI 2006).

Frequent and consistent communication is essential for maintaining organization-wide awareness of performance improvement initiatives. Early in the planning process for spread, a communication plan should be developed in order to update leaders and staff about the spread initiative's progress in a deliberate, organized, and systematic manner. The communication plan is the roadmap for relaying prioritized messages and information to stakeholders and ensures that communications are purposeful and ongoing, thereby promoting an environment of transparency and accountability. The communication plan can take the form of a written document and be developed by performance improvement team members, as well as staff members with marketing, communications, or public relations expertise. The plan should identify objectives of the planned communication, stakeholders that need to or should be informed, modes of communication that will be used, timing and frequency of information release, and individuals responsible for developing and disseminating the various communications. Figure 3.2 provides examples of existing communication tools, along with their intended audience, frequency of usage, and respective content developers (HRET 2014a).

In addition to the communication plan development and implementation, it is recommended to have the "how to" technical knowledge of the intervention communicated through interaction between colleagues. To start this, consider utilizing pilot unit staff or "early adopters," to communicate the "why, what, and how," along with the results and benefits of the intervention being spread (HRET 2014b).

Over the past decade, many organizations have implemented spread initiatives internally and many notable health care stakeholders have funded and supported

Communication Tool	Intended Audience	Frequency	Content Developer
Medical Staff Bulletin	Physicians	Quarterly	Medical Staff Services
General Medical Staff Meetings	Physicians	Quarterly	Chief of Staff and COO
Medical Staff Department Meetings	Physicians	Monthly	Medical Staff Services
Patient/Family Educational Materials	Patients and family members	Ongoing – in displays, waiting rooms	Patient Care Committee
Patient – Family Council	Patient and family council members	Monthly	Chairman
Nursing Newsletter	Nursing staff	Bi-monthly	CNO
Nurse "Huddles"	Nursing staff	Change of shift	CNO
Department Leadership Meetings	Hospital leadership (VPs, Directors, Managers)	Monthly	COO
Medical Center Newsletter	Employees	Monthly	Communications Department
Intranet Bulletin Board	Physicians Employees	Continuous	HR and COO
Staff Meetings	Department employees	Variable	Department Director
Organization Website	Community, Employees, Physicians	Continuous	PR Department
Community Newspaper	Community	Daily	PR Department – press releases
Board Meetings	Board members	Monthly	CEO, COO
Poster Displays/Easels	All	Ongoing – in entry and waiting rooms	PR Department (submit request)

Figure 3.2 Examples of existing communication tools. (Health Research & Educational Trust and Cynosure Health. 2014b. Implementation Guide Part II: Advanced Topics., 2014.)

initiatives to spread best practices within and across states. One emblematic example is the AHRQ-funded initiative to eliminate central line-associated bloodstream infections, the Comprehensive Unit-based Safety Program. The project began with the Intensive Unit Safety Reporting System, developed by the Johns Hopkins University Quality and Safety Group. Given its initial success, *CUSP* was subsequently adapted and implemented in more than 100 ICUs in Michigan. This statewide safety initiative to prevent CLABSI was known as the Keystone Project. In 3 months, the intervention achieved a 66% reduction in CLABSI rates across the participating units (Pronovost et al. 2006).

Because of this statewide success, AHRQ funded *CUSP*: Stop BSI efforts to spread the interventions on a national scale. To date, the over 1000 hospitals participating in *CUSP* have documented a 40% reduction in CLABSI. This translates to an estimated prevention of over 2000 infections, 500 mortalities, and a cost avoidance of over $34 million in health-care expenditures (Sawyer et al. 2010).

CUSP: Stop CLABSI combined both technical and cultural knowledge to facilitate change. The approach includes recommendations related to using a catheter-insertion bundle and other evidence-based interventions to prevent infection, all while focusing on improving communication and safety culture. The approach has had widespread success in reducing health care-associated infections while improving safety culture because of its adaptability and focus on crosscutting strategies to eliminate harm.

Effective Strategies for Executing and Monitoring Spread

Given the success of initiatives such as on the *CUSP*: Stop BSI, the following are recommended as best practices for facilitating spread.

1. **Obtain clear and demonstrated support from senior leadership.** For spread initiatives to be successful, the organization's leadership must be willing to commit to aligning the initiative with organizational strategic priorities, supporting the effort by removing organizational and system barriers, and supplying the required resources. Leaders must buy in and be committed to the initiative and understand how it relates to other organizational priorities. Without a clear link to high-level goals, it is likely the initiative will be abandoned when new priorities arise.

2. **Carefully select units for spread and designate a "spread organizer."** Identify clusters of units with similar needs, processes, or priorities. These can form a first group for spread where the initial intervention will be most applicable. It is also important to identify both official and unofficial leaders within those units who will be allies and champions for the initiative.

3. **Don't start with a resistor or in a chaotic unit.** In the initial stages, it is best to begin with advocates and units that are willing to adopt the change, rather than those units that may have the greatest need but may also be the most resistant. Once the initiative gains momentum, data, and evidence that

demonstrates its success, it will be easier to convince the more resistant units to change.

4. **Designate nurse champions to promote innovations and spread improvements**. Just as it is important to engage physician champions in order to work effectively with physicians, it is also important to find nurse champions. As day-to-day caregivers, nurses have a first-hand understanding of patient needs. They are in a good position to tailor spread efforts based on the existing infrastructure and processes of a unit.

5. **Involve physicians.** Given their inherently high standards, natural propensity for competition, and eye for detail, physicians are important and effective team members for spreading improvement within and across departments. As in all clinical improvement initiatives, clinicians should be involved in all stages of spread to ensure their crucial engagement and support.

6. **Build consensus among staff by showing your data.** As the initiative spreads to additional units, the amount of data, evidence, and momentum for it will build. This enables the spread team to begin approaching people within units that are more ambivalent about the spread effort. Data is a powerful motivator for change.

7. **Ensure ongoing communications.** Designated spread organizers can be important points-of-contact to facilitate mutual exchange of information. More widely, however, the employees throughout the organization should be kept abreast of the progress of the spread initiative. Frequent communication to all stakeholder groups is imperative for success, and improvements in quality, safety, and efficiency should be recognized and celebrated. Recognizing these success stories helps keep staff engaged and motivated.

Case Study: On the CUSP

Barb Edson is the Vice President of Clinical Quality at Health Research & Educational Trust and currently directs the AHRQ-funded *On the CUSP: Stop CAUTI* project, a national initiative to eliminate catheter-associated urinary tract infections. She has held many positions throughout her career in health care, including pediatric nurse and improvement leader. Before joining HRET, Barb led the statewide spread initiative *On the CUSP: Stop BSI*, along with other patient safety collaboratives, as part of the North Carolina Center for Hospital Quality and Patient Safety (On the *CUSP* 2014). The following interview describes experiences from her previous leadership role in achieving spread through the statewide implementation of the AHRQ-funded *On the CUSP: Stop BSI* project as well as other patient safety initiatives.

Q: **What was your approach for assessing readiness for spread?**
A: Observing trends provides a quantitative perspective of an organization's readiness, while survey tools and culture assessments provide an in-depth

qualitative perspective of organizational readiness. To assess specific units' readiness for spread, utilizing bloodstream infection rates and a tool to identify common barriers for improvement help identify greatest need and willingness for spread, respectively.

For hospital/unit data trends, publicly reported data can be used to assess and compare rates with other hospitals/units. For the national *CUSP* project, we deployed a readiness survey that specifically gauged hospitals' technical level of preparedness in avoiding BSI. For instance, the survey asked whether a department implemented a cart to keep line supplies in or whether they used chlorhexidine to clean the site. However, the readiness assessment did not include questions on culture aspects such as whether the cart was used, and if not, why? Were staff members explicitly assigned and held accountable for maintaining the cart? These elements of culture turned out to be very important in a unit's readiness to implement the initiative.

Assessing the culture of an organization can be as powerful as it is challenging. We know that various levels of an organization have different perspectives on culture and safety. For example, senior leaders may view safety more positively than those who are delivering care. We also know that culture can be vastly different from one unit to another within an organization. For these reasons, assessing culture can be very challenging.

In our *On the CUSP: Stop CAUTI* work, the faculty at the University of Michigan developed the CAUTI Guide to Patient Safety Tool through qualitative interviews with over 400 individuals in 43 hospitals. The tool asks questions about important key success factors, such as champions, resistance, and leadership support.

Q: As a clinical leader, what leadership strategies and tools would you advise others to leverage in order to achieve spread?

A: Start small and seek out opportunities while avoiding initial resistors. Next, identify leaders that can be your point-of-contact within units. Utilize coaching skills to assist the team with improvements. Lastly, be vigilant and continuously monitor the progress of spread.

First, analyze your order of spread. Always start very small and look at similar units. In regards to seeking out opportunities, it is sometimes not necessarily better to start with the problem but with an advocate. The first person I would approach was somebody who *wanted* to work with me and champion the efforts. That was more important than going first to departments that clearly had opportunities for improvement. In the beginning, it is also important to not start in a chaotic unit, such as the emergency department, where there are too many unknowns and too many variables.

Personally, I had a difficult time starting the spread work, so I identified someone who could lead from a direct provider perspective (i.e., an unofficial leader). I talked with staff to figure out who the good leaders were. The best way to figure this out is to find out who staff go to when there is a clinical challenge. In other words, whose opinion do they seek? Keep in mind, this leader may be a charge nurse, bedside nurse, or doctor. Regardless of the role, interpersonal and communication skills are key. They don't have to be in official leadership roles as long as they possess the characteristics of a leader and are able to mentor the team members.

After identifying a leader, forming an effective team is crucially important in order to achieve spread. The team should include people involved in every phase of the project. They should also have the characteristics and attributes of high performing teams, which include clear roles, a shared vision, strong leadership and a sense of trust, the ability to communicate, provide regular feedback, and create ways to work together.

Regarding monitoring the spread process, I refer to the data in the units where the process was spread. If the data is showing trends that are within the control limits that were set, then we transition to a monitoring plan. The plan delineates who will monitor the data, how often it will be monitored, the control limits, and what actions will be taken if the data is no longer within the control limits. In spread, monitoring for process variation is a key success factor. There will be many times when a process may need to be varied slightly because the unit that the process was spread to was different in some way.

Q: **What are some important characteristics/functions of an intervention bundle that facilitate the success of its spread?**

A: Integrating technical aims with cultural aims, along with effectively telling the story of "why" these aims are important. Limiting the number of change elements and making them as concise and simplistic as possible. These functions will assist the staff in adoption and facilitate spread.

The *On the CUSP: Stop BSI* project had two aims. The cultural component was to improve safety culture. The technical component was to reduce the infection rate to less than 1 infection per 1000 line days. Although many units achieved zero, we were emphasizing the importance of improvement rather than perfection.

In providing a case on why the intervention is important, showing data and rates is not enough. This requires changing the norm, showing evidence, and talking about the "why." This involves stories that make personal connections, such as who has been adversely harmed due to the current state of operations. Additionally, it involves demonstrating that improvement and successes are attainable and that patient harm is not inevitable.

Q: **Can you describe a time you faced opposition from another clinical leader and were able to persuade them through data?**

A: Even after going through all the steps outlined above, you will typically find someone who doesn't want to do the intervention. This is where use of coaching, monitoring, and meaningful influence is important.

> For example, while working to spread the Surgical Care Improvement Project measures, I was collaborating with a quality improvement professional that was unable to get a department of surgery chair on board with implementation. In response, she first sought the support and participation from other department chairs. She was able to recruit a general surgeon as an advocate, who then piloted the measures, shared evidence, and tweaked and refined them. This took place over a 6- to 8-month timeline. After more sub-specialty surgeons piloted the intervention and built consensus across the organization, it became evident that the department chair, who was in opposition to the SCIP measures, was out of compliance. The data finally convinced him of the need to improve, especially in comparison to his peers. He reached out to the quality improvement professional to seek assistance to implement the measures.
>
> This situation underscores the importance of involving physicians in the process. Personal high standards, paired with natural competition in their environment that facilitates social motivation, work in combination to influence clinicians to implement these interventions to see true results.

Q: **What are roles of leadership and staff in transitioning spread efforts into routine operational responsibilities?**

A: Time and time again, people try to implement through a top-down approach, but this is not often effective. The better method is a top-down framework and bottom-up implementation. Specifically, the hospital leader should support the intervention, through organizational alignment, removal of system barriers, and resource support. However, the direct care providers are very important players on the team. After the intervention is proposed, these leaders drive the improvement work. Nurses, pharmacists, and other clinical staff who are involved in the daily clinical work have the most opportunities to test and modify the intervention until it effectively works within a given setting.

From a leadership standpoint, involve successful people who do the day-to-day clinical work and encourage them lead and support the spread efforts. A team of committed nurses would be a more effective implementation team than individuals in leadership positions who were removed from patient care. A leader can contribute by listening to his or her staff, aligning the organizational priorities, and removing the organizational barriers.

Lessons Learned

Regardless of the quality improvement challenge at hand, from reducing hospital-acquired infections to preventing patient falls, spreading and sustaining improvement is a major challenge. The following are important to address, as they are often poorly addressed before, during, and after the implementation of an intervention (Pronovost et al. 2006):

- **Convincing people that there is a problem.** It is often difficult to convince clinical teams to change if they do not perceive there to be a problem. Important challenges for spread teams are to (1) demonstrate the need for improvement and (2) demonstrate why this particular problem should take priority over other pressing challenges. Possible strategies include using data, using patient stories to emotionally engage the team, prompting clinicians to define what they want to improve, and showing that there is a "relative advantage" in implementing the intervention.
- **Convincing people that the chosen solution is the right one**. More often than not, an improvement intervention will be "essentially contested." That is, even if everyone agreed on the need for good quality, there will likely be disagreement on what defines "good quality" and how to achieve it. Lack of sufficient or consistent evidence for an intervention may lead to resistance from clinicians and other staff. Therefore, it is essential to ensure acceptability by hosting facilitated discussion forums to explore, discuss, and debate the evidence. A "program theory" may provide a helpful framework in which improvement efforts are broken down into actionable activities and the spread team demonstrates causal links between these activities and desired outcomes. This theory will clarify why an intervention is likely to work and better define the focus and strategic direction of the initiative.
- **Excess ambitions and "projectness."** Conversely, it is also common for an improvement initiative to be met with a high and potentially unsustainable level of enthusiasm. This may lead to a subsequent exhaustion of available resources. The scale of resources required to support improvement initiatives is often underestimated, which can quickly cause difficulties in improvement

efforts, especially if the lack of the resources is not diagnosed in a timely manner. Therefore, careful assessment of resources should be conducted at the outset of the project.

Additionally, metrics and measurable objectives should be developed for the post-implementation period and routinely monitored to track progress and identify areas for future development and refinement. This will provide continuous feedback necessary for reevaluation. To continue the momentum of an initiative, organizers should emphasize that the initiative will evolve over time. Otherwise, if an initiative successfully spreads, it may become so standardized that continuous improvement may encounter the barrier of stagnation. In continuous improvement, learning and advancement of new knowledge is not a one-time event, but a culture and ongoing process of continuous improvement (Bristol and Joshi 2014).

Action Steps

The clinical leader should take the following steps in order to achieve spread (Sawyer et al. 2010):

1. **Find opinion leaders and champions.** These individuals can include not only nurses and physicians, but also nurse assistants, pharmacists, non-clinical staff members, and any other stakeholders in the process. Begin identifying champions through discussions with staff on who they look to for advice and expertise. Once identified, assess whether these potential leaders would be willing to advocate for and commit to spread efforts.
2. **Consider the implementation/dissemination model.** Leaders should determine how best to reach and engage the target population for spread efforts. This should include considerations of the hospital's structure, whether infrastructure enhancements could accelerate the adoption of improvements, transition issues and knowledge gaps, and standard operational processes. Then, the leader can adopt an appropriate model that will accommodate all of these aspects.
3. **Use data to demonstrate the effectiveness of the implemented practice.** Data shows whether the intervention is effectively achieving its technical aim. If the intervention is working, it also provides a powerful catalyst for other units to achieve the same improvements.
4. **Use stories to engage other leaders and explain the "why" for spread.** In combination with data, which provides the rationale for spreading an intervention, leaders will be compelled by the human aspect of the intervention's potential impact. Understanding that the intervention could save the life of a relative or friend, or substantially improve their quality of life, will further motivate them to get on board.

5. **Track spread adoption though data.** Measurement is an important part of tracking improvement. Two different kinds of measures that should be used are measures that demonstrate the extent of spread, as well as the outcome of the implemented changes. Furthermore, the rate of spread should be monitored. Self-reporting to a designated data coordinator is a feasible way of collecting and managing data (IHI 2006).

References

Bristol, S., and M.S. Joshi. 2014. Transforming the healthcare system for improved quality. In *The Healthcare Quality Book: Vision, Strategy, and Tools,* Maulik S. Joshi et al. (Eds.). Chicago, IL: Health Administration Press, 541.

Erb, Natalie D., Maulik Joshi, and Jonathan Perlin. Faster by a Power of Ten: A PLAN for accelerating national improvement. *American Journal of Managed Care.* March 2015.

Health Research & Educational Trust and Cynosure Health. 2014a. Implementation Guide Part I: A How-To Guide for Improvement for the AHA/HRET HEN Partnership for Patients.

Health Research & Educational Trust and Cynosure Health. 2014b. Implementation Guide Part II: Advanced Topics.

Health Research & Educational Trust. 2010. HRET Spread Assessment Tool. http://www.hret.org/dissemination/projects/hret_spread_assessment_tool.shtml.

Institute for Healthcare Improvement. 2014. Improvement Standards: Shifting to a Higher Standard. http://www.ihi.org/resources/Pages/ImprovementStories/ShiftingtoaHigherStandard.aspx.

Interview with Barbara Edson, October 31, 2014. Leadership and Spreading Improvement on *On the CUSP*: Stop BSI Project.

Massoud, M.R., G.A. Nielsen, K. Nolan, M.W. Schall, and C. Sevin. 2006. A Framework for Spread: From Local Improvements to System-Wide Change. IHI Innovation Series white paper. Cambridge, MA: Institute for Healthcare Improvement. (www.IHI.org.)

On the CUSP: Stop HAI. About: Barbara S. Edson. http://www.onthecuspstophai.org/about-us/key-personnel/barb-edson-rn-mba-mha/.

Pronovost, Peter, Dale Needham, Sean Berenholtz, David Sinopoli, Haitao Chu, Sara Cosgrove, Bryan Sexton et al. 2006. An intervention to decrease catheter-related bloodstream infections in the ICU. *New England Journal of Medicine* 355(26): 2725–2732.

Rogers, Everett M. 2010. *Diffusion of innovations.* Simon and Schuster.

Sawyer, Melinda, Kristina Weeks, Christine A. Goeschel, David A. Thompson, Sean M. Berenholtz, Jill A. Marsteller, Lisa H. Lubomski et al. 2010. Using evidence, rigorous measurement, and collaboration to eliminate central catheter-associated bloodstream infections. *Critical Care Medicine* 38: S292–S298.

Chapter 4

Physician Champions

The transition to valued-based care will require a transformation of the underlying model of clinical care delivery, including changes to the scope of physicians' clinical practice and behavior. Achieving and sustaining these necessary changes requires a skilled physician champion who can effectively influence his or her physician peers. This chapter explores the context and need for physician champions, their role in important initiatives, selection criteria, and responsibilities as a member of a clinical change team.

The Evidence

"Were any physicians involved?"

This is a question that every health care leader has likely heard at least once during his or her career and it is a question with a lot of weight and implicit commentary. It is a statement that not only asks about the participation of a physician, but of the right kind of physician. The inquirer is not asking if a physician in administration was involved; he or she is asking if a currently practicing peer or clinical colleague participated in the design and implementation of the improvement initiative.

Another way to pose the question is: "Was there a physician champion involved?"

The restatement shows that even physicians themselves recognize the importance of a specific physician in transformation activities. Physician champions are critical in facilitating improvement, due to the history of a physician culture that promotes professional autonomy and independence. This acculturation begins in medical school and is reinforced during training and practice. These elements of typical physician culture can make improvement initiatives that involve physicians very difficult.

Given these cultural challenges, change agents need several tools to influence physician behavior including strong evidence base from scientific literature, performance metrics at the group and individual physician levels and, perhaps most importantly, peer pressure and influence.

The key tactic in the strategy of peer influence is the engagement and development of a physician champion. Although a non-physician can provide the evidence and performance data, the receptivity of the message is heightened when it comes from a respected clinical peer. The role of a physician champion includes:

1. **Communication.** Messaging is at the core of a physician champion's role. Communication includes effective dialog with peers one-on-one and in small group settings. It also includes the ability to communicate in large forums and in settings that are more formal.
2. **Advocacy.** The physician champion should voice his or her individual perspective, and also advocate for the consensus among clinical peers, particularly in regard to clinical matters. In some cases, the physician champion may be the only clinical representative on an improvement team.
3. **Role model.** A physician champion should be in the vanguard with respect to the adoption and the active promotion of new processes and new work flows. He or she should be an active role model whose visibility and communication about an initiative engenders a sense of trust and willingness to change among other physicians.
4. **Translator.** A physician champion serves as the bridge between an initiative and the physicians. The champion must effectively translate the need and basis for the initiative, the individual tactics that are required, and the relevant performance data into a format that is easily received and understood by physicians. This role of translator also extends between physicians and administration. The physician champion must be able to articulate clinical concepts to non-clinicians and similarly may need to translate administrative and business imperatives to clinicians.

It is important to understand a physician champion's role in order to identify and select the right individual. A physician champion is a key opinion leader who is able to influence the behavior and practice of his or her physician colleagues. This does not necessarily require the physician to hold a formal title within an organization. Often, informal leaders without a designated institutional role can be the most effective champions for change. These champions are often widely admired and respected by their colleagues. They are individuals to whom peers turn for counsel and guidance. Use this as an informal gut check of a potential physician champion candidate—it is the physician that others tend to congregate around in the floors, units, and medical staff lounge. It is the physician that other physicians may want to care for them.

This quick visual of physician congregation or an informal dialogue with physicians about who they respect should help to readily identify potential candidates for a physician champion. Going deeper, the search for a physician champion should look for a few additional key characteristics:

1. Enthusiasm and passion for the change initiative
2. Advocacy of patient-centered care and outcome-based care
3. Coachable and responsive to feedback
4. Strong communication skills in group and individual settings
5. A willingness to grow, develop, and mature as a leader

Once a physician champion candidate has been identified, the next step is to convince him or her to provide time and leadership, sometimes uncompensated, toward a clinical change project. It is important to connect to the candidate's "why" in order to identify the underlying passion and drive for the work he or she does. It is important to encourage the proposed champion to talk about his or her interests and concerns at both a personal and professional level. Active listening on behalf of the recruiter is important to accurately gauge potential interest and secure the candidate's engagement. This also forms the basis in subsequent conversations to illustrate the intersection between the champion's "why" and the motivation for the change improvement program.

Active listening and connecting to underlying motivation to identify a potential champion are also motivational tools that the champion will use in his or her role. Tactics to influence behavior include:

1. **Active listening.** There may be an inherent bias by physicians to offer opinions and make decisions quickly and instinctively. The tendency arises from the model of clinical practice wherein a problem is presented in the form of a patient and a course of action must be prescribed quickly. This clinical framework can be adapted, however, and can alternatively be used to reinforce the notion of actively listening and understanding before making a decision. Active listening to clinical peers' concerns and comments is an important step toward promoting engagement and building relationships that ultimately lead to more critical conversations around changing behavior. A dialog between a champion and an individual physician is not possible without this fundamental step of active listening.
2. **Connect to a physician's "why."** In the book *The Happiness Hypothesis*, author Jonathan Haidt articulates the need to appeal to both the emotional and rational sides of the brain to motivate change (Haidt 2006). For the physician champion, the emotional side involves connecting to some of the underlying intrinsic passion of a physician. This can be referred to as a physician's "why" or primary emotive motivation for her actions. This "why" is often connected to promoting the patient's best interest. It is important

for a physician champion to identify this "why" in his or her colleagues and establish a link between this emotional motivation and the change initiative at hand.

3. **Employing anecdotes and stories.** Stories and anecdotes are a powerful way to create a memorable basis for change. Narrative and storytelling are intrinsic within humans (Taleb 2010). These strategies are a key basis for socialization and are essential for the interpretation and distillation of complex information. Stories are a familiar format for the receipt, understanding, and internalization of information. A physician champion should leverage stories in the form of cases of individual patients or personal experiences to engender a familiar and enduring basis for change.

4. **Invoking evidence-based information.** The physician champion should have a ready base of literature and external evidence to support the need for a change. Although some of this evidence base may be strictly clinical, some of it may also be in the realm of health services research, including evidence related to organizational behavior, behavioral economics, incentives, and health care financing. In cases where published literature is scant or unavailable, it is helpful to obtain best practice information from external institutions. Qualitative benchmarking of practice against peers or best-in-class institutions can be an equally powerful substitute for peer-reviewed literature.

5. **Utilizing objective, personalized performance data.** In order to appeal to rational motivation for change, physician champions should utilize data and performance metrics. These measures can be process-oriented or outcome-oriented, aggregated at the level of the hospital or unit, or presented at the individual patient or physician level. Presenting individual physician-level data can be a powerful motivator for change. It is recommended to initially use blinded comparative data, except for in the review of an individual physician's performance. Each physician should receive his or her own unblinded data. For an underperforming physician, a typical reaction includes denial, questioning, and dismissing the accuracy of the data and metrics. With validation and time, however, this resistance should gradually give way to acceptance and an increased intrinsic motivation for individual behavior transformation.

Case Study

The following case study illustrates the application of these concepts around the physician champion role, responsibilities, and motivational tools in performance improvement.

At General Hospital, the leadership team has recently received nationally benchmarked data on length of stay in the intensive care unit. This risk-adjusted data indicates significant opportunity for improvement, prompting a decision to begin a quality improvement initiative dedicated to reducing ICU length of stay. The initiative will be led by the vice president of quality and safety.

This vice president has previously recognized the importance of physician practice and behavior change in improvement work. Accordingly, she begins a search for a physician champion. The vice president recognizes that there are several critical care groups practicing at their hospital and decides to identify at least two champions to balance the mix of practice and potential diversity of opinion.

As a first step, this vice president turns to several physician opinion leaders for guidance. These are individuals with informal leadership roles whose confidence and relationship the vice president has nurtured for several years. This informal "physician cabinet" results in the names of at least four critical care physicians who are well-respected members of the medical staff and have a passion for quality improvement and patient advocacy.

In conversation with the first physician champion candidate, the vice president begins a dialog around some of the physicians' concerns and areas of frustration from a quality and safety perspective related to critical care patients. The vice president spends most of the time actively listening, seeking to understand the physician perspective, and takes notes for future reference. The vice president concludes the brief conversation by saying she would like to process some of this feedback and follow up to see if the conversation might have a connection to some work under consideration for reducing ICU length of stay.

In a follow-up conversation with the physician, the vice president processes the initial physician feedback and explicitly connects it with the proposed project on ICU length of stay. The vice president shares a story of a recent patient that illustrates some of the opportunities for improvement and is purposeful in connecting the dialog to the physician's intrinsic motivation to provide high quality of care. The vice president closes with an offer to the physician to leverage his passion and knowledge as a physician champion for the length of stay transformation. The physician indicates that he is interested and would like additional details.

In their final conversation, the vice president follows up to ensure the candidate has an explicit understanding of the requirements for a physician champion. She emphasizes the key roles around advocacy, communicating with physicians in informal and group settings, role modeling, and serving as a bridge and translator between administration and practicing physicians. They also discuss key characteristics of a physician champion. The vice president assesses the candidate's enthusiasm for the work, responsiveness to coaching, capacity for growth, and communication and speaking abilities. In addition, information is provided to the candidate regarding the time commitment, potential schedule of meetings, and duration of the work.

After selecting and identifying the physician champions, the improvement project formally begins. During the project, the project leader encourages the physician champions to informally dialog with their peers and other clinical colleagues about the work. The champions also provide routine updates at the critical care department meeting to ensure transparency of the work and to solicit feedback from physician stakeholders. The physician champions provide stories and individual cases that illustrate defects in the care process and supply recently published literature and evidence reviews related to the process in question. Throughout the development process, the champions are encouraged to actively listen to feedback and are provided coaching on this technique from the vice president of medical affairs.

Once the review of results from an initial pilot is complete, the project group identifies individual physicians who are not following the new protocol and require individual coaching. The physician champions embrace the role and arrange for a series of informal "cup of coffee" talks in the medical staff lounge. The champions, who have been receiving coaching and guidance throughout the process, use a variety of motivational change techniques to connect and influence their colleagues, especially through using blinded comparison data on performance and evidence-based literature, and through connecting to the physicians' intrinsic passion for patient-centered care. Critical care physician peers provide additional reinforcement for the change. The champions themselves are also diligent about being visible in the ICU and role modeling the expected changes in practice before nurses, house staff, and their colleagues. All of these motivational tools are employed over a series of months, with a continuation of informal physician conversations. After a few months, the initiative is able to identify a sustained impact on the ICU length of stay. The project team continues to monitor the results, track and trend data, and meet on a less frequent basis to ensure sustainment of results.

Lessons Learned

Across many industries, including health care, many change initiatives fail. This is anticipated and inevitable. Professor John Kotter has identified reasons for failure and the corresponding eight success factors for change (Kotter 2007). One of the essential elements is the notion of forming a powerful guiding coalition. Within health care transformation activities, a component of this coalition formation is the selection of an effective physician champion. A physician champion who can articulate the reasons for change and can influence peer behavior is effectively mandatory in any change that will impact clinical care. The physician champion is often the core of the guiding coalition.

The importance of the physician champion in clinical process improvement has been increasingly recognized in the past several years. This is especially true with respect to the implementation of electronic medical records and computerized physician order entry. Both of these technology initiatives have a direct, and in many cases irreversible impact upon physician work flow and practice. As a result, the role of a physician champion is now almost universally recognized as essential for EMR and CPOE success (Poon, Blumenthal, and Jaggi 2004). This experience with health care information technology and the critical importance of the physician champion can be applied to almost all health care change initiatives that require broad physician stakeholder support and engagement. The selection of a physician champion is now a "must" when contemplating an agenda of health care transformation.

Action Steps and Strategies to Lead

1. **Identify key stakeholders to constitute a guiding coalition.** One of the first steps in working through a change is identifying key stakeholders to constitute a guiding coalition. In a clinical transformation, physicians are an essential constituency to be acknowledged and influenced. The physician champion is a bridge role between the change team and the broader medical staff to enact and sustain any process improvement.

2. **Seek guidance and counsel from other physicians.** In identifying and recruiting a physician champion, seek out the guidance and counsel from other physicians. Ask colleagues to whom they turn for advice and whose opinion is widely regarded. In assessing potential candidates, ensure they are not simply key opinion leaders, but individuals who have strong communication skills, a passion for patient-centered care, and an inherent willingness and ability to grow and develop.

3. **Actively guide and assist the physician champion.** Once you have identified a physician champion for your team, it is a leader's responsibility to actively guide and assist the physician champion. As a leader, you should demonstrate the behaviors of change for the physician champion to emulate. This role modeling should include active listening, connecting to the "why," utilizing storytelling, and relying on evidence-based data. These are not just tools in the physician champion repertoire; they are essential levers for any successful clinical leader.

The physician champion is ultimately an extension of the prowess and impact of an organization's senior clinical leadership. As such, the selection and development of the physician champion should be done with prudence and deliberate, active coaching. This will ensure that the physician champion will measure up to the opportunity and potential of the role.

References

Haidt, J. 2006. *The Happiness Hypothesis*. Philadelphia: Basic Books.
Kotter, J. 2007. Leading Change: Why Transformation Efforts Fail. *Harvard Business Review*.

Poon, E.G., D. Blumenthal, and T. Jaggi. 2004. Overcoming barriers to adopting and implementing computerized physician order entry systems in U.S. Hospitals. *Health Affairs* 184–190.

Taleb, N.N. 2010. *The Black Swan: The Impact of the Highly Improbable*, 2nd ed. New York: Random House.

Chapter 5

Building a Culture of Safety

Over the past two decades, health care organizations have focused intensely on patient safety. Goals to eliminate preventable deaths and keep patients free from harm are now commonplace. Although early efforts at increasing patient safety largely focused on clinical processes and improvements at the bedside, it is now recognized that these isolated, front line tactics cannot succeed without commitment to an organizational culture of safety. Building a culture of safety is a prerequisite for high reliability performance, the ideal operating environment for health care organizations. This chapter explores the concept of a culture of safety including key components of the culture, methods to measure culture, and actionable leadership steps for culture change.

The Evidence

Schein defines culture as "a pattern of shared basic assumptions...which has worked well enough to be considered valid and therefore to be taught to new members as the correct way to perceive, think and feel" (Schein 2010). Culture is often manifest by the behaviors of the organization's members, especially leadership. Culture is also understood through unspoken norms and dynamics such as commonly held values and norms. Often, these representations are in fact the more powerful elements of an organization's culture.

The importance of culture is aptly summarized in a quote attributed to management guru Peter Drucker: "Culture eats strategy for lunch." In other words, strategy and the accompanying tactics, work plans, and projects will never succeed in an organization with an incompatible culture. To translate to health care, all of the improvement work with front-line caregivers and providers, such as checklists, decision alerts, and care process redesign, will never succeed in an organization with a culture that does not value safety, reliable system design, and a non-punitive response to human error.

This notion of a non-punitive response to error is considered a foundational element for a culture of safety. Dr. Lucian Leape, regarded as one of the founders of the modern patient safety movement, has stated, "The single greatest impediment to error prevention in medicine is that we punish people for making mistakes." The Institute of Medicine expounds on this concept in the report *Crossing the Quality Chasm*:

> The biggest challenge to moving toward a safer health system is chang-
> ing the culture from one of blaming individuals for errors to one in
> which errors are treated not as personal failure, but as opportunities to
> improve the system and prevent harm.

Both quotes allude to the historical environment in health care organizations where the response to a safety event is to blame specific individuals for the occurrence of the event. Often this blame is accompanied by disciplinary action, punishment, or even termination.

In the short term, this may seem like an effective approach to punish "bad apples" and prevent an event from reoccurring. In reality, this approach is ultimately both unsatisfying and unhelpful. A model of blame and punishment fails to include an examination of the underlying system issues that contributed to an event. As a result, it is a poor prevention strategy. This model also fails to recognize the inherent fallibility of people and that perfection in human performance is an unrealistic expectation. In the absence of a perfectly designed system, human error is a realistic and common occurrence (Marx 2009).

This "names and blames" approach is contrasted with another extreme: no personal accountability for the occurrence of a safety event. Similar to the first approach, a blame-free culture also does not yield meaningful and lasting safety improvements. It does not acknowledge the role of risky or reckless individual human behavior and the contributory impact on safety events. In a culture of safety, there is still an assessment of individual behavior and accountability.

In an organization with a non-punitive response to error, the approach is a balance between the two extremes of individual blame and blame-free responses to error. This is often articulated as the notion of a "just culture" that strikes a balance between total blame and no accountability in the evaluation of individual culpability in safety events. This deliberate approach to establishing individual culpability is a cornerstone of a safety culture.

James Reason is considered a founding thought leader of rigorous, human factors-based approaches to culpability management. His seminal work, *Managing the*

Risks of Organizational Accidents, provides one of the first culpability decision trees developed to assess the role of individual behavior in safety events. According to James Reason:

> Just culture creates an atmosphere of trust in which people are encouraged to provide, and even rewarded for providing, essential safety-related information but in which they are clear about where the line must be drawn between acceptable and unacceptable behavior (1997).

His work was initially used in the nuclear power industry to establish the culpability of individual actions in untoward events. This industry work provides much of the intellectual underpinnings and implementation lessons for the just culture approach within health care (Hobbs 2008).

In the time since Reason's initial publication, his work has been modified and expanded upon in a variety of proprietary and non-proprietary frameworks across many industries. Although the finer points and details may vary in different decision trees, there are common themes across all variations. As Marx has articulated, these frameworks prescribe an approach to culpability that is based on the intention or motivation of the individual's behavior. Marx states that human error should be met with consolation, at-risk behavior should be met with coaching, and reckless behavior should be met with punishment. The behavior should always be met with the same response, regardless of the outcome of the error (Marx 2009).

The just culture is one of the key components of a culture of safety. Other elements include:

■ **Recognition of safety as a fundamental organization value.** For an organization to achieve a culture of safety, safety must be recognized as a core organizational value that is communicated and emphasized on a frequent and visible basis by the most senior leaders. Safety must be recognized as the foremost organizational concern and a value injected into decision-making from the front line to senior management. Paul O'Neill, former CEO of Alcoa, best recognized this primacy of safety within his organization by requiring personal notification of an employee accident within 24 hours of occurrence (Spear 2009). This set the tone within the organization regarding the importance and urgency of workplace safety. Leaders play a pivotal role in shaping their organizational culture and in establishing a culture of safety.

■ **Encouragement and rewards for reporting safety events.** There may be a natural tendency for staff and leaders to hide safety events due to fear of repercussions. This reluctance may be even greater with regard to reporting "near miss" safety events that had the potential to cause patient harm. In an organization with a culture of safety, these tendencies of reluctance to report should be actively discouraged and reversed. The hospital or health system must embody the characteristics of a learning organization and collect data and investigate all classes of safety events, including near misses. In order for this to be successful, there must be a concerted and deliberate effort to promote safety event reporting. The culture must acknowledge and reward the value of reporting, especially self-reporting, of safety events and near misses. One way leaders can promote this is to shift the language to reward and celebrate "good catches" as opposed to "near misses." Leaders should celebrate the important role of humans in recognizing and recovering from potential safety hazards.

◾ **Establishment of a just culture and decision-making algorithm for assessing individual culpability in safety events.** In tandem with the encouragement of event reporting, organizations should have a formal process for establishing individual culpability in the context of safety events. This process should be non-punitive, recognize the occurrence of human error, and establish increasing levels of accountability depending on the motivation and recklessness of the behavior. Such algorithms typically acknowledge the organization's contributory role in providing the correct policies, procedures, training, and work environment for staff to successfully carry out their duties. Though the presumption is often that these culpability algorithms and response processes are within the domain of the organization's safety team, they are in fact most appropriate for oversight and implementation within the human resources function and for use by operational leadership. A common mistake within hospitals and health systems is for a just culture approach/algorithm to be a safety function as opposed to a human resources initiative and organization-wide competency.

Transparency around Safety Events

At an organizational level, there may be a tendency to avoid discussion of adverse events. This reticence among leadership to engage in candid dialog with staff about safety events discourages event reporting and inhibits collective organizational learning. A safety culture requires conversation and learning from safety events. Transparency should be appropriate, ensure patient confidentiality, and not unduly expose the organization to risk. Within these guardrails, it is possible to engender candor about an organization's failings and, most importantly, to collect and disseminate the lessons learned to prevent future safety events.

These domains of safety culture can be measured using survey tools. This assessment of an organization's safety culture can serve several purposes:

1. Provide a thorough assessment of the current state of safety culture with the capability to drill down to identify concerns in specific work areas
2. Benchmark performance against other organizations
3. Encourage leadership attention and the design of interventions to improve safety culture

4. Assess intervention and leadership impact on safety culture
5. Track and trend changes in organizational culture over time

A variety of survey instruments exist for safety culture assessment (Health Foundation 2011). Two of the most popular are the Agency for Healthcare Research and Quality surveys on patient safety culture and the Safety Attitudes Questionnaire.

AHRQ Surveys on Patient Safety Culture

AHRQ provides four surveys on patient safety culture tailored to hospitals, medical offices, nursing homes, and community pharmacies. The surveys can be used to measure the culture of safety across the spectrum from the individual, work unit, and organization. This allows for the assessment of micro-cultures within an organization either by work unit or employee role (e.g., staff vs. leadership; employed medical staff vs. nursing).

The hospital survey measures 12 key organization domains (Table 5.1). and the medical group survey examines 11 domains (Table 5.2).

The survey tools, particularly the hospital survey, have been well validated and are widely used throughout the U.S., allowing for benchmarking and comparison with other organizations. Another advantage is that the survey is freely available

TABLE 5.1 Hospital Survey on Patient Safety Culture: Items and Dimensions

Teamwork within Units
Supervisor/Manager Expectations and Actions Promoting Patient Safety
Organizational Learning—Continuous Improvement
Management Support for Patient Safety
Overall Perceptions of Patient Safety
Feedback and Communication about Error
Communication Openness
Frequency of Events Reported
Teamwork across Units
Staffing
Handoffs and Transitions
Non-punitive Response to Errors

(Agency for Healthcare Research & Quality, 2014.)

TABLE 5.2 Medical Office Survey on Patient Safety Culture: Items and Dimensions

List of Patient Safety and Quality Issues
Information Exchange with other Settings
Teamwork
Work Pressure and Pace
Staff Training
Office Processes and Standardization
Communication Openness
Patient Care Tracking/Follow-up
Communication about Error
Owner/Managing Partner/Leadership Support for Patient Safety
Organizational Learning

(Agency for Healthcare Research & Quality, 2014.)

with a number of open access tools for survey implementation, recruitment, data entry, and analysis (AHRQ).

Safety Attitudes Questionnaire

The SAQ is a survey developed by J. Bryan Sexton, Ph.D. and colleagues at the University of Texas at Austin. It was derived from the Flight Management Attitude Questionnaire, a human factors tool used to assess culture in the cockpit in commercial aviation, allowing for comparisons between health care and other industries.

The SAQ consists of six individual surveys that are tailored to the work settings of the general inpatient floor, intensive care unit, labor and delivery, operating room, pharmacy, and ambulatory setting. Each survey instrument assesses six domains (Table 5.3). The SAQ has been validated and is regarded as quick and easy to complete (Center for Healthcare Quality and Safety).

Case Study

Community General Hospital has recently experienced a preventable safety event involving the death of a young patient. In the event investigation, troubling trends were discovered regarding staff reluctance to speak up about possible errors in care,

Table 5.3   SAQ Survey Domains

Teamwork Climate
Safety Climate
Job Satisfaction
Stress Recognition
Perceptions of Management
Working Conditions

(Sexton, J.B., Helmreich, R.L., Neilands, T.B., Rowan, K., Vella, K., Boyden, J., Roberts, P.R. & Thomas, E.J. (2006). The Safety Attitudes Questionnaire: physchometric properties, benchmarking data, and emerging research. BMC Health Services Research: 6(44)).

fear of retribution for event reporting, and an undue emphasis on staff efficiency, often at the expense of patient safety. Because of these findings, the hospital board has asked the management team to perform an assessment and create an improvement plan to address the organization's safety culture.

After review, the hospital leadership team chooses to conduct an organization-wide safety culture assessment using the AHRQ hospital culture of safety survey. The goal is at least a 30% response rate from the hospital employees. The survey will be conducted during a two-week period in June. In the weeks prior to the survey, the management actively promotes the survey in team meetings and implements a publicity campaign of screen savers. During the survey process, response rates are reported to the leadership team on a daily basis. Frontline leaders and administrative leadership actively promote the survey during routine work rounds.

At the conclusion of the survey period, the hospital has achieved a 34% response rate. Results are stratified and analyzed by unit and employee role, in addition to at the organization level. Results are compared to external benchmarks provided by AHRQ. The analysis reveals an overall composite culture of safety score at the 40th percentile for the organization. Additional drill-down on specific domains reveals opportunities around non-punitive response to error, feedback, and communication about error and frequency of events reported. In addition, the drill-down reveals that there is a 10 to 15% difference between leadership perception and staff perception in any given domain. If the leader responses were to be excluded, the overall organization composite percentile score would decline below the 40th percentile.

Per the direction of the board, these results prompt the creation of a multi-pronged culture of safety action plan. Elements of this improvement plan include:

1. Revision of the hospital mission statement to explicitly message the primacy of safety and the establishment of both patient and associate safety as the first core value of the organization.
2. Under the leadership of human resources, the creation of a non-punitive guide for establishing individual culpability in safety events. This non-punitive guide is based on existing decision trees in the public domain and is customized for the organization. All leaders are trained on how to use the guide and it is reflected in the human resources management policy and is communicated to all front-line staff.
3. To encourage greater transparency around safety events, leadership begins to talk about specific details of safety events, though removing patient-identifying details. Leaders adopt a narrative, story-telling style when discussing events so that the events are accessible and understood by the broadest possible audience in an organization. Each story is closed with lessons learned from the event and an emphasis on creating a platform for organizational change.
4. The initiation of a renewed emphasis on safety event reporting includes a public relations campaign to encourage safety event reporting that is refreshed at regular intervals and a goal of increasing reporting by 40% within a year with specific targets for leaders, public recognition of associates who self-report errors and near misses, and a quarterly organization-wide "life-saver" award.

The improvement plan is expected to take several years to embed within the organization's culture and leadership model. It is now a standing expectation of the board that the culture of safety will be assessed on an annual basis. In addition, leadership will develop an annual improvement plan on the results of the survey and the management incentive will now be tied to both the survey response rate and overall composite performance with the goal of reaching the 75th percentile within four years.

Lessons Learned

Although health care is unique, there are lessons to be learned from industries that have evolved to develop strong cultures of safety and accident avoidance. In these industries, including nuclear power and the U.S. aircraft carrier and submarine fleet, the culture of safety is considered foundational in their high reliability performance.

A culture of safety must be proactively developed and actively managed by organizational leadership; a culture of safety will not evolve on its own. Actively managing culture first requires a basic assessment of the culture. This cultural inventory should be compared against the major components required within a culture of safety, including the primacy of patient and associate safety, the transparency and encouragement of reporting safety events, and a non-punitive response toward error. Without these foundational cultural elements in place and practiced every day, there will be limited return on the other "hard tactics" that focus on the practice and behavior by clinicians, physicians, and others at the front-line patient care.

Action Steps and Strategies to Lead

This chapter outlines some of the essential tactical steps toward measuring and managing culture. There is a fundamental role of leadership in safety culture:

1. **Assess your organization's culture.** Survey tools such as the AHRQ Hospital Survey of Patient Safety Culture and Safety Attitudes Questionnaire help leaders determine gaps in safety culture and identify opportunities for improvement.
2. **Actively manage workplace culture, including the culture of safety.** Leadership and culture are inextricably linked. Management guru Edgar Schein describes culture and leadership as two sides of the same coin. Schein provides a series of primary mechanisms that leaders can use to change, embed, and transmit culture (Schein 2010):
   a. What leaders pay attention to, measure, and control on a regular basis
   b. How leaders react to critical incidents and organizational crises
   c. How leaders allocate resources
   d. Deliberate role modeling, teaching, and coaching
   e. How leaders allocate rewards and status
   f. How leaders recruit, select, promote, and excommunicate
   In improving an organization's safety culture, it is not enough to simply adopt a non-punitive algorithm and change a mission statement. Rigorous attention and examination by leaders is necessary to embed mechanisms and ensure consistency in approach and action toward establishing a culture of safety.
3. **Encourage and reward reporting of safety events.** Particularly when the concepts of a safety culture are new, employees, fearing repercussions, will underreport safety events and near misses. The only way to identify system and process errors, however, is to report them. To support this, leaders must embody the characteristics of a learning organization including investigating the causes of all safety events and near misses.
4. **Utilize a non-punitive policy and decision-making algorithm for assessing individual culpability in safety events.** Without a formal non-punitive policy in place, organizations will not be able to achieve a safety culture. Leaders must develop and adhere to a formal process for establishing individual culpability in the context of serious safety events. Additionally, the

algorithms developed should acknowledge the organization's role in providing the correct policies, procedure, training, and work environment for staff to succeed. This process should not be a quality and safety function, but rather a human resources function applied to the entire organization.

References

Agency for Healthcare Research and Quality. Surveys on Patient Safety Culture. Accessed May 22, 2014. http://www.ahrq.gov/professionals/quality-patient-safety/patientsafetyculture/index.html.

Center for Healthcare Quality and Safety. Safety Attitudes and Safety Climate Questionnaire. Accessed May 22, 2014. https://med.uth.edu/chqs/surveys/safety-attitudes-and-safety-climate-questionnaire/.

The Health Foundation. 2011. Evidence Scan: Measuring Safety Culture. Accessed May 22, 2014. http://www.health.org.uk/public/cms/75/76/313/2600/Measuring%20safety%20culture.pdf?realName = rclb4B.pdf.

Hobbs, Andrew F. 2008. Human Performance Culpability Evaluations, University of Tennessee Knoxville. www.efcog.org.

Institute of Medicine (U.S.). 2001. *Committee on Quality of Health Care in America. Crossing the Quality Chasm: A New Health System for the 21st Century*. Washington, D.C.: National Academies Press.

Marx, David A. 2009. *Whack-A-Mole: The Price We Pay for Expecting Perfection*. Amanda Bray (Ed.). Plano, TX: By Your Side Studios.

Reason, James T. 1997. *Managing the Risks of Organizational Accidents*. Vol. 6. Aldershot: Ashgate.

Schein, Edgar H. 2010. *Organizational Culture and Leadership*. Vol. 2. New York: John Wiley & Sons.

Spear, Steven J. 2009. T*he High-Velocity Edge. How Market Leaders Leverage Operational Excellence to Beat the Competition*. New York: McGraw-Hill.

Chapter 6

Principles and Practices of High Reliability Organizations

Leaders of health care organizations are no longer pursuing incremental change—they are seeking breakthroughs in improvement. To achieve these breakthroughs, organizations must adopt the strategies and tactics of high reliability organizations. In recent years, the science and understanding of HROs has evolved into a codified set of operating components. This chapter explores the underlying principles of HROs, the translation of these concepts to health care, and their real-world implementation within a health care delivery system.

The Evidence

Much of the underlying concepts and literature regarding HROs originated in the book *Managing the Unexpected* by Karl Weick and Kathleen Sutcliffe (2007). In their landmark work, Weick and Sutcliffe identified industries that operate in difficult and unexpected conditions yet have an extremely low level of accidents and injury to workers and customers. In these organizations, the possibility of failure can be overwhelming and catastrophic. Nonetheless, these organizations operate with exceptional records of safety and outcomes. Weick and Sutcliffe deemed this particular set of organizations to be "highly reliable." Examples of HROs include the U.S. submarine fleet, the U.S. air craft carrier fleet, in-flight domestic commercial aviation, and the U.S. nuclear power industry.

Weick and Sutcliffe outlined the characteristics and operating systems of HROs and compared them to non-high reliability industries and organizations. In this comparison, they identify five key principles that define the culture of management and leadership within HROs organizations:

1. Preoccupation with failure
2. Reluctance to simplify
3. Sensitivity to operations
4. Commitment to resilience
5. Deference to expertise

Weick and Sutcliffe refer to these principles as components of a "mindful infrastructure." Another way to convey these ideas is to describe HROs as "always" organizations. These organizations are always mindful, always executing, always safe, and always anticipating the worst, which allows them to perform at an unusually high level despite the high-stakes circumstances. Each of the five HRO principles yields important insights for leadership and operations across industries.

Preoccupation with Failure

HROs treat any lapse or problem, no matter how small, as indicative of a potentially larger issue within an operating system. This manifests as a healthy paranoia that whatever could go wrong will go wrong. The preoccupation with failure is embedded within HRO culture and practiced from the front line to executive leadership. HRO leaders and employees pay great attention to detail, particularly small signals of error, and swarm these issues promptly before they propagate and lead to an error or incident. It is considered a management prerogative to proactively address the small blips within the system.

HROs operationalize this preoccupation with failure by encouraging event reporting and investigating near-miss incidents. For example, in an HRO the discovery of a small, loose part on critical machinery would prompt an investigation of all similar parts throughout the plant and potentially a deeper investigation into the manufacture and installation process.

Reluctance to Simplify

Humans are biologically capable of processing only a fixed amount of facts and information when understanding a situation or solving a problem. As a result, when organizations seek to explain an event or incident, it is a natural and almost an inevitable bias to consider only a limited set of facts and construct a logical explanation from the constrained set of what is known. This cognitive bias in the explanation of past events has been referred to as the narrative fallacy (Taleb 2010). The narrative fallacy occurs because it is appealing to find a simple story that provides order and structure for explaining events that appear random and unpredictable. Unfortunately, this bias limits true, in-depth understanding.

HROs understand this bias and the impact on situational awareness and incident investigation. They actively work against this natural tendency by refusing to simplify explanations of events. HROs consider as broad a set of information as possible from as diverse a group of sources as possible. HRO leaders attempt to preserve the diversity of opinion and perspective when synthesizing their explanations. This approach is a hallmark of high reliability and works against the natural human tendency toward the narrative fallacy and simple explanations.

Sensitivity to Operations

In any organization, the "real work" occurs on the front line. HROs are attuned to the daily situation and environment on the front line of operational work. HRO leaders are attentive, good listeners, and responsive to issues and problems at the operating level. This mode of operation may also be described as routine situational awareness.

Sensitivity to operations requires a process for easy, hassle-free communication of operational status from the front line to leadership. It also requires a leadership commitment to listening to these concerns and to working actively to eliminate the barriers and problems interfering with front-line work. This approach may also be branded as a form of servant leadership within the HRO.

Commitment to Resilience

HROs recognize that problems will inevitably occur and that incidents may elude initial mechanisms for detection and control. HROs actively plan for these contingencies through implementing a system of redundancies at the levels of people, process, and technology. This commitment to resilience, persevering despite errors or failures, mobilizes the system rapidly and effectively to prevent an error from becoming more significant and leading to greater catastrophe. This ability to respond to an error is fundamental to HRO functioning. HRO leadership instills this culture through routine drills and even simulation. This leads to a priority on education and training for associates to ensure competency to respond to a crisis when it occurs.

Deference to Expertise

HROs are flat organizations; that is, they lack the strict hierarchy that is present in many organizations. HROs encourage deference to the individual with the greatest experience or knowledge of a situation, regardless of their official title or position.

HROs push decision-making down the chain of command in the organization and empower those at the front line, where often the greatest knowledge and understanding of a situation lies.

An example of this deference to expertise can be seen in the flight operations on a U.S. aircraft carrier. Within this HRO, any individual—regardless of rank or title—can halt operations for a safety concern that might jeopardize the crew, pilot, or aircraft. The organization places a premium on safety and does not allow hierarchy and rank to interfere with this priority.

To summarize with a quote from Karl Weick and Kathleen Sutcliffe:

> Unexpected events can get you into trouble unless you create a mindful infrastructure that continually tracks small failures, resists oversimplification, is sensitive to operations, maintains capabilities for resilience, and monitors shifting locations of expertise (2007).

Given these guiding principles, the next section focuses on the translation and operationalization of these principles to health care.

Case Study

The literature provides many examples of the real-world practice of high reliability principles within HROs. In contrast, for budding high reliability industries, including health care, there are limited examples of published information on how to implement high reliability principles.

The following are sample tactics to lead to high reliability organizations, organized by each key principle. These examples are based on the authors' experiences and conversations with leaders in health care.

Preoccupation with Failure: Investigating Near Misses and Good Saves

One approach to translating the high reliability principle of preoccupation with failure to health care is to invoke James Reason's "Swiss cheese model" of accident causation (Figure 6.1). This framework explains how although there may be many layers of defense between a hazard and potential safety event, represented as slices of Swiss cheese, an incident may still occur if the holes of the Swiss cheese have aligned to allow an error to propagate through the system. Despite the best intentions, all defenses have opportunity to fail and adverse events occur when all defenses fail simultaneously.

In health care, our current model of safety event investigation is aligned with this approach to thinking. Events or errors are investigated only after harm has

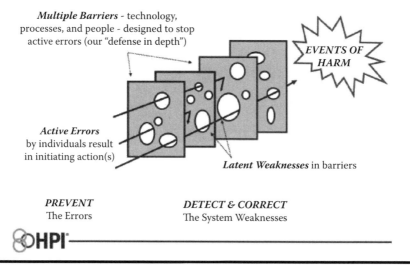

Figure 6.1 The Swiss cheese effect. (Adapted from James Reason, Managing the Risks of Organizational Accidents, 1997.)

occurred. It is only then, after the fact and after an event has occurred, that the individual "holes" in the process are recognized and rectified.

In contrast, if a health care organization were to be preoccupied with failure, leaders would identify the individual holes in the safety systems before a safety event occurred. Once flaws in the system are discovered, they should be proactively addressed to prevent errors. Operationally, the process of identifying the "holes" before a safety event is synonymous with the investigation of "near misses" and "good saves." A "near miss" or "good save" is a safety event that is thwarted by one last barrier of defense. Often, the defense is close to the front line of care. Instead of treating these "good catches" as lucky, a hospital or health system should regard these as small signals of deeper flaws in the system to be investigated and resolved. Consequently, a health care organization that aspires to be an HRO should not just investigate their safety events, but also routinely investigate a sample of near misses and good saves. This proactive approach of attentiveness to small signals helps to solve problems before they lead to significant harm.

Reluctance to Simplify: Thorough Root Cause Analysis and Event Investigation

In a safety event investigation, it is important to resist the tendency to pronounce a simple or single cause of an event. Although finding an easy or unifying answer is intellectually satisfying and allows work to progress, it may cause premature closure of the issue. A simple answer will likely not acknowledge the complexity of the intersection of people, process, and technology that contributes to an event.

To protect against this, hospitals and health systems are urged to adopt a standard and thorough approach to root cause analysis and event investigation. In particular, the complete approach should engage all relevant stakeholders, not just those that were proximal to the event. This approach will pull in groups that may initially feel their participation is irrelevant or not meaningful. Variety and richness of perspective, however, are critical to obtaining a thorough understanding of complex event occurrence.

The investigation team should identify multiple causation threads, each with their own event timeline, which contributed to and converged on the safety event. Establishing this expectation at the start of the event investigation will protect against the temptation to accept simple answers. It will also help to keep an open frame of mind among the investigation team, preserve the diversity of opinion, and enable a richness of perspective. Over time and with repetition of process and stakeholder involvement, this should promote the reluctance to simplify in many aspects of a health care organization's improvement process.

Sensitivity to Operations: Daily Organization Huddle

An approach utilized by the U.S. aircraft carrier fleet to promote sensitivity to operations is the daily operational briefing. This briefing helps to promote organization-wide situational awareness at the beginning of each day. This tactic has been successfully adopted by a number of health care facilities and transformed into a daily safety huddle (Lee and Cosgrove 2014).

Advocate Health Care, a large health system in Illinois, has adopted the daily safety huddle. The daily huddle is a 15-minute briefing by the leaders in the organization to establish situational awareness at the start of the day and is facilitated by the organization president or CEO. Attendees are typically director level and above, though the huddle can include managers, depending on the size of the organization. Each leader participating in the huddle is expected to briefly report on significant safety and quality events that occurred in the past 24 hours, anticipate any safety or quality issues that may arise in the next 24 hours, and provide follow-up to any issues that were identified in previous huddles. The huddle is largely a report out, not a problem-solving session. The leader of the huddle should help to manage the dialog, promote a robust cadence to the huddle, and encourage problem solving at the conclusion of the huddle.

Implementing the daily huddle requires a thorough plan, practice, and a willingness to change and adapt to the daily organizational rhythm. One recommended practice is to establish a meeting-free zone from around 7:00 a.m. to 9:00 a.m. This provides time for leaders to round on their direct reports and collect the information needed for the huddle. It also signals the importance of this time within the organization to establish collective situational awareness. At Advocate, the huddle usually starts around 8:30 a.m. and concludes within 15 to 20 minutes. Even in large organizations this brief timeframe is possible, although it does require practice and role modeling of report outs prior to implementation. Training videos of sample huddles can also be helpful.

Leaders at Advocate Health Care identify two difficult aspects to the implementation of the huddle: encouraging non-clinical areas to report out safety and quality issues, and anticipating safety and quality issues in the future. With regard to the first difficulty, it is important for the organization's leaders to help connect the dots on the critical link between non-clinical support areas and safety/quality issues. Although an occasional "nothing to report" at the huddle is acceptable, it should not be routine. Ongoing responses of "nothing to report" can signal a lack of preoccupation with failure and attention to small signals.

The second difficult issue is the anticipation of future events. To promote this type of thinking, front-line leaders can be encouraged to identify at least one patient that they think could deteriorate in the next 24 hours or whose status is tenuous. The best solution to this barrier is practice, role modeling, and training within the huddle.

A final best practice is to bring front-line associates to attend the huddle on a periodic basis. This has a powerful effect in an organization to enable the individuals delivering care to understand the collective situational awareness, dedication to improving quality and safety, and the responsiveness of the organization to issues directly impacting patient care. Because of the huddle, Advocate has found that problems that would ordinarily take several days to weeks to solve are now resolved in one to two days following the implementation of the daily huddle.

Commitment to Resilience: Simulation

HROs almost universally conduct drills and practice for safety events and worst-case scenarios. In health care, this approach can be replicated with medical simulation. Simulation has already gained acceptance and application within health care. Although a component of it is geared toward procedural competency, simulation can also be utilized for training regarding adverse events, code situations, and rare occurrences. This persistent drilling helps to embed the commitment to resilience within the care delivery setting. It acknowledges that incidents will occur, and emphasizes responsiveness and rapid containment of those occurrences.

In the context of high reliability, simulation does not need to be an expensive or capital-intensive undertaking. Low fidelity simulation of particular events or codes can be an acceptable substitute to practice skills, thought processes, and resilience. Although it may not feel as authentic as a simulation lab, this is an easy way to deploy multiple training scenarios across an organization. It is also important to frame simulation in the broader context of an adult model of learning. Simulation is an education approach for adults to embed skills in their routine work. As such, it should also be accompanied by an organizational commitment to actively developing their workforce, investing in their education, and maintaining competency.

In addition, it is important for physicians to participate in simulation exercises. They are key stakeholders in demonstrating and actualizing the commitment to resiliency. Strategies for the engagement of physicians are provided in Chapter 4. Suffice to say, the impact of simulation is limited without physician participation.

Deference to Expertise: Executive Rounding

Flattening hierarchies within an organization is easier said than done. Within health care, significant power gradients exist between disciplines and roles. There are also disparities between administrators and front-line staff, physicians and nurses, and clinicians and non-clinicians. Eliminating these gradients requires awareness and attentive leadership. It also requires a basis of relationship building and familiarity with front-line staff. This can be actively promoted through intentional executive rounding.

The individual components of executive rounding can take many forms. They can focus on information gathering, influencing behavior, problem solving, or a combination of all of these. Regardless of the emphasis, the foundational component in all executive rounding is relationship building with frontline employees. When rounding is done correctly, leaders and employees develop familiarity and comfort with each other. It enables a diminution of the power gradient between administration and the front line and can become the basis for more meaningful dialog and exchange in the future. Without these relationships in place and the cultural change that accompanies them, there will not be an organizational willingness to seek out guidance and help regardless of title or seniority.

Lessons Learned

It is tempting to distill the process of becoming an HRO into a series of discrete tactics for implementation. However, simply focusing on discrete projects like simulation or daily huddles by themselves will fail to transform an organization into one of high reliability. At its core, an HRO requires a unique form of cultural mindfulness and associated leadership.

For a health care organization that aspires to become an HRO, the first commitment must come from leadership to embrace an approach of mindfulness and a cultural change in management. This commitment needs to be accompanied with articulating a "why" for the change commitment and conveying this to employees up and down the organization. On this journey, it is helpful to highlight and illustrate the practices of exemplars in high reliability, particularly outside of health care, in order to provide an aspirational goal for the organization.

The embodiment of this cultural and leadership mindset is key on the progression toward becoming an HRO. As Weick and Sutcliffe state:

> Change toward greater mindfulness often involves movement toward a more informed culture that is focused on reporting, justice, flexibility and learning (2007).

In the absence of this type of culture, the HRO principles and accompanying tactics will likely not succeed.

Action Steps and Strategies to Lead

1. **Continuously monitor organizational culture.** Without the proper preparation and fortitude, the journey toward high reliability for a health care organization can be daunting and at times seem impossible. The chances of success can be vastly improved by recognizing that an HRO has a unique cultural and leadership mindset that must be owned throughout the organization.
2. **Establish a compelling "why" for the high reliability journey.** Once a level of commitment has been made, the leadership team should establish a compelling "why" for their high reliability journey, accompanied with aspirational goals and examples of HROs.
3. **Educate the organization on the key components of high reliability.** After the leadership team has shared the "why" for the high reliability journey with the organization, there should be efforts to educate employees on the key principles of high reliability.
4. **Generate and celebrate quick wins**. Once the organization understands the "why" and the "what" of high reliability, leaders can begin a rollout of discrete tactics, in particular the daily huddle, which can serve as a powerful initial and visible example of a new organizational process and rhythm of operating. This quick win should be followed with additional high reliability tactics and an ongoing commitment to leading and living HRO principles every day.

References

Lee, Thomas H., and Toby Cosgrove. 2014. Engaging doctors in the health care revolution. *Harvard Business Review* 92(6): 104–111.

Taleb, Nassim Nicholas. 2010. *The Black Swan: The Impact of the Highly Improbable Fragility*. New York: Random House.

Weick, K., and K. Sutcliffe. 2007. *Managing the Unexpected: Resilient Performance in an Age of Uncertainty*. San Francisco, CA: Jossey-Bass.

Chapter 7

Key Quality and Safety Measures

The competitive, dynamic, and increasingly transparent health care landscape in the twenty-first century is motivating organizations to focus on quality and patient safety. More and more, health care organizations are assessing performance across multiple dimensions (i.e., clinical outcomes, preventive measures, patient safety events) with measures that range in complexity and accuracy (NQF "Measures Will Serve Our Future"). Moving forward, a new generation of measures must be developed and implemented to accurately and effectively assess quality across multiple dimensions and across the continuum of care. As health care becomes increasingly data-driven, the ability to develop a bundle of meaningful measures to track and drive organizational improvement will be a critical leadership function.

The Evidence

Performance measurement allows organizations to meet both internal and external needs and demands including guiding department- or hospital-wide performance improvement activities, demonstrating provider accountability, fulfilling public reporting requirements, and facilitating organizational evaluation and decision-making (Schmaltz et al. 2014). As leaders in the field know, health care organizations are required to report on quality, cost, and patient satisfaction measures to fulfill a variety of external requirements. These evaluators then utilize hospitals' performance measurement data for accreditation, calculating reimbursement levels, and public reporting of outcomes to drive transparency and competition (Schmaltz et al. 2014).

Over the past decade, programs from both public (i.e., Medicare, Medicaid) and private (i.e., Blue Cross Blue Shield, United Healthcare) payers have shifted reimbursement policies to incentivize and reward high-quality care. To maximize reimbursement under these programs, organizations must not only provide high-quality care, they must also demonstrate that they have done so through providing accurate and timely data. To this end, hospital leaders must be able to track and use data across a variety of metrics to demonstrate value to consumers and payers, and to guide internal improvement initiatives to remain competitive.

Some examples of programs that are driving the imperative for effective data management and analysis include:

- **Serious Reportable Events**: In 2002, the National Quality Forum published a list of 28 Serious Reportable Events, otherwise known as "never events," that were deemed to be clearly identifiable and preventable medical errors (NQF 2011). In 2008, the Centers for Medicare and Medicaid Services announced it would no longer reimburse facilities for the extra cost of treating these "never events" (CMS 2008). Moving forward, organizations that are unable to identify, track, and eliminate these "never events" will suffer financially.
- **Readmissions**: In October 2012, the Centers for Medicare & Medicaid Services instituted the Hospital Readmissions Reduction Program. Under this program, hospitals with readmission rates higher than the CMS-designated benchmark rate face financial penalties (CMS 2014; KHN 2014). Facilities must implement comprehensive data systems to track readmissions, stratify data, and use predictive modeling to effectively and efficiently reduce readmissions.
- **Affordable Care Act—ACOs and PCMH**: The 2010 Patient Protection and Affordable Care Act creates new incentives for health care organizations to deliver more coordinated, patient-centered care including through accountable care organizations and patient-centered medical homes. In an ACO model, organizations are financially responsible for the cost and quality of care delivered to a defined population of patients. The PCMH model also ties reimbursement to quality outcomes. Gaining status as a PCMH requires the institution of several technologies (i.e., care registries, electronic health records, e-prescribing) and processes to decrease fragmentation in primary care, improve chronic disease outcomes, and increase patient engagement. Similar to ACOs, PCMHs must measure and assess outcomes across a broad range of measures, including both process and outcomes, of its patient population (Nutting et al. 2011). Without systems to accurately measure quality and costs, facilities will be unable to succeed in such financial arrangements.

As programs such as these expand and reimbursement based on cost and quality outcomes becomes standard, organizations must be able to measure their performance across a number of dimensions to both meet external requirements and guide internal improvement projects.

Data for Performance Measurement: The Basics

There are three fundamental purposes for conducting performance measurement, each of which is critical to ensuring a high performing organization (Schmaltz et al. 2014):

1. Assessment of current performance
2. Demonstration and verification of performance improvement
3. Control of performance

These three purposes for measurement complement and support the implementation of internal performance improvement activities (Schmaltz et al. 2014). Organizations assess performance to identify strengths and weaknesses of existing processes and to identify targets areas for intervention. Next, the impact of tested interventions is demonstrated through comparing post-intervention data to baseline data. Finally, ongoing measurement helps to sustain improved performance. Continuous data monitoring can provide early warnings and a correction system that highlights unintended changes in processes (Schmaltz et al. 2014). To succeed in the new era of value-based, consumer-driven health care, clinical leaders must become proficient in utilizing performance measurement to implement ongoing improvement efforts across their organizations, from patient safety initiatives to projects to improve work flow and financial processes.

Types and Dimensions of Measures

Historically, health care "quality" has been very difficult, if not impossible, to measure. A lack of metrics and reporting mechanisms hindered the ability to collect and evaluate data to determine quality. Although challenges remain, over the past decade the availability of metrics, methods, and databases to collect, store, and evaluate quality data has vastly improved.

Avedis Donabedian, often referred to as the father of quality assurance, provided a basic framework of three dimensions of quality (Wyszewianski 2014):

1. **Structure**: refers to characteristics of care providers such as education, training, and professional certification and includes characteristics of care facilities such as adequacy of staffing, equipment, and overall organization.
2. **Process**: quality of process varies across three aspects: (1) appropriateness—whether correct actions were taken; (2) skill—proficiency with which actions were carried out; and (3) timeliness of care.

3. **Outcomes**: refers to indicators of health status such as whether a patient's pain has subsided, whether the patient regained full function, cost of care, and measures of satisfaction.

Health care organizations can and should evaluate performance across each of these dimensions. Particularly when implementing improvement initiatives, organizations should track both process and outcome measures to determine which processes may need to be modified to improve a given outcome.

When implementing improvement initiatives, teams should also consider balancing measures (IHI 2014). Balancing measures help assess whether changes from an intervention designed to improve one part of the system inadvertently cause new problems in other parts of the system. For example, if a hospital is successful in reducing the amount of time that patients spend on a ventilator post-surgery, they should also note whether re-intubation rates have increased. In this example, the time spent on a ventilator is the outcome measure that is targeted for improvement and the rate of ventilation, a process measure, is the balancing measure. If time spent on a ventilator is decreasing yet the rate of re-intubation is increasing, this may indicate that the efforts to decrease time on a ventilator are leading to premature removal, resulting in re-intubation and additional episodes of ventilation and thus undermining the improvement. Another example relates to reducing length of stay. Organizations working to reduce length of stay should monitor readmissions as a balancing measure. If length of stay decreases but readmissions increase, this may indicate that patients are being discharged prematurely (IHI 2014).

Criteria and Standards

Once structure, process, and outcome measures have been established, criteria and standards are used to evaluate performance on each measure. *Criteria* are the specific attributes on which the assessment of quality is based. *Standards* are the quantitative level the criteria are required to meet in order to satisfy expectations about quality. For example, consider process measures related to discharge. The criteria for one such measure may be the percentage of individuals who receive a follow-up phone call from a nurse within 24 hours of discharge. The associated standard might be at least 90% of individuals will have received a follow-up call within 24 hours post-discharge (Wyszewianski 2014). While the criteria define the metric, the standards define how success is determined or evaluated. Figure 7.1 provides additional examples of criteria and standards.

Data Sources

There are many national sources of health care data. Organizations can use these databases to access data on structure, process, and outcome measures. The following

Type of Measure	Focus of Assessment	Criterion	Standard
Structure	Information technology	Achievement of meaningful use standards for electronic health record	100% of physicians' offices to achieve meaningful use requirements
Process	Patient discharge from hospital	Percentage of patients that receive a follow-up phone call within 48 hours of discharge	95% of patients to receive a phone call within 48 hours of discharge
Outcome	Diabetic patients	Percent of patients with HbA1C levels within recommended range	75% of patients within range

Figure 7.1   Examples of criteria and standards of measures.

examples are nationally standardized survey instruments that measure quality of care.

- ▪ **Hospital Compare:** Hospital Compare is a CMS measurement tool that supports hospitals in improving quality of care. The tool contains information on over 4000 Medicare-certified hospitals across the U.S. including measures of structure, patient experience, and measures of timely and effective care, readmissions, complications, and mortality categories. This is a useful source of benchmark data for hospitals to determine their performance relative to peers (Medicare.gov 2014). Hospital Compares also includes quality measures for nursing homes, home health agencies, physician practices, and dialysis facilities. This list continues to grow.
- ▪ **HEDIS:** The Healthcare Effectiveness Data and Information Set is a performance measurement tool developed by the National Committee for Quality Assurance to provide purchasers with information to compare performance of health care plans. HEDIS assesses 81 measures across five domains of care: effectiveness of care, access/availability of care, experience of care, utilization and relative resource use, and health plan descriptive information (NCQA "HEDIS & Quality Measurement"). Currently, more than 90% of health plans in the U.S. use HEDIS to measure performance. Due to the ubiquitous use of HEDIS and the highly specific design of these measures, it is an effective source of data for side-by-side comparison of organizations (NCQA).
- ▪ **NHSN:** The Centers for Disease Control's National Healthcare Safety Network is the most widely used health care-associated infection tracking system in the nation and is known as the HAI surveillance gold standard. It includes four sections: patient safety, health care personnel safety, biovigilance, and long-term care facilities. NHSN provides support to medical facilities, states, regions, and national data collection efforts through providing

reporting tools to identify high rates of HAIs, monitor improvement efforts, and ultimately reduce infection rates. The NHSN website provides hospitals with information to enroll as well as opportunities to participate in state and national HAI collaboratives including CMS-operated HAI reporting programs (CDC 2014).

- **HCAHPS:** The Hospital Consumer Assessment of Healthcare Providers and Systems Survey is a standardized survey, initially deployed by CMS and AHRQ in 2008, that measures patients' experience of care (Hospital Consumer Assessment of Healthcare Providers and Systems 2013). In many instances, HCAHPS scores correlate with quality and mortality outcomes. A 2008 study by Jha et al. that found that hospitals in the top quartile of HCAHPS scores delivered better care for acute myocardial infarction and pneumonia compared to hospitals in the bottom quartile. HCAHPS scores are becoming increasingly important as they contribute to 30% of a hospital's value-based purchasing score (HRET 2012).

In addition to these national databases, organizations can track internal metrics that are relevant for the organization's specific priorities or initiatives. Chapter 8 describes strategies to access additional data sources. When choosing metrics, clinical leaders should prioritize a "critical few" measures that have the greatest impact on driving improvement. Leaders must be aware of data fatigue and ensure that every measure is tied to a report that is important to the organization. This helps to keep teams motivated and engaged in improvement projects and to manage the data burden.

Leaders should select measures that enable benchmarking against peers, competitors, and national standards. Benchmarking involves comparing metrics to other similar organizations to determine relative performance. Improvements in quality and safety are always positive, but organizations may be blind to additional opportunities for improvement if they do not benchmark their performance. For example, a facility may have great success in reducing its rate of early elective deliveries from 20% to 10%, a stunning 50% reduction. However, if the organization benchmarked its performance, it would realize that a rate of 10% still vastly exceeds the national benchmark of 2%. Benchmarking becomes increasingly important as transparency and competition increase in health care and comparative data becomes available to consumers and payers.

Metrics of the Future

As the health care operating model and payment methodologies evolve, so will the metrics used to monitor health system performance. Metrics of the future will include continuum of care metrics, population health metrics, and patient-reported outcome metrics. These types of measures move beyond the amount and type of care delivered and attempt to more accurately evaluate effectiveness and efficiency from the view of the patient.

Continuum of care metrics will reflect quality and cost across multiple facilities. For example, the Medicare cost per beneficiary metric aggregates cost before, during, and after hospitalization. These metrics are a more accurate reflection of the total cost of care and help to identify strategies that truly reduce costs rather than simply shifting costs to another dimension of the system.

Population health metrics will also be important as entities such as accountable care organizations and patient-centered medical homes become responsible for the health outcomes of populations, not merely the medical services provided. Population health metrics will include measures of disease prevalence, the percentage of the population that receives treatment and preventive care consistent with recommended guidelines, and total cost of care metrics. Much investment will be required to develop and test such metrics, but some delivery systems and payers are already beginning to experiment in this area.

A final set of metrics for the future are patient-reported outcome metrics. As clinicians and delivery systems increasingly think in terms of value, an important component is defining what value is from the patient perspective. This will include those outcomes most relevant to patients, including both near-term and longer-term health. Definitions of "quality" will move beyond the use of HEDIS process measures and focus on what is most important to patients: their health outcomes following treatment (Porter 2010).

Effective Strategies: Using Data to Drive Performance Improvement

Choosing metrics to monitor and evaluate quality is a first step. The second step is to use those metrics to drive improvement. To maximize the impact of measurement, three conditions must be met: (1) the measure construct must be sound, (2) the data analyses and interpretation must be scientifically credible, and (3) the data should be reported in a user-friendly, easy to understand format (Schmaltz et al. 2014). If all of these conditions are met, health care organizations can benefit from measurement in many ways (see Figure 7.2).

Selecting Measures

Selecting appropriate measures is foundational for improvement initiatives. Measures can be both adopted from external resources, as described previously, and developed internally to meet specific facility needs. Measures should be selected to meet the specific needs of the initiative goals. Figure 7.3 lists the critical characteristics of all appropriate performance measures (Schmaltz et al. 2014).

Benefits of Measuring Organizational Performance
Provides factual evidence of performance and improvement
Promotes ongoing organizational self-evaluation and improvement
Facilitates cost-benefit analysis
May help facilitate long-term relationships with various external stakeholders
May facilitate differentiation from competitors
May contribute to the awarding of business contracts
Fosters organizational survival

Figure 7.2   Benefits of measuring organizational performance. (Schmaltz, S., Hanold, L. S., Koss, R. G., & Loeb, J. M. 2014. Statistical Tools for Quality Improvement. In Joshi, Ransom, Nash, & Ransom (3rd Ed.), the Healthcare Quality Book: Vision, Strategy, and Tools (135–173). Chicago, IL: Health Administration Press.)

Relevant: measures should directly relate to organization's improvement goals and should align with the organization's overall mission, vision, values, strategic goals and objectives.
Reliable: measures should accurately and consistently identify the events they were designed to identify across multiple health care settings.
Valid: measures should raise good questions about current processes, which also facilitate the identification of opportunities for improvement regarding the services provided and quality of achieved health care results. It's also important to assess how closely the intended use of a measure matches with the measure developer's intended use.
Cost-effective: the costs of any performance measurement versus the benefit must be considered in order to determine whether the measurement activities are worth the investment.
Under the provider's control: performance measures should only collect data on processes or outcomes which the provider is able to influence. Otherwise, an opportunity for improvement identified through a measure cannot be intervened on by a provider or organization.
Precisely defined and specified: in order to ensure uniform application between measurement periods and comparability across organizations, performance measures and their data elements must be specified through precise, predefined and standardized requirements. This will facilitate the reliable collection and calculation of data by various organizations.
Interpretable: the extent to which a user can understand the rationale and results of a measure's data and information.
Risk adjusted or stratified: the extent to which the influence of factors that differentiate comparison groups can be taken into account or controlled for.

Figure 7.3   Critical characteristics of performance measures. (Schmaltz, S., Hanold, L. S., Koss, R. G., & Loeb, J. M. (2014). Statistical Tools for Quality Improvement. In Joshi, Ransom, Nash, & Ransom (3rd Ed.), the Healthcare Quality Book: Vision, Strategy, and Tools (135–173). Chicago, IL: Health Administration Press.)

When selecting measures for an improvement project, clinical leaders should consider:

■ **What measures are currently in use?** An inventory should include mandatory measures that are already reported (i.e., Joint Commission, NHSN, HCAHPS) and facility-specific measures that are being used internally to drive improvement or for other reasons.

■ **Which measures align?** Depending on the purpose of the measurement activities, select measures that align with the particular requirements (e.g., those of CMS, NHSN, or the Joint Commission). Select measures that fulfill multiple requirements to streamline data collection processes and reduce data collection fatigue.

■ **What are the greatest opportunities to improve processes and outcomes?** Are there areas or processes in which performance is inconsistent or not meeting standards? Do any of these adversely affect patient outcomes? Choose those process or outcome measures that are the best indicators of what is driving the targeted outcome.

Lessons Learned

When selecting measures, improvement teams should employ the strategy of "collecting the critical few" and should seek usefulness, not perfection, in measurement (Byrnes 2014). Measurement is a means to an end. Improvement is the primary goal and improvement teams should only collect data that identifies and corrects the process under scrutiny. To achieve this goal, every data element collected should link to a report. This ensures that teams are not collecting excessive, unused data (Byrnes 2014).

From a strategic perspective, clinical leaders should begin moving beyond myriad measures and data sources and toward, at an organizational level, a few, specific measures that drive high performance. An important lesson from the past decade of quality measurement is the need to coordinate and simplify measurement to more effectively drive improvement and to reduce the data burden. There is great opportunity for innovation in this realm.

One example of an innovation in patient safety measurement is the implementation of a total harm measure. Currently the numerous, disparate, and unaligned sources of data and measures lead to measurement fatigue, duplicative efforts, and an abundance of data that is not necessarily effective in driving organizational improvement. One example related to patient safety and quality is the implementation of a "total harm" metric to drive organizational improvement.

Some health systems such as Cincinnati Children's Hospital are utilizing an aggregate system-level measure for all cause harm. Ongoing monitoring and reporting of this measure has enabled the organization to progress toward the goal of eliminating harm (Cincinnati Children's). Although no national metric exists for all cause harm, organizations can begin to aggregate and track data on hospital-acquired conditions in their facilities to show trends over time in pursuit of the goal of zero patients harmed.

Tracking total harm reinforces the imperative to drive all patient harm to zero, emphasizes the connections across multiple areas of harm, provides an opportunity to focus on organization-wide improvement strategies, and engages leadership and boards to drive quality and patient safety through accountability and transparency. Using a total patient harm metric simplifies the current state of quality measurement, one characterized by numerous convoluted measures, enables greater organization-wide engagement, more effectively drives rapid cycle improvement, and builds accountability through transparency.

Case Study: Tracking Total Harm

Nathan Littauer Hospital in Gloversville, NY is leading the way in tracking total harm. Nathan Littauer, a 75-bed rural community hospital, is the only acute care hospital in its county. Given the low census, NLH has relatively few instances of harm. This, however, did not dissuade them from tracking harm, but rather inspired them to track toward zero instances of harm.

In 2012, NLH began tracking total harm across ten topics: surgical site infections, venous thromboembolism, ventilator-associated pneumonia, central-line-associated bloodstream infections, catheter-associated urinary tract infections, clostridium difficile infections, pressure ulcers, falls with injury, early elective deliveries, and adverse drug events.

Since 2013, NLH has experienced a reduction in total harm from 6.5 to 1.0 harms per 1000 discharges in the last quarter of 2014 (Figure 7.4). In the first quarter

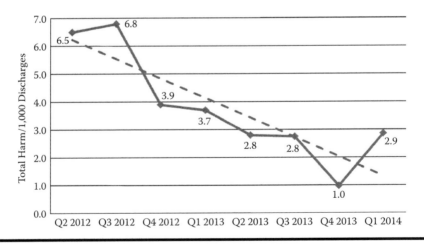

Figure 7.4 Harm across the board: total harm events per 1000 discharges at Nathan Littauer Hospital. (Nathan Littauer Hospital, 2014.)

of 2014, NLH saw an uptick from 1.0 to 2.9 harms per 1000 discharges. Chief medical officer Fred Goldberg has explained that tracking total harm allowed the organization to immediately notice this increase and they were able to act appropriately to identify and eliminate the source. Dr. Goldberg has also described NLH's success in using the total harm rate to engage the organization's board in quality and patient safety work. Because of receiving the information on total harm, the NLH board has collectively adopted a goal of zero harm. The total harm rate is an excellent education tool for the board and promotes transparency and accountability (Goldberg 2014).

Action Steps to Lead

1. **Integrate measurement for improvement into organizational culture.** Clinicians, administrators, and other staff in hospitals are busy providing patient care. Participation in data collection and improvement teams can feel like extra work and time away from patient care. Therefore, it is imperative for clinical leaders to communicate the importance of performance improvement efforts and the relationship to patient care. Clinical leaders have an essential role in creating a culture that is data-driven and focused on continuous improvement. Teams—from management to unit teams—should be equipped and empowered to design and implement their own improvement projects, complete with measures that reflect their projects (Ransom and Ransom 2014).

2. **Choose a few key "big dot" measures to track at an organizational level.** Clinical leaders can focus strategic improvement efforts through intentionally selecting the organization's "big dot" or top outcome measures. When an organization prioritizes things such as total harm, patient satisfaction, and quality of care measures, everyone is held accountable and acts accordingly to meet those goals (Martin et al. 2007). This is an important strategy for preventing both leaders and staff from being flooded with measures and data. Teams must know for which key measures they are responsible.

3. **Connect measurement to action.** All measures should have a purpose and should be connected to action, whether a reporting requirement, improvement initiative, or organizational priority. Connecting data and measurement to the mission of the organization and to an action helps the staff responsible for collecting the data to remain engaged. To this end, clinical leaders should also seek to engage front-line employees in determining which measures to collect and how to motivate others to participate in improvement projects. Those closest to patient care are often the best source of information about what metrics should be used, where and how to collect the data, and how to motivate others to participate in improvement efforts (American Hospital Association and Health Research & Educational Trust 2014).

4. **Monitor the data burden.** Clinical leaders have a role in monitoring the data burden and ensuring that data collection processes are efficient, effective, and purposeful. Given the proliferation of national, state, and local initiatives to improve quality and safety and the lack of coordination around metrics, data burden and fatigue are critical barriers to quality improvement efforts. Clinical leaders should seek ways to streamline and coordinate data collection and be comfortable identifying when collection of a given metric can be discontinued.

5. **Smart analysis: balancing measures and benchmarking.** Clinical leaders have a role is to encourage and guide the selection and analysis of metrics that drive efficient and effective improvement initiatives. When choosing measures, teams should always consider balancing measures and sources for benchmarking the data. Employing these two strategies helps to ensure the improvement efforts are linked to a larger context that informs the true impact of the initiative to maximize the effort and impact of these teams.

References

American Hospital Association and Health Research & Educational Trust. 2014. Implementation Guide Part I: A How-To Guide for Improvement for the AHA/HRET HEN Partnership for Patients.

Byrnes, J.J. 2014. Data collection. In Maulik S. Joshi, Elizabeth R. Ransom, David B. Nash, and Scott B. Ransom (Eds.), *The Healthcare Quality Book: Vision, Strategy, and Tools*, 3rd ed. Chicago, IL: Health Administration Press, pp. 111–133.

Centers for Disease Control and Prevention. 2014. National Healthcare Safety Network (NHSN). http://www.cdc.gov/nhsn/.

Centers for Medicare & Medicaid Services. 2008. Letter to State Medicaid Directors. http://downloads.cms.gov/cmsgov/archived-downloads/SMDL/downloads/SMD073108.pdf.

Centers for Medicare & Medicaid Services. 2014. Readmissions Reduction Program. http://cms.gov/Medicare/Medicare-Fee-for-Service-Payment/AcuteInpatientPPS/Readmissions-Reduction-Program.html/.

Cincinnati Children's. Our Methodology for Achieving Goals. http://www.cincinnatichildrens.org/service/j/anderson-center/safety/methodology/default/. Accessed November 10, 2014.

Goldberg, F. 2014. Engaging the Board in Harm Reduction at a Rural New York State Hospital. Presented at the annual meeting of the Symposium for Leaders in Healthcare Quality.

Health Research & Educational Trust. 2012. Health Care Leader Action Guide to Effectively Using HCAHPS. www.hpoe.org.

Hospital Consumer Assessment of Healthcare Providers and Systems. 2013. HCAHPS Fact Sheet. http://www.hcahpsonline.org/files/August%202013%20HCAHPS%20Fact%20Sheet2.pdf.

Institute of Healthcare Improvement. 2014. Measures. http://www.ihi.org/resources/Pages/Measures/default.aspx.

Institute of Healthcare Improvement. Science of Improvement: Establishing Measures. 2014. http://www.ihi.org/resources/Pages/HowtoImprove/ScienceofImprovementEstablishingMeasures.aspx.

Jha, A., Orav, E., Epstein, A. 2008. Patients' perception of hospital care in the United States. *New England Journal of Medicine* 359: 1921–31.

Kaiser Health News. A Guide to Medicare's Readmissions Penalties and Data. 2014. http://kaiserhealthnews.org/news/a-guide-to-medicare-readmissions-penalties-and-data/.

The Leapfrog Group. 2007. Half of US Hospitals Reporting to Leapfrog Say They Won't Bill for a "Never Event." http://www.leapfroggroup.org/media/file/Release_-_Adoption_of_Leapfrog_Never_Events_Policy_2007.pdf.

Martin, L.A., E.C. Nelson, R.C. Lloyd, and T.W. Nolan. 2007. Whole system measures. IHI Innovation Series white paper. Cambridge, MA: Institute for Healthcare Improvement.

Medicare.gov. What is Hospital Compare? Centers for Medicare & Medicaid Services. http://www.medicare.gov/hospitalcompare/About/What-Is-HOS.html.

National Center for Quality Assurance. HEDIS & Performance Measurement._http://www.ncqa.org/HEDISQualityMeasurement.aspx.

National Quality Forum (NQF). How Measures Will Serve Our Future. http://www.qualityforum.org/Measuring_Performance/ABCs/How_Measures_Will_Serve_Our_Future.aspx.

National Quality Forum (NQF). 2011. Serious Reportable Events in Healthcare–2011 Update: A Consensus Report. Washington, DC: NQF.

Nutting, Paul A., Benjamin F. Crabtree, William L. Miller, Kurt C. Stange, Elizabeth Stewart, and Carlos Jaén. 2011. Transforming physician practices to patient-centered medical homes: Lessons from the national demonstration project. *Health Affairs* 30(3): 439–445.

Porter, M.E., 2010. What is value in health care? *New England Journal of Medicine* 363 26: 2477–2481.

Ransom, S.B., and Elizabeth Ransom. 2014. Implementing quality as the core organizational strategy. In Maulik S. Joshi, Elizabeth R. Ransom, David B. Nash, and Scott B. Ransom (Eds.), *The Healthcare Quality Book: Vision, Strategy, and Tools*, 3rd ed. Chicago, IL: Health Administration Press, pp. 393–421.

Schmaltz, S., L.S. Hanold, R.G. Koss, and J.M.Loeb. 2014. Statistical tools for quality improvement. In Maulik S. Joshi, Elizabeth R. Ransom, David B. Nash, and Scott B. Ransom (Eds.), *The Healthcare Quality Book: Vision, Strategy, and Tools*, 3rd ed. Chicago, IL: Health Administration Press, pp. 135–173.

Wyszewianski, Leon. 2014. Basic concepts of healthcare quality. In Maulik S. Joshi, Elizabeth R. Ransom, David B. Nash, and Scott B. Ransom (Eds.), *The Healthcare Quality Book: Vision, Strategy, and Tools*, 3rd ed. Chicago, IL: Health Administration Press.

Chapter 8

Using Data for Feedback and Improvement

Health care is becoming increasingly data driven. As both the accuracy of measures and the ability to gather and analyze data improve through the adoption of electronic health records, standardization of measures, and increasing organizational capacity for data analytics, clinical leaders must expand their ability to use data to drive improvement. By establishing more effective measures to assess institutional and provider performance, health care organizations have the potential to stimulate greater accountability and improve performance. There are four steps to effectively using data for feedback and improvement: (1) collecting data, (2) displaying data, (3) analyzing data, and (4) using data to drive improvement cycles. This chapter describes Steps 1 through 3. Step 4, using data to implement improvement cycles, is explained in detail in Chapter 2.

Evidence

Individuals and organizations need access to accurate, timely data to drive improvement. External stakeholders, such as hospital accreditors, insurance companies, and governments, also collect and analyze data to develop new products and guide their decision-making. These external databases can also be used to guide improvement programs (see Chapter 7). Currently, hospitals have numerous, disjointed sources of data ranging from administrative databases to patient registries (Byrnes 2014).

Hospitals typically collect data across four key categories or domains:

1. Clinical quality (process and outcomes)

2. Financial performance
3. Patient, physician, and staff satisfaction
4. Functional status/patient outcomes

In order to maintain a balanced perspective of the overall process of care, most mature organizations will deploy teams to improve performance across all four domains (Byrnes 2014). Once an aim has been identified and an improvement team formed, the next step is to collect the data that will guide and drive improvement.

Step 1: Data Collection: Objectives, Sources, and Methods

When beginning a quality improvement project, clinical leaders should consider the following (Byrnes 2014):

1. Identify the purpose of the data measurement activity (e.g., monitoring at regular intervals, investigation over a limited period, one-time study).
2. Identify the most appropriate data sources for the activity.
3. Identify the most important measures to collect.
4. Design a common-sense strategy that will ensure collection of complete, accurate, and timely information.

There are many sources of data, which vary in cost, feasibility, accessibility, and accuracy.

Medical record review is a form of retrospective data collection that is particularly useful in providing detail on links between interventions and outcomes by offering additional data and elements that are not often available in administrative databases. Many national quality improvement database projects, including the Healthcare Effectiveness Data and Information Set, Joint Commission Core Measures, Leapfrog Hospital Survey, and National Quality Forum's National Voluntary Consensus Standards for Hospital Care, require retrospective medical record review for a substantial portion of the data elements included. Disadvantages of medical record review include the significant investments of both of time and money required (Byrnes 2014).

Prospective data collection also relies on the review of medical records but is conducted during a patient's hospitalization as opposed to retroactively. Prospective data collection enables staff to observe trends in patients in real time and intervene accordingly. This method also provides the best insight into how the timely administration of certain therapies contributes to a difference in outcomes, especially when the time window is small. Similar to medical record review, the largest disadvantages of prospective data collection are the expense and time involved.

Specifically, this method is often criticized as taking nurse time away from patient care responsibilities. Therefore, if organizations utilize this method, they should consider hiring dedicated research assistants or data analysts to assist with data collection (Byrnes 2014).

Administrative databases include data elements such as enrollment or eligibility information, claims information, and information on managed care encounters. Examples include hospital billing systems, health plan claims databases, health information management or medical record systems, and registration systems. Administrative data often includes hospital, laboratory, and prescription drug services. The advantages of administrative databases include cost (relatively inexpensive), accessibility (incorporate transaction systems already used in the hospital's daily operations), standardization across administrative databases (simplifies internal comparison and external benchmarking), high volume of available indicators, and accuracy.

However, administrative databases have been developed for financial and administrative purposes rather than for quality improvement. Therefore, some argue that these databases contain inadequate detail, many errors, and "dirty data," meaning that the data makes no sense or appears to have come from another source, potentially compromising the accuracy of the data (Byrnes 2014).

Health plan databases are particularly good sources of data for those quality improvement projects that have a focus on population health management or that focus across the continuum of care because they track all health care received by their enrollees, regardless of provider. This data is electronically available and relatively inexpensive to access. However, there are limitations including questions of accuracy, detail, and timeliness. Additionally, though these databases track events, procedures, and lab tests, they do not contain detailed information on outcomes (Byrnes 2014).

Patient registries allow hospitals to create specialty or condition-specific reports. Patient registries are advantageous due to the ability to collect data over time, ease of customization, and the ability to incorporate multiple data sources and collection methodologies. Though the ability to customize is a significant advantage of registries, the time and costs required for patient registry data collection must be weighed against the insight they would provide (Byrnes 2014).

Patient surveys, a favorite tool of quality improvement professionals, are used to gauge the perceptions of patients in terms of quality of the services provided. Surveys should be administered at the point-of-service, thereby allowing patients to immediately comment on their experience. Survey forms should be concise, and easy to read. Though patient surveys are relatively easy to develop, teams often underestimate the scientific complexity of their design. Poorly designed surveys can undermine the validity and reliability of results (Byrnes 2014). Accordingly, teams should consult an expert in survey design to ensure they are not inadvertently biasing the results.

When choosing a data source and collection method, clinical leaders must balance the investment of time and money with the value that the data will contribute to the improvement effort (Byrnes 2014). Data collection strategies often combine both code- and chart-based sources to optimize strengths and cost-effectiveness while minimizing weaknesses (Byrnes 2014).

Before collection starts, clinical leaders should guide their teams to ask the following questions (American Hospital Association and Health Research & Educational Trust 2014):

a. Why collect the data?
b. What data elements and specific types of data will be collected? Is a sample of data sufficient or are all applicable data necessary?
c. What is the timeframe for data collection? Is the measurement prospective, retrospective, or both? If prospective, is a baseline available?
d. Where do the data reside (e.g., clinical registries, clinical records, administrative systems)? Are there any regulatory or confidentiality issues to address?
e. How will the data be collected and by whom? What data collection resources and tools will be needed? How will the data be coded, edited, and verified?

The Institute for Healthcare Improvement recommends using the following to guide the data collection process (IHI "Measures" 2014):

a. **Aim for usefulness, not perfection.** Measurement is only a means to an end; collect just enough data to determine whether changes are leading to improvement.
b. **Integrate measurement into a consistent routine.** Do not wait until the end of a project to collect patient outcome data. Instead, establish a protocol for who will collect which data and when.
c. **Use both qualitative and quantitative data.** Quantitative data is essential to demonstrate improvement, but qualitative data is often easier to access and can be highly informative. Qualitative data is helpful in determining the story behind the quantitative data, helping to inform more effective strategies for sustainability and spread.
d. **Use sampling.** When patient volume is high, using a sampling method enables teams to accurately track performance in a more manageable way.
e. **Plot data over time (see Step 2: Displaying the Data).** Graphic displays of data over time are effective ways to illustrate trends and patterns. This allows teams to identify what changes resulted in an improvement and to monitor the process for changes.

Once the appropriate source of data and method for data collection have been identified, the next step is to display the data in a manner that is easy to comprehend, and actionable.

Step 2: Displaying the Data

Two important attributes in using data for improvement are transparency and real-time feedback. Thus, teams should display the most current data possible in a manner that is accessible, easy to understand, and actionable. Examples of effective ways to display data to drive improvement include physician profiles, dashboards, and customized run charts.

Physician Profiling

Physician profiles have become more commonplace as greater emphasis is placed on delivering care that is high quality and low cost. These tools provide insight on physician practice patterns, utilization of services, and patient outcomes through analyzing provider-specific and practice-level data. Physician profiles facilitate objective assessment and evaluation of physicians' treatment patterns and can be compared with evidence-based best practice recommendations. Additionally, physician profiles facilitate comparison against peers at the local, state, and national level.

Physician profiles can decrease practice variation through promoting adherence to evidence-based clinical protocols (Nash, Jacoby, and Berman 2013). Comparative data is a powerful motivator as physicians are highly driven, goal-oriented individuals who are motivated to improve their performance against their peers. The use of physician profiles also encourages physician development through the pursuit of credentialing, board certification, and organizational quality improvement initiatives (Nash et al. 2013).

Dashboards

Performance dashboards are an effective tool for driving performance improvement across all levels of the organization—from unit-based quality improvement efforts to governance dashboards used to track high level metrics. Dashboards enable teams to quantify and track progress toward a goal. Effective dashboards incorporate the following (Office of Inspector General):

- **Set ambitious targets.** Teams should set both target and stretch goals. Setting high goals helps drive improvement and keeps organizations from becoming complacent.
- **Avoid color coding to low expectations.** Many dashboard users track progress by updating goals as green (meeting target), yellow (progressing toward target), or red (in jeopardy of not meeting target). However, a dashboard that is colored all green should be examined closely. Meeting targets too early and readily may indicate that those goals were not challenging enough. Though

color coding is a useful tool to track progress, it should not diminish the value and nuances of the dashboard.

- **Simple is better.** This mantra holds true for most displays of data. Keep both the format of the dashboard (e.g., number of measures, display) and the measures clear and concise. Track only the key drivers of success on the dashboard.
- **Align goals with activities of stakeholders.** To engage anyone in improvement initiatives, you must demonstrate value—how does this effort impact something they care about? Dashboard measures should emphasize how all stakeholders contribute to the outcome of the project.
- **Use benchmarks.** Using both internal and external benchmarks helps organizations recognize gaps or blind spots. Though a process may be improving and showing "green," it may still lag behind competitors or other national benchmarks. Whenever possible, organizations should benchmark their data to understand their performance compared to others.
- **Monitor results.** To effectively drive improvement, teams must be reminded of the goal that they are working toward and see the progress. Dashboards should be revisited and shared with the team on a regular basis to monitor progress and make adjustments as necessary.

Run Charts

One of the most effective ways to display data for a quality improvement initiative is through a run chart. Though there are more complex statistical tools that may be utilized (e.g., control charts, statistical process controls), run charts are a relatively simple and accessible method that any team can adopt to track the progress of an improvement initiative.

Run charts display data over time and enable improvement teams to assess how well (or poorly) a process is performing, help determine when changes are truly improvements, and provide information about the value of specific changes or interventions. Improvement teams can create run charts to track both process and outcome measures related to the project's aim. To promote transparency, run charts can be posted in break rooms or even on the unit. At one hospital in Oregon, every unit has a bulletin board that displays the data, run chart, and intervention information related to the unit's current improvement project. For example, a unit working on falls tracked the process measure (completion of hourly rounds) and the outcome measure (total patient falls) using a run chart. The board included information for patients on how to contribute to reducing falls (i.e., using the call light, using non-slip mats) in order to engage patients and family members in the efforts.

There are infinite ways to display data, but teams should choose a method that (1) aligns with the purpose of the project, (2) enables all stakeholders to access and understand the data, (3) promotes transparency and accountability, and (4) is continuously monitored to enable teams to change interventions as appropriate.

Step 3: Analyzing the Data

One of the biggest challenges in improvement is distinguishing between common cause and special cause variation and determining whether a change is actually an improvement. Common cause variation is natural, due to chance, and has no assignable cause. Special cause variation, however, signals an unnatural pattern with an assignable cause. Within a stable process, common cause variation is normal.

As referenced above, there are many complex statistical tools that may be used; however, there are also more simplistic, guiding rules that should be understood and employed by all working on improvement initiatives.

The Institute for Healthcare Improvement has developed numerous modules and tools on using run charts for improvement and specifically to help determine if a change is really an improvement. These "run chart rules" help identify common cause vs. special cause variation and help teams determine whether an intervention is actually driving an improvement (IHI "Better Measurement" 2012).

The key elements of a run chart include the centerline, the median value of the run chart, the y-axis (i.e., the value of the measure), and the x-axis (i.e., time). Run charts can be broken into "runs," defined as one or more consecutive data points on the same side of the median (excluding those points on the median). Refer to these four run chart rules to determine if special case variation is present:

1. **A shift in the process**. Six or more consecutive points above or below the median indicates that there has been a shift in the process and that an intervention has made an impact.
2. **A trend**. Five or more consecutive points all increasing or decreasing indicates non-random variation.
3. **Too many or too few runs.** If a process is stable, there is a predictable number of runs (Appendix at the end of the chapter). If an intervention is successful, the previous process will be disrupted and there will be fewer or more runs in the resulting data. Teams can determine the appropriate number of runs using a table developed by Swed and Eisenhard, included in the Appendix.
4. **An "astronomical" data point.** If a data point is significantly above or below the median, it is considered "astronomical" and indicates non-random variation. These should be investigated for special cause and addressed appropriately. This could be caused by having incorrect data or by some unusual event.

More detail on these rules and methodology is available through the Institute for Healthcare Improvement (http://www.ihi.org/education/WebTraining/OnDemand/Run_ControlCharts/Pages/default.aspx).

There are also many sources of information on statistical process control charts and additional tools for monitoring random vs. non-random variation. As a clinical leader, it is important to develop competencies in this area and to guide teams to understand whether their changes are resulting in an improvement.

Step 4: Implementing Improvement Cycles

The last step in the process of using data for improvement is to conduct improvement cycles; that is, to implement an intervention at first on a small scale and gradually to a larger group as an evidence base develops for its success. Chapter 2 provides detail on improvement methodology including PDSA cycles, Lean, and Six Sigma. Whichever improvement method is chosen, all should be guided by ongoing data collection and analysis.

Lessons Learned

Despite a movement toward more data-driven decision-making, many organizations continue to make decisions based on little or no data, only qualitative or anecdotal data, or inaccurately characterized data. No data is perfect, but organizations and teams must find simple and useful ways to collect, display, analyze, and implement changes based on the data that is relevant to the process they are attempting to improve.

Organizational capacity and capability remain a challenge. Clinicians are already stretched thin completing their patient-care duties. The addition of improvement efforts, particularly those that require skills (i.e., data analytics) that have not been taught, is daunting. To combat this, clinical leaders can support teams through training, designating specific staff time to these projects, or hiring data analysts or research assistants specifically to contribute to these teams.

Another challenge for improvement projects is sustainability, particularly sustaining data collection processes amidst other competing demands. Given the many demands and opportunities for other improvement projects, teams must make decisions on when to scale back or end measurement in order to free up resources and attention to address new projects.

Processes should be monitored beyond the close of the improvement project to ensure that they are sustained and that any issues are addressed as they occur. However, once a process has become stable, monitoring does not need to continue indefinitely.

Finally, when implementing any project that involves data, especially data on individual performance, organizations should expect resistance, skepticism, and denial. For example, common critiques of physician profiling include the lack of consensus around what should be measured, where to pull the data, and how to compare data across organizations. Additionally, many physicians express skepticism claiming that clinical practice does not include "one size fits all" processes and that even generally accepted guidelines may not appropriately apply to their particular population of patients. When implementing new measurement tools or reports, it is important to include physicians in the discussion and development of the tools, acknowledge and address the shortcomings to the extent possible, but also recognize the value despite the shortcomings and emphasize those opportunities to drive improvement and provide safer, more high-quality patient care.

In all efforts to use data for improvement, clinical leaders have a role in (1) demonstrating commitment and support for analytic capability; (2) finding easy, clear ways to display data, and (3) ensuring that data is transparent, current, and relevant.

Interview: Tina Esposito, Vice President, Center for Health Information Services at Advocate Health Care

Tina Esposito is the Vice President for the Center for Health Information Services at Advocate Health Care in Chicago, IL. CHIS provides system-level support related to measurement and analytics including the creation and dissemination of monthly scorecards and maintenance of the Enterprise Data Warehouse. CHIS focuses on quality, safety, and engagement (patient and physician) metrics and guides organizational thinking to consider not only what the numbers are but why they are, which promotes a close examination of the data to drive improvement.

Q: **What criteria do you use to select metrics for the organization?**

A: We've been doing this for a long time now, nearly a decade, and the measure selection process has certainly evolved and gone through many iterations. CHIS focuses on quality, safety, and physician and patient engagement metrics. We do include some financial metrics as part of the monthly scorecard dissemination, but our focus is on the quality, safety, and engagement metric development and analysis.

We have three main criterion or guidelines to identify metrics. First, whenever possible we look for metrics with comparative data. Comparative data helps us determine objective targets and limits or eliminates subjectivity. If you don't have comparative data, you can't know if the targets are correct or feasible. With comparative data, you can increase the rigor of the targets, for example, to be better than 90% of organizations. Comparative data helps make the data and targets meaningful both internally and externally.

Second, we look to ensure that the goal or measure is meaningful in itself. For example, if it touches a lot of lives or is an area in which we have a good level of opportunity for improvement; it has to be worth the effort associated with tracking it.

Finally, we look for metrics that have some level of external exposure or visibility, whether that is public reporting requirements or payer-driven metrics. Many organizations focus on exactly what Medicare focuses on. Medicare requirements are certainly a guideline for us, but it's not our only compass. Whether or not a measure is publicly reported is only one guideline for use. For example, Medicare has certainly recently emphasized readmissions. We decided years ago that as a fully integrated delivery system and accountable care model it was in our best interest to focus on all readmissions, not only those that Medicare has identified. So we move beyond public reporting requirements to consider how the measures can be most valuable for us.

Overall, it's important to be proactive in identifying and selecting measures and really understand what the issue or opportunity is. The comparative piece has evolved and continues to. For many things, we're in uncharted waters where we don't have comparative data (i.e., much of our safety work). However, we use these three rules to provide boundaries and help focus.

Q: **What is the process used to select these metrics and how do you ensure appropriate engagement and buy-in?**

A: Before we began the current measure selection process, we had a very top-down approach where the chief medical officer or other leaders would identify five or six metrics on an annual basis based on what they thought was important. We've evolved to a now very collaborative process driven by a subgroup of the Health Outcomes Council. This subgroup includes representatives from clinical leadership (chief medical officers and chief nursing executives) and vice presidents of quality from each site of care. This group works all summer to identify organizational priorities through a process that allows individuals to propose potential metrics, look closely at opportunities, and identify areas with a large patient impact or external visibility. The process begins in April, and by August, the group presents the proposed metrics to the full Health Outcomes Council. The council then provides feedback and revisions, which are incorporated before the measures next go to the senior leadership group, which includes leadership representatives from each hospital and at the system level. Finally, the package is presented to the executive management team at the system level. Once approved, those measures go to human resources to cascade down the goals, which wraps up by November.

As we've transitioned to this new collaborative process, the big change is that they've become "our" measures, which helps with buy-in. Everyone knows about the process and every month we release a "close," similar to a financial close, to disseminate the latest quality, safety, and patient satisfaction measures. These results include a front narrative cover, index score that rolls up all the metrics, performance compared to targets, and notes changes in performance. The report also includes details at the site level and by measure. For example, a site will be able to see the index score, each measure, and their performance. The report also includes a link to the Enterprise Data Warehouse, which enables additional drill down. The report also includes a "watch list." This includes metrics that are not large enough to be included as weighted performance metrics but are still things we should be tracking, such as publicly reported metrics or those that support a large internal initiative. Finally, the last page of the report includes all operational definitions and the CHIS department serves as a resource for anyone who has questions.

Q: **Over time, how has your process of metric selection evolved and what are some of the most significant challenges you see?**

A: The process has absolutely evolved and I think we've found the right level of engagement and have pretty good representation across the organization for the process to identify metrics. We have had a few evolutions. Back in 2011, we had 17 or 18 safety and quality metrics. It became clear that if we were going to raise these as organizational priorities, we needed to focus. We narrowed the list down to 7 or 8 using the criteria referenced above. We also incorporated the watch list to allow the organization to continue monitoring measures beyond those items included on a weighted scorecard.

One ongoing challenge is sustainability. We know that when metrics are reported on, incorporated into scorecards, and are part of incentives, they tend to improve. We've struggled with ensuring that performance is sustained, however, beyond the year that the measures are included at that high level. This year, we've included three sustainment metrics. These are weighted less than other metrics, but we still see them as important enough to continue to include on the scorecard. This is a good first step, but it's unclear what we'll do once the list of sustainment metrics grows.

The second challenge relates to how to measure safety culture. Advocate is very focused on safety culture and it's a challenging thing to measure. There's absolutely no comparative data. The easiest way to reduce the number of safety events is to decrease reporting, but we don't want to disincentivize people from being transparent. We want to incentivize transparency and openness in reporting and incentivize driving down the number of safety events. Given the lack of comparatives, it's difficult to determine what an appropriate target is for safety. We're working through this though and have tried to tell the organization that it's okay if we don't have comparative data; we just need to be thoughtful and at times creative with setting up targets.

Q: **How is the use of data integrated into feedback and improvement? What have been some lessons learned?**

A: The monthly close and monthly scorecard process are the two main ways that we disseminate data. For us, the goal has been to ensure the data is actionable. To do this, it must be available at your fingertips and in a format that makes it very easy to identify opportunities for improvement.

Take a readmissions example. We need to display at a high level what readmission results are, but we also need to understand why that number is what it is in order to drive improvement. We need to figure out how to change that number. To do this, we created a front end for the Enterprise Data Warehouse that allows people to click through and slice and dice the data across different characteristics. They can investigate where readmitted patients are coming from more frequently, for example, skilled nursing facilities or home health. They can stratify by age range, how soon patients are being readmitted, and more. We tried to make the data easy to understand and actionable through enabling users to drill down.

When we started working on the data warehouse in 2007, we assumed "if we build it, they will come." That wasn't the case. We learned that we couldn't give a data-dump to people and assume they will know what questions to ask or how to navigate through it. We had to focus in on how and what information we were providing people based on different skill levels. For those who are less technical and savvy with both data skills and business questions, we need to provide data in different forms (i.e., rolled up, through ad hoc reports). For those who are very analytical, we built an Advocate Data Intelligence tool which gives access to a master Excel sheet with all the data that they can pivot, slide, dice, and data mine at their own pace. We learned that we had to provide the data in different ways and customize based on roles and ability.

Q: **How do you see the use of data for improvement evolving within your organization—and what are the next steps to get there?**

A: As we move along on the journey to accountable care, value, and population health, the next step is to get to real population health metrics that span the care continuum. We have a set of "true north" metrics, the board-level metrics that tell how we're doing on big metrics like mortality. In 2015, we're implementing a true north population health metric. This will follow a patient cohort, diabetic patients, who are in the clinical integration program through one of four payer groupings: Health Maintenance Organization, Centers for Medicare and Medicaid Sharing Savings Program, Blue Cross Blue Shield Accountable Care Organization, and Medicare Advantage. This metric will examine for this group whether they met various clinical integration metrics in the physician's office (e.g., HbA1c and blood pressure control); were admitted; if the admission was appropriate; did those admitted meet the length of stay goal; did they get an infection; they did go to home care; did those who went to home care meet the appropriate diabetic metrics, require post-acute care; and if they were readmitted, what was their length of stay in post-acute? This is where I see metrics changing. All of this activity that's now stratified across settings will bleed into one level of service.

Right now accountable care is very much about utilization and dollars. There are some quality metrics, but they are nowhere near where they need to be. Moving forward, the industry will hopefully start thinking differently about what a population health metric is and how quality metrics will be different in a population health framework.

Advocate is on a big data journey. For health care organizations, big data includes all of the metrics referenced above. This kind of reporting and analysis is not possible unless all the data is in one place. You need data from all electronic health records at all sites of care, plus all the claims data from all sites in one data warehouse that is also tied to an enterprise patient index. This needs to be the foundation before you can begin to think of new ways to measure quality or population health. This organization of big data and linking to the enterprise patient indices needs to happen first.

Action Steps and Strategies to Lead

1. **Support teams in developing plans for data collection, reporting, and analytics.** Finding and analyzing the relevant and accurate data involves commitment and resources. Clinical leaders can help teams to develop feasible plans that add value and efficiency to their projects.
2. **Provide ongoing feedback through dialog and draw clear connections between the data and recommendations (i.e., clinical guidelines) or what actions are necessary to improve the process.** Data is not useful if it is not reviewed on an ongoing basis to check for changes and opportunities. If clinicians do not understand the data or do not see it as valuable, discontent, skepticism, and rebellion against the data and reports can undermine the project. As a clinical leader, your role is to promote transparency, explain the data, including the strengths and caveats, and guide your colleagues to engage with the data in a productive way.
3. **Use graphical methods to display data.** Find simple, concise ways to display data that show the relationship between action and results. Clinical leaders should find ways to make data accessible to all who are working on the improvement projects. It should not require an advanced degree in statistics to

understand the data required to implement an improvement project. Leaders should seek new and innovative ways to display data to drive improvement.

4. **Explain change and variation in terms of special cause vs. common cause.** This is a core element of using data for improvement. Leaders must demonstrate an understanding of the difference in special vs. common cause variation in order to effectively and efficiently drive improvement work. As a clinical leader, if you explain changes in these terms, it becomes embedded in the organizational culture to think of processes in this way.

References

American Hospital Association and Health Research & Educational Trust. 2014. Implementation Guide Part I: A How-To Guide for Improvement for the AHA/HRET HEN Partnership for Patients.

Byrnes, J.J. 2014. Data collection. In Maulik S. Joshi, Elizabeth R. Ransom, David B. Nash, and Scott B. Ransom (Eds.), *The Healthcare Quality Book: Vision, Strategy, and Tools,* 3rd ed. Chicago, IL: Health Administration Press, pp. 111–133.

Centers for Medicare & Medicaid. 2014. Physician Quality Reporting System. http://www.cms.gov/Medicare/Quality-Initiatives-Patient-Assessment-Instruments/PQRS/index.html?redirect=/PQRS/.

Health Research & Educational Trust and Kaufman, Hall & Associates, Inc. 2013. Value-Based Contracting. www.hpoe.org.

Hospital Value-Based Purchasing Program. 2014. https://questions.cms.gov/.

Institute for Healthcare Improvement. Science of Improvement: Establishing Measures. http://www.ihi.org/resources/Pages/HowtoImprove/ScienceofImprovementEstablishingMeasures.aspx.

Lloyd, R., Mary Seddon, and Richard Hamblin. 2012. Better Quality Through Better Measurement. http://www.ihi.org/education/conferences/apacforum2012/documents/i5_presentation_lloyd.pdf.

Nash, D.B., R. Jacoby, and B. Berman. 2014. Physician and provider profiling. In Maulik S. Joshi, Elizabeth R. Ransom, David B. Nash, and Scott B. Ransom (Eds.), *The Healthcare Quality Book: Vision, Strategy, and Tools,* 3rd ed. Chicago, IL: Health Administration Press, pp. 175–192.

Office of Inspector General. Driving for Quality in Acute Care: A Board of Directors Dashboard. Government Industry Roundtable. http://oig.hhs.gov/fraud/docs/complianceguidance/RoundtableAcuteCare.pdf.

Schmaltz, S., L.S. Hanold, R.G. Koss, and J.M.Loeb. 2014. Statistical tools for quality improvement. In Maulik S. Joshi, Elizabeth R. Ransom, David B. Nash, and Scott B. Ransom (Eds.), *The Healthcare Quality Book: Vision, Strategy, and Tools*, 3rd ed. Chicago, IL: Health Administration Press, pp. 135–173.

Swed, F. S., Eisenhart, C. 1943. Tables for teaching randomness of grouping in a sequence of alternatives. *The Annals of Mathematical Statistics.* 14: 66–87.

Appendix: Table for Testing Randomness of Grouping in a Sequence of Alternatives

Total Number of Data Points on the Run Chart that do not Fall on the Median	Lower Limit for the Number of Runs (< than this number runs is "too few")	Upper Limit for the Number of Runs (> than this number runs is "too many")
10	3	9
11	3	10
12	3	11
13	4	11
14	4	12
15	5	12
16	5	13
17	5	13
18	6	14
19	6	15
20	6	16
21	7	16
22	7	17
23	7	17
24	8	18
25	8	18
26	9	19
27	10	19
28	10	20
29	10	20
30	11	21
31	11	22
32	11	23

(Continued)

Appendix (Continued): Table for Testing Randomness of Grouping in a Sequence of Alternatives

Total Number of Data Points on the Run Chart that do not Fall on the Median	Lower Limit for the Number of Runs (< than this number runs is "too few")	Upper Limit for the Number of Runs (> than this number runs is "too many")
33	12	23
34	12	24
35	12	24
36	13	25
37	13	25
38	14	26
39	14	26
40	15	27
41	15	27
42	16	28
43	16	28
44	17	29
45	17	30
46	17	31
47	18	31
48	18	32
49	19	32
50	19	33
51	20	33
52	20	34
53	21	34
54	21	35
55	22	35

(Continued)

Appendix (Continued): Table for Testing Randomness of Grouping in a Sequence of Alternatives

Total Number of Data Points on the Run Chart that do not Fall on the Median	Lower Limit for the Number of Runs (< than this number runs is "too few")	Upper Limit for the Number of Runs (> than this number runs is "too many")
56	22	36
57	23	36
58	23	37
59	24	38
60	34	38

Table is based on about a 5% risk of failing the run test for random patterns of data. Adapted from Swed FS, Eisenhart C. Tables for Testing Randomness of Grouping in a Sequence of Alternatives. Annals of Mathematical Statistics. 1943;XIV:66-87, Tables II and III.

Chapter 9

Leading Effective Teams: For Clinical Care and for Performance Improvement

Delivering safe, high-quality, efficient, and effective health care requires multidisciplinary teams that are proficient in coordination and collaboration. Fragmented care is a key contributor to poor quality outcomes including preventable readmissions, medication errors, and adverse drug events. Care is fragmented both within facilities and across facilities, leading to miscommunication, and duplicative care, and missed opportunities, often to the detriment of the patients. Strong teams—both clinical care teams and performance improvement teams—are necessary to improve care coordination and reduce the fragmentation that leads to low-quality, high-cost health care. An important role for leaders is to "get the right people on the bus" and lead and coach teams to success through promoting open communication and transparency, maximizing the skills and contributions of all team members, and focusing on execution toward the goal of delivering safe, high-quality care.

Evidence

Teams and teamwork are often hailed as solutions to much of what ails the U.S. health care system. There is certainly much potential to improve quality, safety, efficiency, and the patient experience through team-based care. Not all teams are created equal, however. Creating effective teams requires an informed and intentional approach.

A team is defined as involving two or more people who differentiate their roles, share common goals, interact with each other, and perform tasks that affect others (Taplin, Foster, and Shortell 2013). Specifically, work teams accomplish tasks on an ongoing basis in a specific organizational setting (e.g., primary care team, surgical team, emergency department team). Other types include parallel teams to address shared challenges, project teams to focus on a one-time deliverable with a limited term, and management teams for oversight. This chapter includes strategies for clinical leaders to create effective work teams (i.e., clinical care teams) and project teams (i.e., performance improvement teams with specific, measureable aims).

Clinical Care Teams

Currently, much of U.S. health care is delivered in silos with physicians and practice staff isolated from one another. Practices are often designed around supporting physicians' routines, not around patient needs or preferences. As a result, practices struggle to meet the increasingly diverse needs of patients (Chesluk and Holmboe 2010) and, in many cases, patient satisfaction and outcomes suffer.

National efforts such as accountable care organizations and patient-centered medical homes incentivize hospitals and practices to re-organize to be team-based and to have processes and work flows that are dictated by patient, not provider, needs. Both local and national efforts are also increasingly emphasizing the role of patients and their family members as active and important members of care teams.

Research shows that effective teams have the following characteristics: strong leadership, a clear division of labor, adequate training for team members in their respective roles, and organizational policies that support the team structure. To build and maintain effective care delivery teams, organizations must invest in training, creation of protocols, adoption of rules related to decision-making and communication, and granting of designated, non-patient care time for team meetings (Bodenheimer 2007). Clinical leaders have unique insights into the importance of these components and can be advocates for creating protocols and rules that effectively guide and streamline patient care work processes and allow all members of the team to maximize their contribution to patient care. Without organizational support and a culture that values teamwork, care will remain siloed and uncoordinated.

Two key mechanisms that leaders can use to support teams are: (1) providing training and support (i.e., designated non-patient care time) for teamwork; and (2) aligning incentives and interdependent functions of team members to achieve patient goals (Taplin et al. 2013). Support and training includes creating an organizational culture that promotes teamwork, providing teamwork training for employees on specific skills, emphasizing hiring and promotion based on both team and technical clinical skills, prioritizing ongoing coaching, providing time for non-patient care, and ensuring that all team members are recognized and reimbursed for their time and contributions (Taplin et al. 2013). Aligning incentives also involves creating policies and reward and recognition systems that focus on patient outcomes. Leaders can create alignment through emphasizing and publicly recognizing the roles of all team members in achieving good patient outcomes. Increased understanding of the various roles of team members creates trust and respect, both of which are important to enabling high-functioning teams.

Performance Improvement Teams

Performance improvement teams are project teams that are time-limited and organized to achieve a specific improvement aim. A clinical leader's first role in leading improvement teams is to recruit a multidisciplinary group of individuals to comprise the team. Performance improvement teams can vary in size and composition; both factors should be dictated by the needs of the project. Leaders should begin by reviewing the project's aim and considering which systems and departments contribute to the process under review (Health Research & Educational Trust 2013). The team should include representatives from all relevant disciplines, which may include: nurses, physicians, administrators, patients, receptionists, environmental services, pharmacy, social workers, behavioral health, billing and finance, or others. The optimal size of an improvement team is five to eight individuals, but will vary based on the needs of the project. Improvement teams should include a patient or family member whenever possible ("Science of Improvement: Forming the Team").

The Institute for Healthcare Improvement recommends that quality improvement teams include at least one individual with each of the following expertise: clinical leadership, technical expertise, day-to-day leadership, and project sponsorship ("Science of Improvement: Forming the Team").

- *Clinical leaders* have the authority to test and implement changes and can provide insight related to how proposed changes may inadvertently impact other parts of the system. They also provide insights into how proposed changes will impact clinical care.
- *Technical experts* provide the best insight into the specific process or subject at hand. For example, experts in performance improvement can guide teams in choosing measures and collecting and analyzing data. A project to improve discharge planning may include nurses as technical experts—those who deliver the discharge instructions—but also electronic health record technicians who may have intimate knowledge in regard to technical pieces of the discharge planning process.
- The *day-to-day leader* on the quality improvement team ensures the implementation of small tests of change, data collection, and monitoring of results. This individual is the driver of the project and must work closely with the

physician champion (see Chapter 4) to effectively engage clinicians and other frontline staff.

■ Finally, every improvement team should have a *project sponsor*, someone with the executive authority to provide resources, address barriers, and provide a link to senior management and the strategic aims of the organization. Project sponsors need not participate in the day-to-day activities of the project but should be regularly updated so they can effectively address barriers that arise.

Strategies for Success

Implementation science and research on effective teams is an emerging field. One program that has produced great success in changing organizational culture and building effective clinical care teams is the Team Strategies and Tools to Enhance Performance and Patient Safety. The following case study highlights the key components of the TeamSTEPPS curriculum. Organizations can access tools online and enroll in the training program for more information.

Effective Strategy: TeamSTEPPS

In 2006, the Department of Defense Patient Safety Program released Team Strategies and Tools to Enhance Performance and Patient Safety. TeamSTEPPS is a collection of tools, strategies, and training curriculum focused on establishing high-performing teams through:

■ Producing highly effective medical teams that optimize the use of information, people, and resources to achieve the best clinical outcomes for patients;
■ Increasing team awareness and clarifying team roles and responsibilities;
■ Resolving conflicts and improving information sharing; and
■ Eliminating barriers to quality and safety.

The Agency for Research in Quality and Safety funds a national implementation plan for TeamSTEPPS, which includes support for six regional training centers. Individuals who complete training at these facilities become master trainers and in turn facilitate the TeamSTEPPS training to frontline providers in hospitals and other health care facilities (TeamSTEPPS*: National Implementation).

The TeamSTEPPS curriculum includes five key principles: team structure, communication, leadership, situation monitoring, and mutual support. As depicted in Figure 9.1, the curriculum emphasizes the dynamic, two-way relationship between outcomes (performance, knowledge, attitudes) and skills (leadership, communication, situation monitoring, and mutual support), encircled by the patient care team.

Figure 9.1 TeamSTEPPS framework and competencies. (Agency for Healthcare Research & Quality, 2014.)

The patient care team includes not only those directly responsible for providing medical care, but also all of those on and off the medical staff (i.e., family members, caregivers) who are involved in the patient's care.

Effective Strategy: Patient and Family Engagement

One emerging and promising practice in health care is the emphasis of engaging patients and families on teams, both clinical care teams and improvement teams. A growing body of evidence (more in Chapter 10) suggests that initiatives to promote patient and family engagement in care lead to better outcomes. Effective clinical care teams will include patients and family members through best practices such as shared decision-making, hourly rounding, and bedside shift change.

Additionally, patients and families can also serve as advisors in quality and patient safety initiatives. Patient and family advisory councils are one promising practice that leverages the experience and insight of patients to improve care. Patient advisors can also serve on standing quality and safety committees or participate in governance meetings to share their stories and experiences.

Communication • SBAR – Situation, Background, Assessment, Recommendation and Request • Call-Out • Check-Back • Handoff – I PASS THE BATON
Leadership • Tools: Team Events – Brief, Huddle, Debrief

Situational Awareness
• Situational Monitoring (Individual Skill)
    • STEP – Status, Team, Environment, Progress
    • I'M SAFE Checklist – Illness, Medication, Stress, Alcohol and Drugs,
      Fatigue, Eating and Elimination
• Situational Awareness (Individual Outcome)
• Shared Mental Model (Team Outcome)

Mutual Support • Task assistance • Feedback – Timely, Respectful, Specific, Directed towards improvement,   Considerate • Advocacy and Assertion • Two-Challenge Rule • Assertve Statements: CUS • DESC Script • Team Performance Observation Tool

Case Study: Building an Improvement Team

The following case study provides an example of how an improvement team might be identified and formed and emphasizes the role of the clinical leader in supporting such a team.

Roger, a nurse, notices a high rate of falls on his unit and, wanting to improve patient safety, shares this data with the department quality officer, Sharon. Sharon recently filled this leadership role after practicing as a physician for 20 years. She is new to the role but is committed to supporting this team in their goal of reducing patient harm.

After analyzing the data and comparing the unit's fall rate to others in the organization and to other similar facilities, Sharon determines that a performance improvement team to reduce falls will be a worthwhile effort that aligns with the hospital's mission of providing safe, high-quality care. As a clinical leader, she agrees to be the project sponsor and begins gathering information to bring to senior leadership to convince them to allocate the resources the team will need to be successful. Sharon provides a crucial link to leadership and has the important role of advocating for resources and removing barriers for her team to be successful.

Meanwhile, Roger begins assembling the rest of the team, including a day-to-day leader, technical experts, and clinical leaders. Roger and Sharon determine the aim of the team to be "to reduce patient falls on the unit by 50% in six months."

Based on baseline data, they suspect that many patients on the unit are falling due to lack of ambulation, side effects of medications, and slippery floors. Given his knowledge of and commitment to this issue, Roger agrees to take on the role of day-to-day leader of the team. He will ensure that data is collected, displayed, and used to drive rapid cycle improvement and small tests of change. Roger recruits additional clinical experts including the pharmacist (he suspects some falls may be due to medication side effects), a physical therapist, and a facilities manager who is responsible for ordering hospital beds and floor mats. Roger also recruits the husband of a patient who recently fell while staying at the hospital. The man was visibly and understandably upset that his wife suffered harm while in the hospital, and expressed his desire to work with the hospital to ensure that a similar situation did not happen again.

Once the team is assembled, Sharon, the clinical leader and project sponsor, attends monthly update meetings and checks in with Roger regularly to receive updates on the team's progress. One of the team's recommendations, which was proven successful through a series of small tests of change, is to add non-slip mats in the rooms of patients who are at high risk for falling. Sharon, as the team's liaison to leadership, brings this recommendation and the accompanying evidence and data to the leadership team. With Sharon as their advocate, the team feels engaged, supported, and valued and continues this important effort, even though it requires additional work beyond their usual responsibilities.

After the six-month project, it becomes clear that the implementation of non-slip mats in patient rooms is an effective strategy to reduce falls and one that can be spread throughout the organization. As a clinical leader, Sharon's next role is to advocate for and facilitate the spread of this intervention throughout her facility to other units that are experiencing high rates of patient falls. Through working with the executive team, she is able to demonstrate the value and success of the project and succeed in sharing the results and spreading the intervention to additional units, which results in a significant decline in falls across the organization.

Voice from the Field: Ken Anderson, MD, Chief Operating Officer, Health Research & Educational Trust

Q: **What makes a successful team?**

A: There are three key components that contribute to team success: skills, commitment, and accountability. Team members should have complementary skills including problem solving, technical skills, and interpersonal skills (e.g., communication). Strong teams rally around a common purpose and common goals and have structures for accountability.

Q: **What are some common misconceptions about teams?**

A: Teams need to be put in place with a clear goal and purpose; creating a team should be directly associated with solving a problem. If the team does not have a clear challenge, aim statement, goals, and measures, it is unlikely to succeed. Many people believe that the success of the team is directly attributable to the team leader. The team leader has the important role of building commitment and identifying and filling gaps on the team, but the largest driver of success is not the leader, but rather the ability of all team members to engage in the common purpose and hold one another accountable. A similar misconception is that all the expertise lies with a few key people on the team. In fact, opportunities are often missed when teams do not allow all members to contribute. The final misconception is that successful teams have a few hard-working people who drive the team's success. In fact, teams that have a more balanced and distributed approach to their work are more likely to create richer, more sustainable solutions.

Q: **What are some useful tools for teams to use in implementing clinical quality improvement projects?**

A: The tools will be dictated by the needs of the project and the speed of change required. For example, larger process improvement projects to address throughput or staffing patterns will require tools such as Plan–Do–Study–Act cycles, Lean, or Six Sigma. These tools promote incremental change over a long time horizon. When a critical clinical event occurs, such as a patient fall, wrong site surgery, or hospital-acquired infection, shorter horizon tools should be used. Tools such as the 5 Whys,* workout sessions (daylong sessions to brainstorm and come up with a solution to the problem), and "just do it projects" drive more rapid, small-cycle change. Most importantly, the tools should match the problem.

Q: **One important role for a clinical leader is "getting the right people on the bus." What characteristics do you look for in recruiting team members? What strategies do you use to recruit and engage people?**

A: Roger's diffusion of innovation model identifies five groups: innovators, early adopters, early majority, late majority, and laggards. Teams often aim to recruit innovators and early adopters but they should also look among the late majority to find skeptics. It is important to distinguish between skeptics and cynics. Cynics are not good team members because they are not willing to change. Skeptics, however, are great people to have on a team. Skeptics ask the difficult questions but are amenable to change if convinced with data that the change will produce a positive result. Often, skeptics can become the strongest advocates of a program with

---

* The "5 Whys" is an exercise where a team asks "why" five times when a failure has occurred to get to the root cause of the problem.

which they initially disagree. It is also important to recruit from the frontl ine and to have team members who are authentic spokespersons for the process.

Q: **Creating effective teams has a lot do with culture. As a clinical leader, how can you promote a culture of teamwork and collaboration?**

A: A good place to start is to give the front line a voice. Often there is too much deference to physicians because of perceived expertise, even outside their area of focus. This leads to a less robust discussion than is possible and the exclusion of other important voices from the front line. A skilled facilitator will enable everyone's voice to be heard. A critical first step is setting and agreeing to ground rules as a team.

Q: **What are some common barriers to effective teamwork?**

A: The first mistake is to assume that all the right people are in the room. There may be people in the room who do not contribute to the process, or there may be people left out of the room that do have intimate knowledge of the process at hand and should be included in the discussion. It is important to begin any project by asking, "Do we have everyone in the room that we need?" The clinical leader has a key role in holding pre-screening meetings to ensure that everyone on the team is a good match.

The second barrier is lack of direction. When teams do not have a clear aim and charter with measures and goals, they are likely to struggle. It is important to establish who will do what by when. Third, accountability is very important. Team leaders must have strong interpersonal and communication skills to promote a culture of accountability. A good tool to drive accountability is to end each meeting outlining the 3 Ws: "who will do what by when." The biggest mistakes are made in the assembly of the team, not getting the right people in the room, or creating a team when there is no need for one. When projects lack a well-disciplined plan from the start, they are likely to fail. A strong team leader is efficient with people's time, promotes open dialogue and inclusion of all perspectives, and promotes accountability to each other and to the team's goal.

Lessons Learned

Over the past decade, the increased focus on teams and team-based care has yielded many lessons learned. Key lessons for implementation include:

1. **Form drives function.** Teams—both for delivering clinical care and for driving improvement—must be built with the function or aim in mind. Emergency room teams will differ from primary care and surgical teams. Similarly, improvement teams to reduce hospital-acquired infections within

a unit will differ from those working to reduce readmissions across a hospital system. Efforts to de-silo and coordinate care across the continuum will require new representation from home health to public health. Similarly, improvement efforts across the continuum of care—from unit-based interventions to community-level interventions—will require different teams that include different perspectives (Health Research & Educational Trust 2013). The two key features of all teams, however, are that they should be interdisciplinary and engage a patient representative.

2. **Clinical leaders and executive sponsors are keys to securing resources and removing obstacles.** As a clinical leader, your primary role is to get the right people on the team and then advocate to senior leadership to secure the necessary resources (human, financial, time) for the team to succeed. As a leader, your team should come to you with barriers and your energy should be focused on removing those barriers, not on micromanaging the day-to-day activities of the team.

3. **Culture change is essential.** Simply grouping individuals together and calling them a team is not sufficient. To truly promote both team-based care and a culture of continuous improvement, organizations must re-orient to focus on the needs of the patient, not those of clinicians or administrators. Leadership plays a crucial role in initiating and supporting ongoing culture change through providing training in teamwork, engaging individuals throughout the organization in decisions that affect them, and modeling the behaviors associated with effective teamwork (i.e., the principles of TeamSTEPPS).

Action Steps to Lead

1. **Define the aims and objectives of the team first and then build the team accordingly.** For both clinical and improvement teams, the composition and size of the team should be dictated by the purpose or aim of the team. In both instances, teams should be multidisciplinary with individuals representing all key processes affected by the team's work and should include a patient or family member perspective.

2. **Prioritize training and support for teamwork.** Leadership should provide both initial training in specific teamwork skills as well as ongoing coaching to promote a culture that encourages and supports teamwork. Other forms of support can include, but are not limited to, designating non-patient care time for team meetings, reimbursing individuals for team activities, and developing communication plans and decision protocols that reinforce teamwork.

3. **Engage patients and their families in both care and improvement teams.** Patients and family members provide important insights related to safety, quality, and efficiency. Teams should focus on and be built around the needs of the end user—the patient.

References

Bodenheimer, Thomas. 2007. Building Teams in Primary Care: Lessons Learned. *California Health Care Foundation.* http://www.chcf.org/~/media/MEDIA%20LIBRARY%20 Files/PDF/B/PDF%20BuildingTeamsInPrimaryCareLessons.pdf.

Cheslick, Benjamin, and Eric Holmboe. 2010. How Teams Work—Or Don't—In Primary Care: A Field Study on Internal Medicine Practices. *Health Affairs* 29.5:874–879.

Health Research & Educational Trust. 2013. *Leading Improvement Across the Continuum: Skills, Tools and Teams for Success.* Chicago, IL: Health Research & Educational Trust. Accessed at www.hpoe.org.

Science of Improvement: Forming the Team. Institute for Healthcare Improvement. http://www.ihi.org/resources/Pages/HowtoImprove/ScienceofImprovement FormingtheTeam.aspx.

Taplin, Stephen, Mary Foster, and Stephen Shortell. 2013. Organizational Leadership for Building Effective Health Care Teams. *Annals of Internal Medicine.* 11:279–281.

TeamSTEPPS®: National Implementation. Agency for Healthcare Research and Quality. http://teamstepps.ahrq.gov/abouttoolsmaterials.htm.

Chapter 10

Engaging Patients and Families

Patient and family engagement is an important strategy for building organizations that deliver safe, high-quality, patient-centered care. This chapter provides an overview of the range of activities, policies, and strategies that constitute PFE, strategies for success, case studies, and action steps to create more patient- and family-centered organizations.

The Evidence

A growing body of evidence supports the practice of patient and family engagement at both the direct care level and at the organizational level as an effective strategy to improve outcomes in patient safety, quality, and patient satisfaction (Carman et al. 2013; Epstein and Street 2008; Coulter and Ellins 2007; Charmel and Frampton 2008). A report from the Health Research & Educational Trust summarizes the ways in which patient and family engagement can positively impact health care facilities (HRET 2013):

1. Contributes to better clinical outcomes (Weingart et al. 2011).
2. Reduces institutional and individual costs of care (Hibbard, Green, and Overton 2013; Institute of Medicine 2012).
3. Increases adherence to recommended treatment regimens, which can lead to fewer complications and readmissions (McCarly 2009).

4. Improves patient satisfaction with care coordination and other patient experience measures that impact hospital reimbursement rates (Sorra et al. 2012; Weingart et al. 2011).

Engaging patients and families as active partners in care improves the experience of care, promotes patient activation, and leads to improved outcomes—all goals that health care organizations should strive for as places of healing. There are also additional financial motivations for PFE. Reimbursement is increasingly tied to measures of patient satisfaction, experience, and outcomes. PFE can have an obvious impact on improving satisfaction and experience, and can impact health outcomes as well. For example, PFE is an effective strategy to ensure the success of the treatment and medication regimens that are necessary to achieve optimal outcomes.

Research suggests that patients who are more actively involved in their care experience better outcomes. The measure of "patient activation," which refers to a patient's knowledge, skills, ability, and willingness to manage his or her own health and care, is predictive of both outcomes and cost (Health Affairs 2011). Studies have shown that patients with the lowest patient activation scores (i.e., those with the least skills and confidence to actively engage in their own health care) incurred costs up to 21% higher than those with the highest activation levels (Health Affairs 2011). Engaging patients and families in care to increase activation levels shows promise as a strategy to achieve all three dimensions of the Triple Aim: better care, better health, and lower costs.

Patient engagement can take many forms: at the direct care level, in organizational design and governance, and in policymaking in the larger community. A framework developed by Carman et al. (2013) describes a continuum of patient engagement across these settings segmented by "how much information flows between patient and provider, how active a role the patient has in care decisions and how involved the patient or patient organization becomes in health organization decisions and in policy making" (Carman et al. 2013). This continuum provides a framework to strategize and prioritize initiatives to build more patient- and family-centered health care facilities. For example, at the direct care level, the lowest level of engagement, "consultation," involves patients simply receiving information about a diagnosis. At the highest level of engagement, "partnership and shared leadership," the same opportunity would be approached through encouraging treatment decisions made based on patients' preferences, medical evidence, and clinical judgment.

Prevalence of Patient and Family Engagement Practices

Despite the strong and increasing evidence base supporting PFE, the prevalence of PFE practices is relatively limited in U.S. hospitals. In 2013, the Gordon and Betty Moore Foundation and Health Research and Educational Trust surveyed hospitals to determine the prevalence of PFE practices in U.S. hospitals, identify which strategies hospitals use, and identify the largest challenges in implementing PFE practices. Survey results showed that few hospitals have fully implemented the majority of recommended PFE strategies and that there is much variability in the number of strategies currently being used. The survey results also provided insight on the barriers that hospitals face in implementing PFE practices. The top three barriers cited were: competing organizational priorities, the time required to set up and implement advisory programs, and the time available for change of shift reports at the bedside and multidisciplinary rounds at the bedside (HPOE 2014).

Researchers concluded that while some variability in PFE can be explained by hospital characteristics, much seems to be attributable to leadership choices or other factors, not hospital type or location (HPOE 2014). As a clinical leader, it is important to understand common barriers in order to motivate and enable the organization to overcome them. There is great opportunity for clinical leaders to innovate and lead in the area of PFE. The following sections describe the key strategies organizations should implement to increase patient and family engagement.

Effective Strategies for Patient and Family Engagement

Strategies at the Direct Care Level

When patients and families are active participants in their care, patient satisfaction, adherence to treatment and medication regimens, and care outcomes improve. Patient engagement at the direct care level includes "integrating patients' values, experiences, and perspectives in relation to prevention, diagnosis, and treatment" (Carman et al. 2013). Organizations and health care teams should create environments that enable and encourage patients and their families to become active members of the care team. Examples of "must do" strategies at the direct care level include:

- Providing patients unrestricted access to their medical records
- Implementing bedside change-of-shift reports
- Involving patients and families in multidisciplinary rounds
- Using patient- and family-activated rapid response
- Using patient teach-back, having patients repeat back what the provider has explained to ensure effective communication
- Developing online personal health records
- Transitioning policies on "visiting" to be inclusive, welcoming, and patient-driven to include individuals identified by the patient to be "partners in care"

One important policy emphasized by the Institute for Patient- and Family-Centered Care that encourages greater engagement not only from patients but also from their family members and caregivers is to revise visiting policies to move from "families as visitors to families as members of the care team" (IPFCC). Evidence shows that the presence and participation of families as partners in care leads to cost savings, improved patient experience, and reduced readmissions (IPFCC). The evidence is so compelling, in fact, that the Joint Commission has recommended that patients bring a family member or trusted friend with them to the hospital as a safety strategy (McGreevey 2006).

To promote this practice, hospital visiting guidelines should consider the importance of language and proactively invite patients to decide which family members and important friends should participate in their recovery. The definition of "family" should not be dictated by the facility, staff, or traditional conceptions. Instead, hospital staff should ask the patients to define their family and other "partners in care" and determine how they will be involved in care and decision-making.

The Institute for Patient- and Family-Centered Care has developed a brief that includes recommendations for health care leaders with respect to changing hospital visiting policies and practices:

- Ensure that senior executives provide leadership and support to change restrictive visiting policies and practices.
- Involve patient and family advisors in revising visiting policies and practices as well as in orienting, training, and supporting hospital staff for change in practice.
- Use language of partnership, support, and mutual respect. Avoid terms like "visit," "visitors," and "visitation." Use words such as "welcome," "encourage," or "invite" instead of "allow," "permit," or "authorize."
- Develop systems and processes to determine which family and friends the patient designates as "partners in care" and how they will be involved in care.

The full report on visiting policies from IPFCC may be accessed at http://www.ipfcc.org/visiting.pdf.

Strategies to Engage Patients in Organizational Design and Governance

Beyond the direct care experience, health care organizations can engage patients and families in organizational design, quality improvement initiatives, and governance structures in order to more completely and proactively integrate the patient perspective into the organization's operating model (Figure 10.1). The key to PFE at the organizational level is to intentionally, consistently, and meaningfully engage patients and families as advisors through inclusion on ad hoc, short-term projects;

Policies and Procedures	Personnel
Policies in place related to key patient and family engagement efforts	Commitment to patient and family engagement in position descriptions
Mechanisms for employees, patients and families to report concerns about failures to engage patients or families	Patient engagement embedded in new employee orientation and other staff and physician training with patients and family as faculty
Processes for acknowledging and correcting engagement failures	Support for patient and family engagement evaluated in employee reviews
Defined ways to review and improve patient and family engagement processes over time	Incentives linked to meeting patient and family engagement goals
Meetings and Committees	**Data Systems**
Routine inclusion of patients and families as advisors	Patient experience data collected and reviewed
Agendas with topics directly related to patient and family engagement	Evaluation data collected about patient engagement efforts and training
Minutes to reflect substantive discussion of patient and family engagement	Monitoring targeted outcomes for improvement linked to engagement initiatives

Figure 10.1   Integrating a vision for patient- and family-centered care. (Health Research & Educational Trust. 2013. A Leadership Resource for Patient and Family Engagement Strategies. Accessed at www.hpoe.org)

enduring patient and family advisory councils; and quality and safety committees and the board of trustees. Strategies include:

- Building patient and family advisory councils
- Inviting patients to serve on boards or other committees.
- Engaging patients in the design and execution of quality improvement projects
- Engaging patients to assist with staff hiring and training
- Integrate a vision for patient- and family-centered care throughout all policies and procedures, personnel decisions, meetings and committee structure, and data systems

Working with Patients/FamilyAdvisors

The Agency for Healthcare Research and Quality has published a series of toolkits that outline strategies for engaging patients and families. The number one strategy identified is to work with patients and families as advisors. Hospitals must be intentional and thoughtful about recruiting and engaging patient/family advisors and maximizing their contributions. The AHRQ toolkit identifies the following steps in engaging patient and family advisors:

1. Identify a staff liaison
2. Identify opportunities for working with patient and family advisors
3. Prepare hospital leadership, clinicians, and staff to work with advisors
4. Recruit, select, and train patient and family advisors
5. Implement and coordinate advisor activities

In addition to working with individual PFAs, organizations can also form patient/family advisory councils to provide ongoing mechanisms for interaction with PFAs. PFACs are freestanding committees that serve as an advisory resource to the organization. PFACs provide patients with a venue to offer input into policy and program development at the hospital, express challenges or concerns, and provide new ideas and a patient perspective. Hospitals benefit from new insights that may improve care processes and develop stronger relationships with their patients and the larger community. PFACs are not simply venues for patients to bring personal grievances to be addressed and resolved. Rather, PFACs provide opportunities to use stories and experiences, both negative and positive, as catalysts for change.

The following should be considered when developing a PFAC:

■ **Size:** Smaller groups encourage greater discussion and engagement while larger groups promote greater diversity of experience. IPFCC recommends 12 to 18 members as a manageable size.
■ **Composition:** The council should be reflective of the patient community and be diverse in race, ethnicity, gender, age, and experience. Staff members may serve on the council but should not dominate the group. It is recommended that no more than three to four staff members participate on a council.
■ **Structure:** For a formal PFAC, bylaws, terms, officers, committees, and reimbursement for participants should all be considered. Alternatively, if the purpose is to create a time-limited work group to address one specific issue, a formal PFAC may not be necessary or appropriate. The structure should be reflective of the institution's purpose and goals for engaging patients.
■ **Orientation:** When new advisors join the council, they should receive an orientation to the group and the PFA role. This orientation can include information about the organization, the council, its members, roles and responsibilities, expectations, and strategies to be an effective council member. Additionally, some orientation on the basics of health care quality and patient safety may be helpful. For example, an explanation of basic improvement methodology, the organization's structure and methodology for improvement, safety or quality priorities within the institution, and common acronyms, terms, and medical jargon may be helpful to address.

There are many ways to engage patients, from individual care encounters and through board committees to improve safety. The following case studies provide examples of organizations that are highly committed to PFE.

Case Studies

Developing a Patient and Family Advisory Council

BayState Health in Springfield, Massachusetts established a patient/family advisory council for its children's hospital in 2007 and for its adult inpatient hospital in 2010. The children's hospital PFAC comprises 30 members; the adult inpatient hospital PFAC comprises 18 members.

BayState Health describes its PFAC as serving to:

- Ensure the consumer's point of view, perspective, and experience are not only heard but also integrated into all aspects of care
- Promote the delivery of high quality, safety, and positively memorable health care experiences
- Provide a vital link between BayState Health and the community.
- Promote patient centeredness as a fundamental principle to flip the conversation from "what's the matter" to "what matters to you"

The PFAC provides insight into changes that improve services for patients and families; evaluates practices, programs, and services and provides recommendations based on patient- and family-centered principles; voices needs, concerns, and recommendations to be reviewed by hospital leadership; and advises on aspects of hospital operations such as admission/discharge practices, facility design, physician and staff education, patient safety, quality improvement, and communications. Council advisors serve many roles including as advisors, faculty, mentors, ambassadors, and organizational partners.

Partnering with Patients and Families to Achieve High Reliability

In North Carolina, Vidant Health, a regional health system with 8 hospitals and 350 primary and specialty care providers in more than 70 locations, is leading the way in providing patient- and family-centered care. Vidant takes a comprehensive approach by integrating PFE and patient/family advisors from the bedside to the boardroom. Figure 10.2 provides an overview of the roles of patient and family advisors at Vidant. Chief Medical Officer at Vidant, Dr. Mark Rumans, has described key takeaways for leaders related to patient and family engagement:

- **Purposeful rounding:** bedside report, hourly rounds
- **Storytelling and education:** board presentations, videos, staff meetings, conferences, resident and employee orientation
- **Quality teams:** falls with harm, catheter-associated urinary tract infection, hospital-acquired pressure ulcers, ventilator-associated pneumonia, central line-associated bloodstream infections, hand hygiene, pain, long-range planning
- **Review of patient materials**
- **Safety** — safety summit, safety rounds, RCA teams
- **Facility design** — all patients facing construction and renovations
- **Patient portal development and enhancements**
- **Care coordination**
- **Advisors to the board**

Figure 10.2   Patient and Family Advisor Roles at Vidant. (Vidant Health, 2014.)

- ◼ **Leadership:** Get leaders involved and committed early to promote buy-in.
- ◼ **Integrate into existing work:** Don't reinvent the wheel—integrate patient and family advisors to build on existing work.
- ◼ **Transparency** is powerful.
- ◼ **It takes time:** It takes time to change culture; don't estimate the amount of time necessary to make changes. Leadership must create a culture of "no excuses" where there is a sharp focus on execution.
- ◼ **Take a system approach:** For example, Vidant has adopted the Wagner's Chronic Care model, which provides a structure for organizational change through integrating six elements, and has embedded reliability principles to outline patient engagement strategies.

Because of these organization-wide efforts and commitment embedding PFE throughout the system, Vidant has achieved HCAHPS performance in the top 20% across all dimensions of care, an 83% reduction in serious safety events, a 62% reduction in hospital-acquired infections, and many quality awards.

Lessons Learned

A narrow focus on patient satisfaction and patient experience metrics is not sufficient to truly partner with patients and families. Patient and family engagement extends beyond individual care encounters; it is a concept that must be embraced and integrated throughout leadership and governance decision-making processes. Patient experience, satisfaction, or engagement should not be a siloed activity, but rather one that is integrated across all initiatives and departments in the organization.

Results from initial efforts by hospitals to effectively and meaningfully engage patients have been mixed. While some institutions have had great success, others have struggled to overcome barriers. The following lessons represent key learnings from past efforts in PFE that should be noted and translated to improve the effectiveness of future interventions.

Beyond the Bedside

Patient and family engagement extends beyond the medical encounter. Historically, organizations have focused on increasing patient satisfaction scores related to the experience of care (i.e., noise levels, proximity of parking, and overall aesthetics of the facilities). Gradually, patient satisfaction measures have expanded to include measures of patient engagement in the care process, albeit still while in the facility during treatment. These patient engagement initiatives include hourly rounding to include the patient and family, teach-back, effective discharge planning, shared decision-making, and less restricted visitation policies. All of these are important and notable priorities to improve activation and engagement; however, most of these policies focus on the one-on-one interactions between patients, families, and clinicians when the patient presents for treatment. At this point, it is too late to modify the design of the facility (i.e., signage, dietary offerings, care processes) and the patient safety and quality protocols that may significantly impact that patient's stay.

Recognizing this shortfall and the need to move beyond the direct care interactions, the national focus has now shifted again to emphasize partnering with patients and families to proactively build patient- and family-centered care facilities. Increasingly, hospitals and health systems are even extending beyond the walls of the facility to engage patient and family advisors in community-based initiatives and in advocacy and policymaking.

Engage Patients as Partners

Patients and families must be engaged as equal partners in the care process. The concept of patient- and family-centered care is built on the covenants of respect and dignity, information sharing, participation, and collaboration (Johnson et al. 2008). Particularly when patients and family members serve in advisory roles, they should be regarded as equal partners and not as special guests or one-time participants who are quickly dismissed or forgotten. To truly build patient- and family-centered organizations, the patient perspective must be systematically integrated throughout decision-making processes.

Provide Meaningful Opportunities for Patients and Families to Contribute

Individuals who commit to serving in an advisory role aspire to contribute in a significant and meaningful way. Often, organizations build PFACs or invite PFAs to serve in advisory roles but lack the infrastructure or capacity to maximize the input of these advisors. As a result, councils or individuals feel underutilized or ignored. Many PFAs have expressed frustration with working on projects such as "selecting the paint color for the maternity ward" or "reviewing building plans after they are already drawn and approved." They do not feel that these efforts are meaningful or contribute to creating safe spaces for patients to heal. Leadership must demonstrate an ongoing commitment to engage patients in new and meaningful initiatives early and often and should periodically report to the advisors on how patient feedback has been incorporated into decision-making.

Patient and Family Engagement as a Strategy to Eliminate Harm

Patient and family engagement should not be a siloed initiative; it should be a cross-cutting strategy to improve care, including patient experience, safety, and quality. In particular, patient and family engagement should be recognized and utilized as a key strategy to eliminate harm in facilities. As demonstrated in the case studies and examples provided in this chapter, PFAs can be effective advisors and advocates to improve safety and quality. PFAs can serve to improve quality and safety in many capacities: through formal PFACs, as members of standing quality and safety committees, or through participation in board meetings.

Barriers to Engagement

Despite the substantial evidence that supports PFE, many leaders and organizations continue to cite significant barriers to engaging patients and families. A guide from the Health Research & Educational Trust outlines potential barriers (Figure 10.3) at the provider, organizational, and patient level.

As a clinical leader, one important role is to effectively communicate the evidence that supports the implementation of PFE initiatives in order to persuade and motivate the organization to adopt these policies. Figure 10.4 includes a checklist for leaders related to integrating patient and family engagement throughout the organization.

Provider Barriers:

• Perception that involving/engaging patients takes more time
• Limited availability to recognize decision aid opportunities and follow through
• Weak interpersonal skills (communication skills as well as strategies for appropriately involving patient/family members) of care team members
• Uncertainty about what bedside reporting should entail
• Uncertainty about how to involve the patient appropriately

Organizational Barriers:

• Patient privacy/HIPPA concerns
• Risk management concerns
• Liability issues that may arise from sharing data with patients and multiple providers
• Competing priorities for scarce resources in a system that does not consider patient and family engagement to be a top priority
• Lack of resources to set up advisory councils
• Foreign language/cultural barriers
• Lack of senior leadership understanding of and involvement with patient and family engagement issues
• Limited financial support/resources
• Insufficient training of clinical providers about how to engage with patients
• Limited availability and high cost of patient engagement technology and clinical information systems
• Time it takes to set up and implement advisory programs
• Disagreements about when patients should be provided with access to certain data

Patient and Family Barriers:

• Unwillingness of patients to participate in care activities
• Reluctance of patients and family to share personal, sensitive information
• Intimidation felt by patients in the traditional patient/provider relationship

Figure 10.3 Potential barriers to patient and family engagement. (Health Research & Educational Trust. 2013. A Leadership Resource for Patient and Family Engagement Strategies. Accessed at www.hpoe.org)

Action Steps and Strategies to Lead

1. **Determine your organization's current state of patient and family engagement using an assessment tool.** All improvement initiatives should begin with an assessment of the problem; PFE is no different. There are several tools available to help determine your organization's current state and priorities for improvement. For example: Strategies for Leadership: Patient- and Family-Centered Care–A hospital self-assessment inventory; Patient- and Family-Centered Care Organizational Self-Assessment Tool or Checklist for Attitudes about Patients and Families as Advisors.

1. Develop a Clear Vision for Patient Engagement	2. Assess Strengths and Gaps in Your PFE Efforts
1. Ensure your organization has a clear definition of patient and family engagement.	1. Elicit feedback from your senior leadership team, staff, patients, and families about various patient engagement efforts.
2. Discuss patient and family engagement with your senior leadership team so that they understand it matters to you and the organization.	2. Use one or more formal patient engagement assessments to identify strengths and gaps.
3. Elicit input from your board, your staff and representative patients about what your organization will look like if you are successfully engaging patients and families.	3. Inventory policies, processes, position descriptions, and training programs to determine whether patient and family engagement is appropriately included.
4. Make improving patient and family engagement an organizational goal.	
5. Allocate time in meetings with senior leadership, staff, and the board to hear and tell stories about engagement successes and shortcomings.	4. Discuss findings and conclusions with leadership, staff, and patients to create awareness and lay the groundwork for improvement efforts.
3. Implement Your Plan to Strengthen PFE Efforts	**4. Monitor Your Progress in Improving PFE**
1. Assess options for strengthening patient and family engagement at your hospital.	1. Select measures that will allow you to see whether processes and outcomes are changing.
2. Prioritize initiatives based on needs, opportunities, and input from key stakeholders.	2. Ensure systems are in place to collect, analyze, and share data on an ongoing basis.
3. Equip and empower your staff to support the engagement strategies you are implementing.	3. Compile results in a format that is easy to understand and monitor.
4. Anticipate barriers and proactively intervene to overcome them.	4. Share results with staff, senior leadership, the board, community, and the public.

Figure 10.4 Checklist for leading patient and family engagement. (Health Research & Educational Trust. 2013. A Leadership Resource for Patient and Family Engagement Strategies. Accessed at www.hpoe.org)

2. **Develop a clear vision of how your organization will engage patients and families.** Efforts to increase PFE should not be isolated initiatives but rather should be integrated throughout the organization's culture and work systems. Beginning with the organization's mission, leadership should develop and communicate a comprehensive vision for what patient- and

family-centered care means at their facility. Leaders have a key role in communicating and role modeling this vision for partnering with patients and family members.

3. **Demonstrate commitment through providing resources and infrastructure to support patient- and family-centered care.** Many of the barriers to PFE relate to time and limited resources. PFE is often seen as one more initiative that takes away from patient care. Leaders must not only communicate the evidence for PFE and publicly commit to these initiatives but also must support that commitment through providing the resources and infrastructure necessary to support these practices.

References

Benjamin, E., and L. McShane. Patient & Family Advisory Councils: A Valuable Resource to Support Excellent Patient and Family Experiences. Symposium for Leaders in Healthcare Quality. http://www.aha-slhq.org/resources/resources/AHA_SLHQ_Roadmap_PFAC.pptx.

Carman, K.L., P. Dardess, M. Maurer, S. Sofaer, K. Adams, C. Bechtel, and J. Sweeney. 2013. Patient and family engagement: A framework for understanding the elements and developing interventions and policies. *Health Affairs* 32(2): 223–231.

Charmel, P.A., and S.B. Frampton. 2008. Building the business case for patient-centered care. *Healthcare Financial Management* 62(3): 80–85.

Coulter, A., and J. Ellins. 2007. Effectiveness of strategies for informing, educating, and involving patients. *BMJ* 335(7609).

Epstein, R., and R. Street. 2008. *Patient-Centered Care for the 21st Century: Physicians' Roles, Health Systems and Patients' Preferences.* Philadelphia, PA: ABIM Foundation.

Health policy brief: Patient engagement, *Health Affairs* February 14, 2011.

Health Research & Educational Trust. 2013. *A Leadership Resource for Patient and Family Engagement Strategies.* Accessed at www.hpoe.org.

Hibbard, J.H., J. Greene, and V. Overton. 2013. Patients with lower activation associated with higher costs: Delivery systems should know their patients' "scores." *Health Affairs* 32(2): 216–222.

HPOE Live Webinar Series. 2014 The current state of patient and family engagement strategies in American hospitals. July 30.

Institute for Patient- and Family-Centered Care. Changing hospital "visiting" policies and practices: Supporting family presence and participation. http://www.ipfcc.org/visiting.pdf.

Institute of Medicine. 2012. *Demanding Value from Our Health Care: Motivating Patient Action to Reduce Waste in Health Care.* Washington, D.C.: National Academies Press.

Johnson, B., M. Abraham, J. Conway, L. Simmons, S. Edgman-Levitan, P. Sodomka, J. Schlucter, and D. Ford. 2008. *Partnering with Patients and Families to Design a Patient- and Family-Centered Health Care System: Recommendations and Promising Practices.* Bethesda, MD: Institute for Patient- and Family-Centered Care.

McCarly, P. 2009. Patient empowerment and motivational interviewing: Engaging patients to self-manage their own care. *Nephrology Nursing Journal* 36(4): 409–414.

McGreevey, M. (Ed.). 2006. *Patients as Partners: How to Involve Patients and Families in Their Own Care.* Oakbrook Terrace, IL: Joint Commission Resources, Inc.

Rumans, M., and D.H. Handron. Engaging Patients and Families in Quality and Safety Performance Improvement. Symposium for Leaders in Healthcare Quality. http://www.aha-slhq.org/resources/resources/AHA_SLHQ_Roadmap_Pt_Family_Eng_HRO.pptx.

Sorra, J., K. Khanna, N. Dyer et al. 2012. Exploring relationships between patient safety culture and patients' assessments of hospital care. *Journal of Patient Satisfaction* 8(3): 1–9.

Weingart, S.N., J. Zhu, L. Chiapetta et al. 2011. Hospitalized patients' participation and its impact on quality of care and patient safety. *International Journal for Quality in Health Care* 23(3): 269–277.

Chapter 11

Improving Care Coordination and Reducing Readmissions

Over the past decade, significant attention and funding have been devoted to reducing readmissions in an attempt to both improve quality and reduce costs. Readmissions are frequently occurring, expensive, and sometimes life-threatening events that can often be attributed to a lack of care coordination, including gaps in care transitions and follow-up care (HRET 2014; Jencks, Mark, and Coleman 2009). Investments in pilot interventions to reduce readmissions have led to some consensus around promising practices that result in better care coordination, reduced readmissions, and better outcomes for patients. This chapter provides a summary of the most successful efforts in care coordination and reducing readmissions, identifies the most effective strategies, and concludes with action steps for clinical leaders to successfully implement those strategies.

Evidence

In 2009, a study by Joynt and Jha published in the *New England Journal of Medicine* concluded that readmissions among Medicare beneficiaries were not only costly to the U.S. health care system but also very common. Almost one fifth (19.6%) of Medicare beneficiaries during the study period were re-hospitalized within 30 days of discharge. Within 90 days of hospital discharge, the readmission rate increased to 34%. Most importantly, the study estimated that merely 10% of readmissions were planned, suggesting that there is significant opportunity to reduce the number of unplanned readmissions (HRET 2014).

Readmissions have recently come under scrutiny from payers and patient advocates due to a growing body of literature that suggests unplanned readmissions are associated with lower quality of care (Benbassat and Taragin 2000). Encouragingly, research and pilot programs have demonstrated the effectiveness of interventions such as patient education, pre-discharge assessment, care coordination strategies, and strategies to target social determinants of health in reducing unplanned readmissions.

In addition to concerns about quality, readmissions are very costly for the health care system and for patients. In 2010 alone, the rate of hospital readmissions was 19.2% and cost Medicare $17.5 billion (CMS 2012). Though readmissions are a cost for payers, prior to 2012 hospitals were reimbursed in full for readmissions under the fee-for-service system. Thus, hospitals were not incentivized to reduce readmissions, but rather to increase the number of patients admitted in order to maintain revenue and operations.

In 2012, the Centers for Medicare and Medicaid Services implemented the Medicare Hospital Readmissions Reduction Program to correct this misalignment of incentives. This program penalizes hospitals for excess readmissions through a reduction in their Medicare reimbursement rate. In 2015, the maximum penalty for inpatient hospital payments will increase to 3%, up from 2% from 2013, a nontrivial incentive for hospitals (HRET 2014). This program begins to correct the perverse incentives of the fee-for-service system to reward high-quality care and reduce readmissions, though many challenges remain.

Recent data suggests that the resources, attention, and investment in reducing readmissions are beginning to yield results. From 2007 to 2011, the national 30-day, all cause, hospital readmission rate averaged 19%. In 2012, that rate dropped noticeably for the first time to 18.5% (HRET 2014). Many organizations have successfully addressed readmissions. Those efforts are now beginning to register on a national scale.

In 2010, the Health Research & Educational Trust, in partnership with the Commonwealth Fund and John A. Hartford Foundation, developed a health care leader action guide to reduce readmissions, which includes summaries of the most promising interventions and pilot programs to date. The following section provides summaries for four key programs that have the strongest evidence for success: Project RED, the Care Transitions Program, Evercare Care Model™, and the Transitional Care Model.

Boston Medical Center Re-Engineered Discharge

Project Re-Engineering Discharge is an intervention developed by researchers at Boston University Medical Center that is based on 12 discrete, mutually reinforcing components (Figure 11.1) that aim to improve communication and streamline the

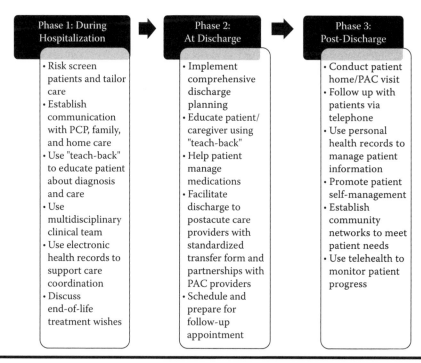

Phase 1: During Hospitalization	Phase 2: At Discharge	Phase 3: Post-Discharge
• Risk screen patients and tailor care • Establish communication with PCP, family, and home care • Use "teach-back" to educate patient about diagnosis and care • Use multidisciplinary clinical team • Use electronic health records to support care coordination • Discuss end-of-life treatment wishes	• Implement comprehensive discharge planning • Educate patient/caregiver using "teach-back" • Help patient manage medications • Facilitate discharge to postacute care providers with standardized transfer form and partnerships with PAC providers • Schedule and prepare for follow-up appointment	• Conduct patient home/PAC visit • Follow up with patients via telephone • Use personal health records to manage patient information • Promote patient self-management • Establish community networks to meet patient needs • Use telehealth to monitor patient progress

Figure 11.1 Strategies for improving care coordination and reducing readmissions. (Osei-Anto, A., Joshi, M., Audet, A.M., Berman, A., Jencks, S. Health Care Leader Action Guide to Reduce Avoidable Readmissions. Health Research & Educational Trust, Chicago, IL. January 2010.)

multiple components that contribute to a successful discharge. The initial implementation of Project RED resulted in a 30% reduction in readmissions and emergency room visits (Project RED). As a result, the Agency for Healthcare Research and Quality funded the creation of a toolkit that enabled others to adopt and replicate the success of the program. This toolkit is available free of charge online at www.bu.edu/fammed/projectred/toolkit.html.

Key elements of the Project RED approach include patient education, comprehensive discharge planning, an after hospital care plan, and a post-discharge phone call for medication reconciliation.

Care Transitions Program

The Care Transitions Program was developed to address the need for an interdisciplinary, patient-centered transition that improves continuity of care across multiple settings and providers. This 4-week program pairs older patients that have complex care needs with a Transitions Coach (Coleman 2007). The Transitions Coach, typically a discharge nurse, visits the patient prior to discharge and at home or a skilled nursing facility two to three days post-discharge. In addition, they have three follow-up telephone calls with the patient over the first 28 days post-discharge (Alper, O'Malley, and Greenwald 2014).

The role of the Transitions Coach is to empower the patient and caregiver to actively build self-management and care skills for the transition process from hospital to home. This includes encouraging the patient to maintain a discharge preparation checklist, a personal health record that consists of interdisciplinary communication elements during the care transition, as well as set up timely follow-up appointments (Alper, O'Malley, and Greenwald 2013; Coleman 2007). Furthermore, they help the patient develop problem-solving and communication skills for addressing common challenges in care transitions (Coleman 2007). A study that evaluated the Care Transitions Program demonstrated that it reduced 30-day readmissions from 11.9% to 8.3% and 90-day readmissions from 22.5% to 16.7%, with an average cost reduction of $500 per patient caseload (Coleman et al. 2006).

Note that the role of the Transitions Coach is not to provide skilled care or to directly fix the patient's problems, but rather to provide guidance and tools. This intervention is fundamentally a self-management model based on the premise of adult learning and skills transfer and works to sustainably address a patient's current and long-term needs (Coleman 2007).

Evercare™ Care Model

A home and community-based program, Evercare's At Home Model provides an alternative to traditional nursing homes. This program is designed for elderly and disabled Medicaid patients and patients with long-term or advanced illnesses (Evercare 2010). It was originally developed when two nurse practitioners in Minnesota observed that elderly patients were having difficulty in seeing their primary care provider regularly, which often led to emergency department visits and hospital admissions. They hypothesized that patients would benefit from personalized, compassionate, and highly responsive care and developed the Evercare Model to deliver such care. The Evercare Model includes the following key elements (UHC 2014; Kappas-Larson 2008):

■ Pairing of a patient with a nurse practitioner to help coordinate and provide care that focused on the patient's psychosocial well-being.
■ Holistic monitoring of the patient's physical, social, and psychological needs while focusing on prevention.
■ Minimized patient care transfers.
■ Care teams to advocate for patients and assist in maximizing health insurance benefits.

■ Stronger and more consistent communication among the patient's family, care team, and nursing home staff.

Currently, the Evercare model is used by clinicians across the country, in nursing homes and in the community, to care for elderly patients who live independently or have special medical needs (Kappas-Larson 2008).

Transitional Care Model (TCM)

Elderly adults who have chronic co-morbidities and receive complex therapies are at particularly high-risk of experiencing mismanagement of care (Transitional Care Model 2013). Major factors contributing to this risk include uncoordinated care, fragmented communication between providers, inadequate patient and caregiver education, and insufficient access to services. TCM was developed to address the transition from a hospital to a post-acute care setting or home.

TCM equips patients and family caregivers with strategies to more effectively manage the patient's multiple chronic illnesses. Essential elements of the program include:

■ A transitional care nurse who uses advanced knowledge and skills to coordinate the care of high-risk patients within and across all health care settings.
■ Holistic and comprehensive assessment of each elderly patient's prioritized needs, preferences, and goals.
■ Regular home visits by the TCN with ongoing telephone support available.
■ Multidisciplinary approach involving the patient, family caregivers, and health care providers as members of the same team.

Studies have proven TCM to be effective in reducing hospital readmissions, improving post-discharge health outcomes, and enhancing patient and family caregiver satisfaction (TCM 2013).

Strategies for Success

Figure 11.1 outlines interventions to reduce readmissions pre-discharge, at discharge, and post-discharge. These strategies vary in complexity and the amount of resources required. A hospital's existing infrastructure and capacity may or may not support the implementation of these interventions; some may require additional resources, installation of new technologies, formation of new partnerships, or culture change.

In addition to adopting these specific strategies, the role of clinical leaders is to develop a comprehensive, customized approach to care coordination and read-missions reduction at their facility and within their community. The overarching strategies in Figure 11.1 can guide the development of such an approach.

Identify Patients at High Risk for Readmission

Screening patients to identify those at higher risk of readmissions can help provid-ers tailor interventions to them in a timely manner. No risk stratification tool is perfectly accurate, and patients with highly advanced disease or at-risk socioeco-nomic situations will likely have unpreventable readmissions (Alper, O'Malley and Greenwald 2013). However, one risk stratification tool that has been used success-fully is the LACE index. Upon admission, this tool assesses information on the patient's acute admission, comorbidities, length of stay, and emergency department visits during the previous six months, which can be pulled from the patient's medi-cal record. The LACE risk score for readmission is then calculated. A patient's score assigns them to a risk level, which suggests tailored interventions for them promptly after admission. If necessary, charge nurses can modify a patient's risk level based on their clinical judgment (Nataraja 2014).

Build Self-Management Skills

Many patients return to the hospital, often repeatedly, because they lack the skills and understanding needed to adequately manage their condition. Initiatives to improve health literacy and patient activation levels, educate patients on their medi-cations, provide clearly written instructions, and educate patients on symptoms and red flags for complications can all improve self-management skills. However, stud-ies have shown that patients immediately forget 40 to 80% of the medical infor-mation they receive (Dewalt et al. 2010). To ensure that the health care provider communicated information clearly to the patient and family caregiver about self-management skills, the teach-back method is an effective tool that should always be used prior to discharge. The method involves asking a patient or family mem-ber to explain in his or her own words what they need to know or do to care for the patient. In order to competently use teach-back, the provider should use plain language, a caring tone of voice and attitude, comfortable body language and eye contact, and non-shaming, open-ended questions that avoid yielding simple "yes" or "no" answers. To recheck understanding, the provider can ask them to re-explain the information or clarify information if it was initially misunderstood (Dewalt et al. 2010). Evidence has shown that teach-back improves patient-provider com-munication and patient outcomes (Dewalt et al. 2010). Furthermore, in a study on patients with heart failure, patients who underwent the teach-back method correctly answered 75% of self-care teach-back questions 84.4% of the time while hospitalized. During follow-up calls seven days following discharge, 75% of teach-back questions were answered correctly 77.1% of the time (White et al. 2013).

Discharge Planning

Care coordination is a significant challenge and one of the primary drivers of readmissions. In order to adequately prepare a patient for a transition to home, a skilled nursing facility, or other post-acute care setting, the provider must develop a discharge plan, ideally at the start of a patient's hospitalization. Discharge planning is a complex process that involves determining the appropriate post-discharge site of care, a patient's functional self-care abilities, medication reconciliation, and should produce a discharge summary. Medication reconciliation is a process that verifies a patient's list of medications prior to hospital discharge, by identifying medications that have been added, discontinued, or changed. In order to perform accurate medication reconciliation, a provider should have an accurate: (1) pre-admission medication list, (2) list of medications that the patient is taking at the time of discharge, and (3) knowledge of medication changes during hospitalizations and the reasons for the changes. It is critical to perform an accurate medication reconciliation for a successful discharge transition. In a 2012 systematic review, medication reconciliation was associated in most studies with a decrease in potential and actual adverse drug events. Furthermore, many initiatives focus on medication reconciliation in order to prevent avoidable readmissions. The discharge summary is the primary communication tool between hospital and post-acute care providers and should communicate the hospitalization outcome, the patient's disposition, and the necessary provisions for follow-up care (e.g., appointments, care need specifications) (Alper, O'Malley, and Greenwald 2013).

Follow-Up and Community Resources

Many hospital readmissions are unavoidable; however, many readmissions are due to factors that occur either during or after the transition from the hospital to post-acute care. These factors include premature discharge or failed handoffs, insufficient follow-up, adverse drug events, and patient falls (Alper, O'Malley, and Greenwald 2013). To keep patients from returning, it is essential for hospitals to not only identify and educate patients about resources, but also to truly connect patients with the community-based resources they can access for support. Many patients are readmitted because of social or economic barriers including lack of transportation, inadequate nutrition, lack of social support, or inability to access a pharmacy to fill prescriptions. Hospitals have a role in preemptively identifying these barriers and connecting patients with those organizations and social services agencies that can help. Multi-faceted interventions that are comprised of follow-up telemonitoring, home visits, scheduling convenient follow-up appointments for the patient, and follow-up medication reconciliation with a clinical pharmacist over the phone are effective strategies for assessing and addressing patient status, needs, and barriers to adequately receiving and self-administering care following hospital discharge (Alper, O'Malley, and Greenwald 2013).

Case Study—Collaborative Effort to Reduce Readmissions at Griffin Hospital

Griffin Hospital is a 160-bed hospital in Derby, Connecticut (HPOE 2013). Hospital leadership stratified their data and identified an excessively high readmissions rate for patients with congestive heart failure (CHF). The CHF population is largely comprised of the elderly, so hospital leaders partnered with nursing homes, home health agencies, and skilled nursing facilities to better understand each organization's role and potential factors that contributed to readmissions. Through these conversations, the hospital discovered these reasons for CHF readmissions: overconsumption of dietary sodium, lack of consistency in services provided by post-acute home care, lack of follow-up with primary care and cardiac physicians, and differences in teaching tools and protocols used by each organization.

Because of this process, Griffin Hospital created the Valley Gateway to Health collaborative and invited skilled nursing facilities and home health agencies to join in efforts to reduce readmissions. This collaborative resulted in the development of a shared transitional care model that included standardized teaching tools and protocols for providers and patients. The new protocol consisted of the following:

- **Multidisciplinary Team:** Every patient admitted from the emergency department with congestive heart failure is seen by a multidisciplinary team.
- **Discharge Planning:** Prior to discharge, each team member meets with the patient to ensure that he or she understands medical prescriptions, diet and exercise plans, and can recognize symptoms that would require calling the cardiologist or primary care physician.
- **Follow-Up**: After discharge, the hospital follows up with the patient and nursing homes every week for one month.
- **Teach-Back:** Provide patients with information on actions they can take to prevent readmissions. In order to maintain standardized messaging, nursing homes and home health facilities used the same brochure in their conversations with patients.

Because of the collaborative, CHF readmissions decreased from 15% in 2010 to 7% in 2011. Furthermore, internal heart failure readmissions decreased by 34.8% and heart failure readmission to any facility decreased by 23.8% (HPOE 2013).

Lessons Learned

1. **Engage multiple stakeholders across the continuum of care.** To successfully reduce readmissions, any initiative must include practitioners across the continuum of care. This may include representatives from the hospital, primary care, hospice, home health, and long-term care settings. It may also include social services, behavioral health, and community-based organizations that target the social determinants of health.
2. **Engage patients, families, and caregivers.** Patients, their families, and their caregivers are crucial partners in reducing readmissions. The patient and his or her designated family member or caregiver should be included in discussions throughout the care episode. Clinicians must be especially attuned to the needs, concerns, and potential barriers voiced by the patient or his or her family members. Common barriers include lack of transportation to a follow-up appointment, incomplete inventory or medication reconciliation, a lack of access to nutritious foods, or other non-medical causes. Clinicians should listen to the concerns of the patient to recognize and address those avoidable barriers early in the process.
3. **Prioritize interventions.** As with any improvement project, organizations should start small and incrementally add interventions once others have become integrated into the workflow. This will help prevent improvement fatigue. Figure 11.1 provides key interventions to implement during hospitalization, at discharge, and post-discharge. Hospitals can begin with the during-hospitalization and at discharge processes and expand to the post-discharge interventions once they have identified partners in the community as willing participants.

Action Steps to Lead

1. **Start with the data.** Any improvement project, particularly one focused on readmissions, should begin with a thorough examination of the organization's data to identify root causes, patterns, and drivers of readmissions. Clinical leaders should stratify and examine data:
   - **For different conditions:** examine correlation with patient's severity, such as diagnosis and significant co-morbidities.

- **By practitioners:** assess readmission rates by physician to determine appropriateness or if any practitioner type is associated with unexpected readmissions.
- **By readmission source:** examine rates by provider source (e.g., skilled nursing facility, rehabilitation center) to determine the places from which patients are most frequently being readmitted.
- **At different time frames:** readmission rates can be examined at time points such as 7, 30, 60, and 90 days. Earlier time points may reveal gaps in effective transitions to the ambulatory setting, whereas later time points could demonstrate flaws with follow-up care and patients' understanding of discharge instructions.

Patterns in the data will reveal which processes to target. Eventually, sophisticated risk stratification and prediction tools can also help facilities identify patients at high risk of readmission before they are discharged, so that additional measures may be taken as appropriate. Using data and targeted analysis can ensure that interventions are both cost-efficient and effective.

2. **Assess and prioritize your improvement opportunities.** The clinical leader's role is to prioritize interventions and devote resources accordingly based on what the data reveals. Leaders should prioritize interventions that leverage immediate opportunities for improvement within the hospital. For example, clinical leaders could focus on specific patient populations, stages in the care delivery process, leveraging other quality improvement efforts in other areas, or building on the organization's established strengths.

3. **Engage key stakeholders.** Reducing readmissions and improving care coordination requires working with partners inside and outside the hospital. Clinical leaders must engage partners across the care continuum, not only in the implementation process but in the development process as well. Stakeholders should be included in the planning from the beginning of the project to create buy-in and to develop the best strategies. Stakeholders may include patients, physicians, pharmacists, social services, nutritionists, physical therapists, community providers, community-based organizations, and local government. Community partners become increasingly important as interventions move beyond the hospital walls. Community organizations are often better equipped than hospitals to address non-medical factors that put patients at risk of readmission, such as behavioral, health literacy, and cultural issues.

4. **Monitor your hospital's progress.** As with any quality improvement initiative, monitoring the hospital's efforts is the key to sustaining progress in reducing readmissions. Monitoring could shed light on which individual strategies are efficacious and help guide leaders in implementing additional strategies.

References

Alper, Eric, Terrence A. O'Malley, Jeffrey Greenwald, Mark D. Aronson, and H. Nancy Sokol. 2013. Hospital discharge and readmission. *Up To Date.* http://www.uptodate.com/contents/hospital-discharge-and-readmission.

Benbassat, J., and Mark Taragin. 2000. Hospital readmissions as a measure of quality of health care: Advantages and limitations. *Archives of Internal Medicine* 160(8): 1074–1081.

Berenson, Robert A., Ronald A. Paulus, and Noah S. Kalman. 2012. Medicare's readmissions-reduction program—a positive alternative. *New England Journal of Medicine* 366(15): 1364–1366.

Berkowitz, Randi E., Zachary Fang, Benjamin K.I. Helfand, Richard N. Jones, Robert Schreiber, and Michael K. Paasche-Orlow. 2013. Project ReEngineered Discharge (RED) lowers hospital readmissions of patients discharged from a skilled nursing facility. *Journal of the American Medical Directors Association* 14(10): 736–740.

Centers for Medicare & Medicaid Services. 2012. National Medicare Readmission Findings: Recent Data and Trends. Office of Information Product and Data Analytics. Accessed at http://www.academyhealth.org/files/2012/sunday/brennan.pdf.

Centers for Medicare & Medicaid Services. Readmissions Reduction Program. Accessed at http://cms.gov/Medicare/Medicare-Fee-for-Service-Payment/AcuteInpatientPPS/Readmissions-Reduction-Program.html/.

Coleman, Eric A., Carla Parry, Sandra Chalmers, and Sung-Joon Min. 2006. The care transitions intervention: Results of a randomized controlled trial. *Archives of Internal Medicine* 166(17): 1822–1828.

Coleman, Eric A. 2007. The Care Transitions Program. Accessed at http://caretransitions.org/.

Dewalt, Darren A., Leigh F. Callaghan, Victoria H. Hawk, Kimberly A. Broucksou, Ashley Hink, Rima Rudd, and Cindy Brach. 2010. Health literacy universal precautions toolkit. Chapel Hill, NC: North Carolina Network Consortium.

Evercare by United Healthcare. 2010. Physician and Health Care Professional Administrative Manual: Evercare At Home. http://caretransitions.org/.

Health Research & Educational Trust. 2014. Readmissions Change Package: Improving Care Transitions and Reducing Readmissions. 2014 Update.

Hospitals in Pursuit of Excellence. 2013. Collaborative Effort to Reduce Readmissions at Griffin Hospital. Accessed at http://www.hpoe.org/resources/case-studies/1260.

Jencks, Stephen F., Mark V. Williams, and Eric A. Coleman. 2009. Rehospitalizations among patients in the Medicare fee-for-service program. *New England Journal of Medicine* 360(14): 1418–1428.

Joynt, Karen E., and Ashish K. Jha. 2013. A path forward on Medicare readmissions. *New England Journal of Medicine* 368(13): 1175–1177.

Kappas-Larson, P. 2008. The Evercare Story: Reshaping the Health Care Model, Revolutionizing Long-Term Care. Accessed at http://www.medscape.com/viewarticle/571071.

Nataraja, Sruti. 2014. Leverage existing tools to predict readmissions. The Advisory Board Company. Accessed at http://www.advisory.com/Research/Physician-Executive-Council/Expert-Insights/2011/Leverage-existing-tools-to-predict-readmissions.

Osei-Anto, A., M. Joshi, A.M. Audet, A. Berman, and S. Jencks. 2010. *Health Care Leader Action Guide to Reduce Avoidable Readmissions.* Chicago, IL: Health Research & Educational Trust.

Project Red (Re-Engineered Design). A Research Group at Boston University Medical Center. Accessed at http://www.bu.edu/fammed/projectred/.

Transitional Care Model. 2013. Overview of TCM. Accessed at http://www.transitional-care.info/about-tcm.

UnitedHealthcare Medicare Solutions. 2014. Our Story—Our Difference. Accessed at https://www.uhcmedicaresolutions.com/health-plans/special-needs/nursing-home-placement.html.

UnityPoint Health, Picker Institute, Des Moines University, and Health Literacy Iowa. Always Use Teach-back! 10 Elements of Competence for Using Teach-back Effectively. Accessed at http://www.ihi.org/resources/Pages/Tools/AlwaysUseTeachBack!.aspx.

White, Matthew, Roxanne Garbez, Maureen Carroll, Eileen Brinker, and Jill Howie-Esquivel. 2013. Is "Teach-Back" associated with knowledge retention and hospital readmission in hospitalized heart failure patients? *Journal of Cardiovascular Nursing* 28(2): 137–146.

Chapter 12

Addressing Variation in Utilization

There is significant regional and small-area variation in cost, quality, and utilization of health care services in the U.S. (AHRQ 2002). Utilization, broadly defined, is the usage of available health care services that include treatments, diagnostic tests, and surgeries. Clinical leaders must be able to distinguish between warranted and unwarranted variation in cost, quality, and utilization, as well as develop plans to address variation appropriately. This chapter provides an overview of the causes and scope of variation within the hospital setting and provides direction on how to measure and manage variation.

Evidence

Variation is not a new phenomenon. In a now classic study conducted in 1938, Dr. J. Allison Glover uncovered geographic variation in tonsillectomy procedures in schoolchildren in England and Wales. Dr. Glover was unable to identify a cause for the variation other than providers' preferences in performing surgery (Ballard et al. 2014). Decades later, in 1973, Jack Wennberg, who would become a pioneer and leading researcher in variation in health care, published his first paper on small area variation (Wennberg and Gittelsohn 1973). Since then, identifying and explaining variation has been the subject of many studies, including the Dartmouth Atlas of Healthcare, a series of reports dedicated to analyzing health care utilization in the U.S. (Newhouse et al. 2013; Ballard et al. 2014).

Variation in health care spending and utilization generates interest and concern because of its implications for cost and quality. There are many documented instances of systematic variation in Medicare spending and utilization that are seemingly unrelated to health outcomes. In these instances, higher costs do not necessarily correlate with higher quality (Combes and Arespacochaga 2013). Furthermore, research has demonstrated that unexplained variation persists even when controlling for individuals' age, sex, income, race, and health status, and that the unexplained variation is significant (Newhouse et al. 2013). In 2012, Medicare spending per beneficiary averaged at $9,503, and ranged from a low of $6,569 in Grand Junction, Colorado to a high of $15,957 in Miami, Florida (Gnadinger 2014).

As health care costs continue to grow, the potential for savings through reducing unwarranted variation is increasingly becoming a focus of policymakers and health care leaders. In 2009, Peter Orszag, then director of the Office of Management and Budget, cited data that indicated health spending could be reduced by $700 billion annually if high-cost areas incorporated low-cost area practice patterns (Gnadinger 2014). Given the potential to provide care that is higher quality at a lower cost, clinical leaders must develop competencies in identifying and addressing unwarranted variation at their facilities.

Understanding Warranted vs. Unwarranted Variation

Not all variation is inappropriate. Variation may be warranted or unwarranted. Warranted variation occurs because of differences in patient preference, disease prevalence, or other patient-related factors. Alternatively, unwarranted variation is not explained by patient preference or condition. Unwarranted variation implies inefficiency including underuse, overuse, or misuse of services (Gnadinger 2014; Ballard et al. 2014). Potential causes of unwarranted variation include underuse of effective care, misuse of preference-sensitive care, and overuse of supply-sensitive care (Ballard et al. 2014). Preference-sensitive care includes treatments that involve significant tradeoffs that affect the patient's quality or length of life, but for which there is no clear evidence-based recommendation for practice. In these cases, treatment decisions should reflect patients' personal values and preferences (Dartmouth Atlas Project 2007). In many instances, however, there is unwarranted variation in the use of preference-sensitive care due to a failure to accurately communicate the risks and benefits of alternative treatments. As a result, the treatment choice is not based on the patient's values and preferences, but on those of the physician.

Research suggests that the extent and degree of unwarranted variation in the U.S. is a result of the empirical nature of clinical practice and the lack of a foundation in evidence-based medicine. No facility is exempt; even top academic medical centers experience unwarranted variations in delivery and outcomes of care (Wennberg 2002). To provide high value, patient-centered care, leaders must guide their facilities to recognize the systematic underuse, misuse, or overuse of care and to modify practice patterns to provide care that is evidence-based and consistent with patient preferences and values.

There are many reasons to reduce unwarranted variation. Specifically, payment reform and new reimbursement models are designed to reward high value care. Reimbursement is increasingly tied to quality and patient experience outcomes. Facilities that are over- or under-providing care will be penalized under value-based reimbursement. As the health care system shifts from a fee-for-service model to one based on value, providers will be incentivized to deliver appropriate, effective care at a reduced cost to maximize reimbursement and minimize financial penalties. Furthermore, research demonstrates that reducing unwarranted variation improves quality of care and leads to increased patient satisfaction—both important components in the triple aim of health (AHRQ 2002).

In recent years, many stakeholders in health care have sponsored initiatives or educational campaigns promoting evidence-based care and reduction of unwarranted variation. Two examples are the Choosing Wisely Campaign and the American Hospital Association's education related to the appropriate use of medical resources.

Choosing Wisely®

In a 2014 survey funded by the Robert Wood Johnson Foundation, 75% of physicians reported that the frequency of unnecessary medical tests and procedures is a somewhat or very serious problem. To combat this, the ABIM Foundation's Choosing Wisely® Campaign promotes conversations between patients and providers in order to choose care that is evidence-based, not duplicative, free from harm, and truly necessary. This campaign engages medical specialty organizations to identify commonly used tests or procedures that should be questioned and discussed concerning their necessity (ABIM Foundation 2014; Choosing Wisely 2014).

Because of this campaign, leading health care provider organizations across the nation have developed specialty-specific lists on "Things Providers and Patients Should Question." These lists provide evidence-based recommendations for patients and providers to discuss regarding decision-making on the most appropriate care for each individual patient. These recommendations include information such as whether tests and procedures are appropriate in specific situations (http://www.choosingwisely.org/doctor-patient-lists/). In addition to these lists, participants in the campaign have developed patient-friendly materials that use plain language to educate patients on various medical topics, as well as resources on physician-patient communication. These resources empower patients to understand their condition and to initiate conversations with their physicians regarding the appropriateness of care. Physicians can also access a suite of communication education models to help them engage with their patients in these conversations. The campaign equips both physicians and patients to tackle these challenging but important conversations. These resources can be found at http://www.abimfoundation.org/Initiatives/Choosing-Wisely.aspx.

American Hospital Association: Appropriate Use of Medical Resources

Given the exponential increase in medical knowledge, technology, and costs of health care in the U.S., it is important to determine when providers are doing more than is necessary. Particularly, it is important to identify when unnecessary treatment is actually harming instead of helping patients.

The American Hospital Association's Physician Leadership Forum has published a white paper, "Appropriate Use of Medical Resources," that outlines steps for utilizing health care resources in an appropriate and consistent manner. This paper examines the drivers of health care costs, explores the contributing factors, and suggests ways in which hospitals and health systems can lead a movement to more appropriately utilize medical resources. This white paper aims to help delivery systems achieve the triple aim: improved health outcomes, quality patient experience, and lower costs, specifically through reducing utilization of non-beneficial care and educating providers on how to better communicate with patients on these issues. This white paper includes a list of the top five hospital-based procedures and interventions that should be reviewed and discussed between a patient and physician prior to administering that treatment. Similar to the Choosing Wisely® initiative, the AHA's efforts to promote appropriate use of medical resources focus on fostering discussion between patients and providers to ensure that care is not only medically necessary, but also aligned with patients' preferences and values.

Strategies for Success

Many recommendations and evidence-based tools are useful in reducing unwarranted variation. For example, tools that facilitate shared decisionmaking between providers and patients not only ensure high quality of care for the patient but also make more efficient use of clinicians' time (HRET 2011). In 2011, the Health Research and Educational Trust published an action guide for health care leaders on understanding and managing variation and outlined five steps for clinical leaders aiming to reduce unwarranted variation (Figure 12.1) (HRET 2011).

1. **Determine your strategic focus for reducing variation.** Leadership must be clear on the strategic imperative for reducing readmissions: to reduce operational costs, reduce spending on hospitalization, improve patient safety and satisfaction, or strengthen shared decision-making and patient engagement.
2. **Set measurable goals.** Adhering to the adage "what gets measured gets managed," leadership should set measureable goals related to the aim of reducing variation and track progress toward those goals on a regular basis.
3. **Acquire and analyze data.** The first step in addressing variation is to identify it. To do so, organizations must have high-quality data on their own

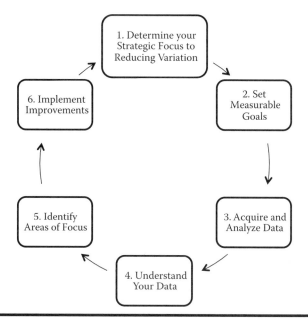

Figure 12.1 Steps to understanding and addressing variation. (Health Care Leader Action Guide: Understanding and Managing Variation. Health Research & Educational Trust, Chicago, IL. February 2011. www.hret.org/variation.)

performance as well as local, regional, state, and national data for comparison. Data acquisition and analysis is necessary to identify and prioritize opportunities to reduce variation. The collection process should focus on a few critical metrics that are most relevant to the operational or clinical processes under scrutiny. Data should be collected from both internal and external sources, and should incorporate multiple sources to minimize the potential shortcomings of various data sources. Sources for comparison and benchmark data include the Dartmouth Atlas, University Health System Consortium, Premier, and the Veterans Health Administration.

4. **Identify areas of focus.** One of the crucial roles of the clinical leader is to prioritize interventions to manage variation. Once variation is identified, leaders should investigate (a) whether the organization's performance varies in a way that positively or negatively impacts patients, the health system, and the community and (b) the drivers and root causes of variation. If it is determined that the variation should be addressed, leaders can identify interventions to reduce variation. Based on national trends, the following areas may yield the greatest opportunity for improvement: readmissions, emergency room utilization, intensive care unit utilization, obstetrics utilization, surgical procedures, appropriateness of admission, diagnostic and treatment procedures, imaging, and end-of-life care. Alternatively, leaders may use the following to

guide the decision of which areas' initiatives to prioritize: those areas with the highest volume of services, that have the greatest financial impact, that are most likely to result in avoidable injury, or have been identified by leadership as a high priority for the organization.

5. **Implement improvements.** As with any improvement initiative, there should be substantial planning before any intervention is implemented. The following questions can help guide the planning process:

   — *Communication:* Has there been visible and sufficient communication focused on the initiative? Are the communications frequent, relevant, and compelling?

   — *Consensus:* Is there adequate buy-in among senior leaders, mid-level managers, and clinical staff at the point-of-care to address the issue? Has utilization management and reduction of unnecessary treatment become part of everyone's job (including the front line)? Or are these efforts isolated and being encouraged only by a few managers?

   — *Leadership:* Is there sufficient leadership to drive improvement and internal decision making that supports change and innovation?

   — *Accountability:* Have improvement initiatives on variation been tied to overall performance metrics? Will senior leaders of key areas be evaluated on their ability to drive improvement?

   — *Timelines:* Has the organization categorized and established several levels of targets (i.e., short-, medium-, and long-term goals and strategies?) Has the organization's leadership agreed on the improvement initiative's timeline and does it include identified milestones?

   — *Micro-centers for change:* Have demonstration sites been selected to serve as models?

   — *Utilization improvement officers:* Are there a sufficient number of utilization experts throughout the organization who can act as resources? Are there available training programs and resources that are designed to maintain the focus and drive for improvement?

   — *Overarching guidelines:* Has the organization adopted the appropriate and current CMS, AHRQ, or other federal guidelines related to utilization? Does the organization's plan look three to five years ahead to maintain a competitive position in the industry?

Interview: Dr. Debra O'Connor, Vice President of Clinical Effectiveness, Advocate Health Care

Dr. Debra O'Connor is the vice president of clinical effectiveness at Advocate Health Care, an integrated delivery system in Chicago. Prior to her current position,

Dr. O'Connor practiced family medicine for over 30 years and has served as medical director at many sites within Advocate Health Care.

Q: **Why did Advocate decide to examine variation in utilization? What are the major drivers for this initiative?**

A: This goes back to the philosophy, mission, and vision of Advocate Health Care, which is to be a high reliability organization with zero safety events by 2020. Advocate recognized the changes in and evolution of health care, including the shift in reimbursement from fee-for-service to population management, growth in capitation, bundled payments, and patients becoming wiser consumers of services. This has created the perfect storm that Advocate wants to get ahead of and we need to get everyone on board, including our leadership team and all our associates, so we can move forward effectively.

Utilization was one area where we noticed physician variation that wasn't tied to better outcomes. Variation drives up costs. For example, the cost of certain products is higher than others, so we're trying to standardize what physicians are using. We also see a lot of waste. If a physician wants to try a product and decides he doesn't like it, he might end up with a lot of unused inventory. There is also additional cost associated with training for different products. If we're using different products for the same service, there is an additional cost to train staff on a variety of products. We've seen that variation in products leads to variation in outcomes, so our focus is on standardizing care because it can lead to better outcomes.

The key to success is to make sure that everyone across the Advocate system is focused on our value proposition: better care and exceptional patient satisfaction delivered in a cost effective way. We do this by looking at the best evidence behind what we're doing, developing guidelines, and continuously looking for ways to improve our processes.

Q: **How have you gone about tackling this throughout the organization? In particular, how do you scale across so many different physicians at so many different sites of care?**

A: The Advocate Clinical Effectiveness team was created in part to address the need for a system approach to tackle variation and utilization. It is a way to look at standardizing care across the system by focusing on physician-driven care with a mission to continuously improve the standard of care across the system. To do this, we've created eight service teams to examine the evidence and discuss guidelines, standards, and the best products to use. Right now, we have teams in transfusion safety, orthopedics, spine, OB/GYN, oncology, cardiology, hospitalist, and general surgery. We're moving into neonatology by beginning to standardize infant formula and will also focus on cardiovascular surgery in the next year. These teams have physicians and representatives from ten sites and include both employed and independent physicians. The teams examine comparative effectiveness data, come to a consensus on effectiveness, and select the best products for use across the system.

We have additional initiatives related to variation in utilization including a medical decision-making team, a sepsis early detection system collaborative, a time-driven activity-based costing initiative to examine total hip and knee replacement (with the Institute for Healthcare Improvement and faculty at Harvard), and diagnostic utilization activities like imaging and laboratory utilization.

Another way we tackle variation is by working with our supply chain partners. We have local supply chain representatives on all of our service teams to share opportunities in supply utilization and acquisition, including new technology.

We are also a partner in an external sourcing collaborative, SharedClarity, which includes not only Advocate, but also Dignity Health System, Baylor, Scott and White Health System, McLaren Health System, and United Health Group, to look at best products in multiple supply areas. The collective partners develop local clinical review teams to come to consensus around best products based on a review of evidence-based research and literature as well as safety data. So far, we have been working on items in cardiology (i.e., DES, bare metal and peripheral stents, as well as cardiac rhythm devices), in radiology (contrast media), and on the surgery front (hernia mesh). Future projects include orthopedic trauma, hip and knee implants. The purpose of the Advocate clinical review team is to engage our physicians' representatives to come together to look at evidence around product selection. For example, for cardiac rhythm devices, we visited the offices of our electrophysiology cardiologists to get their individual opinions on best products and to see what they felt were the new products in development that we should be aware of. We showed them the evidence-based literature and data around the devices being discussed, so they could review current research, literature, and safety information, and then provide their opinions individually. We shared a synopsis of the opinions and comments from those meetings with all EP cardiologists across the system, and then we invited all the EP cardiologists to come together to participate in a few group meetings to collectively discuss their opinions and utilization preferences with their peers. This allowed them to share opinions further and come to consensus around best products. Each of the other health system partners did the same thing locally. The CRT leaders from the separate health system partners then participated in a collaborative meeting to share our local physicians' opinions and preferences, and then see if we could come to a consensus as a 4-system partnership around best products. Once consensus was reached by all, this was shared with the sourcing group, who would then go out to source and negotiate the contract. What is nice about this way of engaging physicians is that it looks at the evidence around best products first in order to drive better health outcomes, and then on the back end, sourcing negotiates the contract using that information. It puts what's best for the patient first, and the value and cost side of the equation as a secondary consideration.

Q: **What are some notable wins that you have achieved?**

A: It's a win that we have active physician engagement, which drives value. The collaboration with the supply chain also drives value. On the service team for transfusion safety, which is the longest standing service team, we've created significant value in terms of safety and appropriate blood use. Over two years, we've saved 51,000 units of blood and blood products, 404 lives, repurposed 98,809 nursing hours, and achieved 67,369 fewer inpatient days (based on NSQIP data).

On the time-driven activity-based costing project, we're looking at total hip and knee replacement through a collaborative across multiple health systems. We are mapping patients' paths across the continuum of care and looking at the amount of time the patient spends with each resource, cost, and efficiencies during each area of care. We have improved resource efficiency, process design improvements, have new bundled payment options, reduced length of stay, have fewer readmissions, a lower complications rate, improvement in pre-surgery education and post-surgery education, and removed Foley catheters and CTM devices that were unnecessary. We also rearranged the hours of physical therapists so we could see patients sooner after surgery. This has reduced length of stay, reduced pain, and increased patient satisfaction.

On the orthopedic service team, we were seeing 6% to 95% variation in antibiotic impregnated bone cements, used to prevent infection in high-risk patients. We brought our orthopedic surgeons together to look at the evidence, talk about the guidelines, and discuss what was driving some physicians to use that product at a high rate. We found that for many, it was simply easier to put the product on the table and use it on almost every patient with the rationale that if they gave it to everyone then they wouldn't miss the high-risk patient that might slip through the cracks. Physicians sitting across the table from each other had frank dialog about their disagreement with that philosophy and countered that patients can be harmed by giving an antibiotic they don't really need. It is the surgeon's job to review the patient history to determine risk status ahead of surgery. Physicians on the orthopedic service team then unanimously decided to uphold the guidelines set forth by their orthopedic society, and we are now seeing significant improvement across the system in appropriate use of this product and better safety and value for our patients.

Q: **What have been some of the key lessons learned in the process?**

A: Physicians want timely and accurate data to help move toward best practice. We also learned to communicate with caregivers with focused messages and actionable items. Additionally, most physicians don't know the cost of supplies and equipment and if they did, they would make better choices.

We learned we need to streamline processes and efficiencies in the workspace of physicians. This helps them to improve efficiency and quality and improves engagement. Physicians also respond to positive reinforcement. Through our clinical integration program, we reward high performance on patient satisfaction and quality. We also learned that we need to be very transparent, develop a culture that manages risk, and continuously focus on innovation and improvement.

We learned that we need to partner together to effect change. This can't just be leadership or physicians or nursing. We need to work as a team to provide high quality care. We need to be connected through IT platforms and share information across the continuum in order to reduce variation. We also found that there is not great alignment in the way insurance plans are designed. Advocate is hoping to have a national voice to help drive alignment between insurance plans and what patients are expected to do to create their own value. Finally, we've seen that to drive change in these population management initiatives, you need a certain volume of patients across the system. This is a work in progress and will take time to fully achieve.

Q: **Any advice for organizations that are thinking of tackling similar initiatives?**

A: This work is about transforming the culture of the organization. We need to move from volume-based to value-based, align key stakeholders, standardize processes, build infrastructure to support changes, and design projects to improve quality, safety, and value. We use PDSA (Plan–Do–Study–Act) cycles to see if we can achieve improvement in one unit before we roll something out across the system. Finally, any strategy needs to put patients and patient interest at the forefront. Leaders need to make the case for a cause to action. For us, that's been to drive value, specifically health outcomes, in a cost-effective manner.

Through all the work we've done, we've learned that it's crucial to engage physicians in the process. They need to feel valued, respected, and a part of the decision-making process. It should be easy for them to participate. For example, we go out to their offices, have meetings or calls early in the morning or in the evenings because it's easier for surgeons to get together and participate. We also pay physicians if they come to late meetings because we respect their opinions and recognize that their time is important. This is a really important part of the process.

Finally, it's important to get really good evidence out there so you can have a dialog of different opinions. This has been a huge lesson. If we just take one person's opinion here or there, physicians don't feel like they're a part of the process. Therefore, we start with a few opinion leaders to develop a baseline opinion, and then expand the process and dialog to include all physicians in that particular discipline.

Lessons Learned

Given the influx of new research related to the extent and causes of variation as well many ongoing initiatives to identify and reduce unwarranted variation, there is immense, ongoing learning in this area of research and practice. The following insights from research and initiatives over the past decade should inform future efforts in this area.

Defining Variation: Warranted vs. Unwarranted. Not all variation is unwarranted or inappropriate (Ballard et al. 2014). Any variation must be investigated to determine whether it is appropriate. Initially, there may be resistance from clinicians when unwarranted variation is identified. As a clinical leader, your role is to drive consensus through data, evidence, and guidelines.

Generating Clinician Buy-In. Particularly for initiatives that target practice variation, clinicians may be resistant to change. Clinicians often believe that variation is explained by the specific demographics of their patients; they are sicker, older, or poorer and cannot be compared to others. Alternatively, you may receive resistance to "cookbook medicine," or fears that implementing clinical guidelines and protocols will eliminate the value of physicians in diagnosing and treating patients. For these reasons, it is important to involve clinicians from the beginning of the project in identifying opportunities to reduce variation, developing guidelines or protocols, and implementing those recommendations. It is important to choose clinicians who are opinion leaders and who will be good ambassadors for the initiative. Persuasion and engagement should rely heavily on ongoing data and feedback, and comparison to published evidence and guidelines.

More than adherence to clinical protocols and evidence-based guidelines. Though reducing variation often does involve the development of and adherence to clinical protocols and evidence-based guidelines, those are not the only strategies. Despite the growing body of evidence-based treatments, there are still many conditions for which the recommended course of action is preference-sensitive. That is, there are important tradeoffs between treatment options and a significant impact on quality of life, yet there is no evidence-based recommendation. In these instances, the course of treatment should be determined by the patient's values and preferences, and only once the patient has been given access to all the appropriate information. Thus, in many instances, reducing unwarranted variation involves the intentional engagement of patients in shared decision making (Center for the Evaluative Clinical Sciences 2007).

Regional intervention vs. targeting decision-makers. The 2013 Institute of Medicine Report on variation in health care spending recommends targeting decision-making to reduce variation (Newhouse et al. 2013). To date, many policy interventions that aim to reduce variation have included geographically based payment policies to encourage high-spending regions to behave more like low-spending ones. Additionally, regional multi-stakeholder initiatives have made significant progress in addressing the local economic, social, political, and environmental drivers of health care utilization. This is one important approach. At an organizational level, key approaches include promoting clinical and financial integration and maintaining robust information systems, including electronic health records.

Action Steps and Strategies to Lead

1. **Engage clinicians with data-driven feedback.** In any initiative to improve care delivery, physicians and clinical stakeholders should be engaged early and often. As a clinical leader, you can convene a group of peer physicians to review data and hypothesize drivers of unwarranted variation. Often, the solution may be the development or adoption of an evidence-based clinical guideline. Clinicians must be engaged throughout the development and adoption process to generate buy-in. All decision-making should be based on evidence and reinforced through data (HRET 2011).

2. **Standardize operational processes using quality improvement interventions.** Variation may be addressed through standardizing processes through quality improvement initiatives. Interventions and tools such as checklists, Lean, Six Sigma, and Plan–Do–Study–Act (see Chapter 2) can guide projects to improve quality, patient satisfaction, and efficiency (HRET 2011).

3. **Implement evidence-based clinical guidelines and appropriateness criteria.** A recent Congressional Budget Office report indicated that less than 50% of medical care in the U.S. is supported by good evidence (HRET 2011). Greater adherence to evidence-based guidelines would result in fewer unnecessary treatments, lower cost, and an increase in appropriate, high-quality care. Appropriateness criteria for certain procedures are important components of evidence-based guidelines and can be used to improve care on a prospective basis.

4. **Initiating and sustaining a culture change toward safety, improvement, transparency, and excellence.** Efforts to reduce variation in utilization should be integrated into everyday processes. External benchmarks by top-performing states have been established and provide examples of collaborative leadership. Aside from clinical and administrative stakeholders, patients

can also play an integral role in helping reduce unwarranted variation. By communicating with patients and learning why they needed to undergo surgery or utilize emergency department services, needed resources or education in the community can be identified in order to reduce unnecessary medical utilization (HRET 2011).

References

ABIM Foundation. 2014. Choosing Wisely®: An initiative of the ABIM Foundation. http://www.abimfoundation.org/Initiatives/Choosing-Wisely.aspx.

Agency for Healthcare Research and Quality. 2002. Improving Health Care Quality. http://archive.ahrq.gov/research/findings/factsheets/errors-safety/improving-quality/improving-health-care-quality.pdf.

Ballard, D.J., B. Graca et al. 2014. Variation in medical practice and implications for quality. In *The Healthcare Quality Book: Vision, Strategy, and Tools*, 3rd ed. Maulik S. Joshi, Elizabeth R. Ransom, David B. Nash, and Scott B. Ransom (Eds.). Chicago, IL: Health Administration Press, pp. 55–82.

Barclay, L. and Désirée Lie. 2009. Surgical checklist may improve outcomes for noncardiac surgery. http://www.medscape.org/viewarticle/586780.

Center for the Evaluative Clinical Sciences. 2007. A Dartmouth Atlas Project Topic Brief: Preference-Sensitive Care. http://www.dartmouthatlas.org/downloads/reports/preference_sensitive.pdf.

Choosing Wisely®: An initiative of the ABIM. 2014. http://www.choosingwisely.org/about-us/.

Combes, J.R., and E. Arespacochaga. 2013. Appropriate Use of Medical Resources. American Hospital Association's Physician Leadership Forum, Chicago, IL.

Gauld, Robin, Jedediah Horwitt, Sheila Williams, and Alan B. Cohen. 2011. What strategies do US hospitals employ to reduce unwarranted clinical practice variations? *American Journal of Medical Quality* 26(2): 120–126.

Gnadinger, Tracy. 2014. New Health Policy Brief: Geographic Variation in Medicare Spending. Health Affairs Blog. http://healthaffairs.org/blog/2014/03/06/new-health-policy-brief-geographic-variation-in-medicare-spending/.

Gregoire, C.O. 2009. A Message from the Governor. http://www.scoap.org/wp-content/uploads/2011/12/SCOAPgovmsg.pdf.

Health Care Leader Action Guide: Understanding and Managing Variation. Health Research & Educational Trust, Chicago, IL. February 2011. www.hret.org/variation.

Joshi, M.S., and Donald Berwick. 2014. Healthcare quality and the patient. In *The Healthcare Quality Book: Vision, Strategy, and Tools*, 3rd ed. Maulik S. Joshi, Elizabeth R. Ransom, David B. Nash, and Scott B. Ransom (Eds.). Chicago, IL: Health Administration Press, pp. 3–29.

Newhouse, J.P., and A.M. Garber. 2013. Geographic variation in health care spending in the United States: Insights from an Institute of Medicine Report. *JAMA* 310(12): 1227–1228. doi:10.1001/jama.2013.278139.

Newhouse, Joseph P., Alan M. Garber, Robin P. Graham, Margaret A. McCoy, Michelle Mancher, and Ashna Kibria, Eds. 2013. *Variation in Health Care Spending: Target Decision Making, Not Geography*. Washington, D.C.: National Academies Press.

Surgical Care and Outcomes Assessment Program (SCOAP). 2014. Surgical Checklist Initiative. http://www.scoap.org/checklists.

Wennberg, John E. 2002. Unwarranted variations in healthcare delivery: Implications for academic medical centres. *British Medical Journal* 325(7370): 961.

World Health Organization. 2014. http://www.who.int/patientsafety/safesurgery/en/.

Chapter 13

Physician Alignment and Clinical Integration

Payers, employers, and the government are implementing new payment models and incentive programs to actively drive the health care delivery system to produce safe, high-quality care at a lower cost. This shift in reimbursement, from a focus on volume to a focus on value, is compelling hospitals and health care systems to improve coordination across the continuum of care. One approach to achieve this alignment between delivery system and provider stakeholders is through clinical integration. This chapter explores the rationale for clinical integration, required elements and infrastructure, and action steps to ensure successful physician alignment.

The Evidence

The call for increased value in health care is embodied in the Institute for Healthcare Improvement's Triple Aim: improved patient experience and better population health outcomes at a reduced cost. This movement toward achieving the Triple Aim has led organizations to identify ways to better align all providers, especially physicians, in the pursuit of high value care.

One strategy to promote alignment is for hospitals and health systems to employ physicians. Employing physicians is the truest form of vertical integration between the delivery system and providers. Some of the most highly regarded integrated delivery systems in this country, including Kaiser Permanente, Mayo Clinic, and Geisinger Health System, have adopted an employed physician model. This model, with its accompanying internal alignment and significant infrastructure, can make care seamless, efficient, and well coordinated. Despite the many advantages, it is a model that cannot be easily replicated in most markets and settings. One of the difficulties in vertical integration through physician employment is the significant investment required to acquire clinical practices. This may be cost prohibitive or completely unfeasible depending on the extent of consolidation by providers in a given market.

As a result, many hospitals and health systems are looking to other models that are short of direct physician employment but still promote alignment between the delivery system and physicians. One popular approach is clinical integration. Clinical integration is an arrangement between two or more distinct health care entities with the explicit goal of ensuring the coordination of care and interdependence of services in order to control costs and improve quality. Clinical integration arrangements are vehicles to link providers across the continuum of care. Stakeholders can include preventive services, inpatient care, and post-acute and ambulatory care centers.

It is important to differentiate true clinical integration from the traditional physician hospital organization arrangement. Historically, PHOs were entities to connect the hospital and medical staff for purposes of joint managed care contracting. In these early PHOs, stakeholders often continued to practice in separate silos and there was little sharing of clinical and financial information and limited coordination of care.

Clinical integration builds upon the PHO framework through incorporating elements of pay-for-performance contracting to benefit the health system and physicians. These value-based incentives are a key differentiator from the legacy PHO model. Financial incentives provide an impetus for stakeholder alignment, encourage integration of care, and serve as the foundation for population health initiatives. As a result, these aspects allow clinical integration programs to evolve from mere pay-for-performance contracting vehicles to entities that support more advanced iterations of pay-for-value programs, including the facilitation of shared savings, bundled payments, or accountable care arrangements.

In addition to serving as reimbursement vehicles, clinical integration programs often also serve as the platforms for health care delivery transformation across the continuum of care. Among physicians, this may include standardizing protocols and guidelines, developing care pathways, ensuring compliance with required technology and, most importantly, creating new care-team models that actively engage other non-physician clinicians. Promoting these tactics can be difficult given the traditional mindset of physicians in which independent practice is emphasized. The best way to mitigate this barrier is to institutionalize physician leadership and governance within the clinically integrated organization. Physician leaders must serve both the roles of champion and peer-influencer to encourage behavior modification. Physician governance structures guide the entire change management process at both the levels of practice and culture.

The Federal Trade Commission requires clinical integration programs to be independently governed entities. Clinical integration programs must have a legal

Figure 13.1 Clinically integrated network: sample organizational chart.

structure that explicitly links payment to outcomes and not to referrals. As a result, it is recommended that clinically integrated organizations create a separate board with equal representation between the delivery system and physicians. It is important to appoint several independent physicians (i.e., not employed) to the board, particularly those who are regarded as opinion leaders within the medical staff. This creates a strong basis for the culture change and transformation of care that is ultimately required for program success.

In addition, the governance model should include several standing board committees with at least 50% physician representation. A sample organization chart is provided in Figure 13.1. In this example of a clinically integrated entity, four permanent committees report directly to the board:

- Contract Finance Committee: This group bears responsibility for the review of all clinical integration program finances and managed care contracting.
- Utilization Management Committee: This committee serves as an extension of care management with a focus on patterns of utilization, care coordination, and overall cost.
- Credentialing Committee: This group recommends criteria for membership, reviews applications from physicians for inclusion in the clinically integrated organization, and provides guidance on potential membership terminations.
- Quality Improvement Committee: This standing committee focuses exclusively on the clinical aspects of the organization, including developing protocols and guidelines, clinical integration metrics and methodologies for scoring, and areas for targeted quality and safety improvement.

The work within a clinical integration program is supported by metrics and incentives. The incentives often arise from some pay-for-performance contracting with payers. Depending on the market and circumstances, securing these arrangements can be difficult. It may require the providers to agree to some reduction in reimbursement in exchange for the payer to fund a physician performance incentive fund.

If this approach is not feasible, an alternate possibility is to start a clinical integration program focused on one's own employees, using self-funding by the health system to build a physician incentive fund. The physician performance incentive fund should be tied directly to performance metrics. In many clinical integration programs, the initial metrics focus on primary care and ambulatory measures and often draw upon pre-existing measures from the Health Effectiveness Data and Information Set. As a clinically integrated network matures, the program should explore the inclusion of additional metrics for specialists as well as measures that promote alignment between physicians and the delivery system. For example, metrics such as length of stay, readmissions, obstetric elective inductions, and the CMS core measures explicitly link physician practice and hospital performance. In the most evolved models of clinical integration, metrics will expand to focus on true population health. This metric expansion often occurs when the clinical integration program engages in some type of shared savings or accountable care contracting. Population health metrics include total cost of care, in-network care coordination, utilization of preferred post-acute providers, and admissions per 1000 patient-days. Regardless of the stage of a clinical integration program, measures should be calculated and scored on multiple levels: an individual basis, by practice group, specialty, and PHO. One recommended practice is to weight the scores in each of these tiers to promote cooperation and collaboration between individual physicians, groups, and specialties within the clinically integrated organization.

The calculation of clinical integration scores should be accompanied by transparency of results and a process to provide and solicit timely physician feedback. Organizations often utilize an electronic registry tool to promote compliance with clinical integration metrics and to track performance in real time. This can be augmented with monthly dashboards and routine meetings with physicians (see Chapter 8). This intensity and visibility of feedback is essential so that physicians can understand their practice patterns and make the appropriate adjustments in their approach to care.

The launch of a clinical integration program requires significant investments in infrastructure with respect to people, processes, and technology. The case study highlights the components necessary to build a successful clinically integrated network.

Case Study

General Health System is a two-hospital health system with an employed medical group. In response to declines in their traditional fee-for-service reimbursement, the organization has decided to embark on an aggressive path to capture more revenue from fee-for-value payment arrangements. The health system leadership understands that the transition to value-based care will require greater alignment with their physicians. They also realize that they lack the financial capacity to acquire additional physician practices, the truest form of vertical integration. As a result,

General Health System has decided to pursue the strategy of developing a clinically integrated network.

Each of General Health System's hospitals has a PHO that have been folded into a super-PHO which has a primary focus on joint contracting for the physicians and health system. Under the new clinical integration strategy, the PHO will actively seek some form of pay-for-performance contract to fund a physician performance initiative. The system leadership envisions this as a prelude to the eventual formation of an accountable care organization and participation in some type of shared risk contracts with both Medicare and commercial payers.

As the organization begins to formulate its approach toward payers, it recognizes that there are several key pieces of infrastructure that will need to be developed and implemented simultaneously.

Physician Hospital Organization Field Support Team

The health system leadership understands that clinical integration requires a transformation to the existing model of care delivery. One key to this change will be the ability to communicate frequently with independently practicing physicians. This communication must be data-driven, easy to understand, and convenient for physicians to receive and access. The leading approach is to develop a PHO field support team.

The PHO field support team consists of physician relations representatives who are assigned to support specific physician practices. Their interactions with the practices include providing feedback on current clinical integration metric scores, educating on tactics that will lead to improved performance and general assistance in navigating the clinical integration program. Potential candidates for this role include individuals who are relationship-driven and who have some understanding of analytics, performance improvement, and health care operations. The PHO field support team essentially becomes the "boots on the ground" for the clinical integration program to ensure timely communication and support for front-line physicians. All selected individuals will be provided with an extensive orientation on the clinical integration program, including education on coaching techniques with physicians.

Clinical Programs

The underlying premise of clinical integration is to promote care coordination. This requires the implementation of clinical programs that focus on high-risk patients, utilization opportunities, and population health concerns. High-risk patients should be identified through a data-driven approach by examining population clusters with frequent hospitalizations or readmissions. This will likely lead the organization to identify individuals with multiple comorbidities, behavioral health problems, and challenging economic and social circumstances.

Opportunities to address utilization include programs that measure generic prescribing rate of medications and the use of high-cost ambulatory imaging. Population health concerns may include diseases that are particularly prevalent in the community served. In the General Health System service area, underutilization of mammography screening and obesity among adolescents are two areas of particular concern.

The leadership of General Health System realizes that these new clinical programs will require the development of new capabilities and hiring for new positions. For example, the high-risk patient program will require staffing by outpatient care managers to visit patients at the home and after their physician visits. These care managers will help ensure smooth care transitions by assisting with medication compliance, scheduling, and transportation to physician visits. They will also support with self-monitoring and treatment plans, and ensure adequate social and economic support for the patient. The utilization program for generic prescribing rates will be driven through a new ambulatory pharmacy program. Pharmacists will perform academic detailing of physicians regarding generic prescribing options and will provide feedback on their generic dispensing rate. The programs around adolescent obesity and mammography will be enabled through the newly created position of community health workers. These are trusted individuals within the community who have received some training in peer coaching and will work to motivate individuals to engage in self-care and health promoting behaviors. Community health workers also connect community members directly with health system resources and assist in organizing screening events and educational sessions in collaboration with religious and community organizations.

IT Solutions

General Health System has an inpatient electronic health record and ambulatory EHR for their employed physicians. There is an acknowledgment that additional IT products and data sharing will be required as they embark on clinical integration. Accordingly, the health system decides to provide incentives for clinically integrated physicians to purchase a specifically identified ambulatory EHR, thus promoting alignment across the network. These incentives essentially subsidize the IT investment required by an independent practice. The EHRs of the health system and its aligned physicians will be linked through an internal health information exchange that will enable data sharing and views of a longitudinal patient record. The health system leadership also decides to invest in an electronic disease registry. These disease registries will enable physicians to identify the relevant measures for each individual attributed patient, and provide prompts and alerts for screening and performance of certain critical tasks. The disease registries will also display real-time clinical integration metrics.

General Health System intends to use clinical integration as a bridge toward population health. With an eye toward this future, the leadership recognizes that patient engagement will be very important in delivering greater value. The health system decides to make additional investments in a patient portal that will enable patients to view information from the EHR, schedule appointments, and participate in e-visits.

As the organization assesses these infrastructure requirements and costs, the team begins to build a physician-led platform for governance. A seasoned leader and former medical staff president is selected to serve as the president of the clinical integration program. A 20-member board is formed with 10 physician representatives and 10 health system representatives. All but two of the physician representatives are independent physicians. In addition, the board establishes several standing committees to address clinical integration metrics, utilization management, finance, and audit.

The launch of the clinical integrated network is heralded by the signing of a pay-for-performance contract with the leading commercial insurer in the market. During the course of the negotiation, the health system and physicians sought a rate increase of 5%. The payer was initially only willing to provide a 2% increase. However, the parties compromised to a 2% rate increase and an additional 2% to be devoted to a physician incentive fund. In addition, the health system agreed to place its employees within their self-insured plan as participants in the clinically integrated network.

Lessons Learned

As the case study demonstrates, building a clinical integration program requires the pursuit of multiple initiatives simultaneously. An organization must establish a governing body, identify leadership for the entity, create an organizational structure, engage in preliminary discussions with payers for funding the pay-for-performance incentive fund, and assess current capabilities, required technology, and personnel investments. It can be difficult for an existing leadership team to manage all of these projects given their additional job roles and commitments. As a result, many organizations create an executive role that is specifically focused on building and launching the clinical integration program. This is often the best and most simple place to begin such a complex undertaking.

Clinical integration entities should be physician-led. The amount and difficulty of change required in the transition to a care coordination model and population health cannot be underestimated. True physician leadership with sound, clinically oriented decision-making is a powerful influence to garner support among other front-line physicians. A non-physician led and governed clinically integrated network is unlikely to develop the grassroots-level support from practicing physicians that is needed to produce the necessary practice and cultural changes.

In clinical integration initiatives to date, organizations have often realized that they began the endeavor without an adequate appreciation of the magnitude of work and investment required to build a clinically integrated network. Organizations are often in a rush to launch these networks. To be successful, the leadership model, levels of trust, and culture all need time to evolve and develop within a program.

In this rush to launch, organizations also too quickly adopt shared savings contracts under the mistaken assumption that it is an easy and fast way to fund the physician performance incentive. However, a new clinically integrated network is often too immature in its leadership, culture, and infrastructure to be able to assume this type of risk and generate sufficient savings. If it can be avoided, new clinically integrated networks should not begin with a shared savings program. A better approach for a new clinical integration program is to structure pay-for-performance contracts with commercial payers, even if that requires a smaller increase in reimbursement rates in future years.

Action Steps and Strategies to Lead

A successful clinical integration program requires strong physician leadership and a commitment to a future focus on population health. The following are recommendations for forming a clinical integration program:

1. **Understand why you are forming the clinical integration network.** Both the physicians and health system should agree that health care is definitively moving away from volume-based reimbursement and gravitating toward pay-for-value. This understanding of the future provides a shared basis for change among all stakeholders.

2. **Identify physician opinion leaders and organization champions.** The care coordination and outcome-driven approach of clinical integration requires physician partnership at every level in the network. A clinically integrated network that is created exclusively by one side or predominantly by non-physicians will not engage clinicians and will often fail. Identify physician champions, especially independent physicians, early in the planning process and involve them in all aspects of conception, design, and decision-making.

3. **Set up the right governance structure.** The composition of the board and the standing committees set the tone for the entire clinical integration program. At least half of the board representation should consist of physicians and, specifically, with a particular majority of independent physicians. The standing committee structure should have a similar composition. The charters and authority of these committees should also be clearly established at the start. Physicians may be new to the notion of serving on a board and the committee structure. Education in organization governance is an important investment to consider for physician board and committee members.

4. **Select the right metrics for your stage of development.** The journey of clinical integration can be compared to a marathon, each with its own stages and challenges. The metrics selected to measure physician performance should be appropriate for the stage in the journey. A new clinically integrated organization, still building trust and models of governance and leadership, should look toward well-established quality metrics, particularly in primary care and ambulatory practice, as these kinds of practitioners will likely comprise the majority of membership. As trust and collaboration increases between hospital and physicians, metrics should evolve to reflect and promote aligned goals. Finally, the most mature organizations that are ready to engage in true population health should consider metrics that look to drive the triple aim of better patient experience and improved population health at a lower cost.

5. **Make the necessary investments in infrastructure.** Clinical integration is more than simply the payer contracts and the metrics. It is also about providing the administrative support, technology, tools, and clinical roles to enable coordination of care and excellence in patient outcomes. These associated costs need to be established and recognized upfront along with a commitment to funding the infrastructure necessary for success.

Launching a clinical integration program requires a deliberate strategic approach with a concerted effort toward engaging physician leadership. As with any major change management initiative, it is not just the tactics but also the culture and its response to change that are the ultimate drivers of success.

Chapter 14

New Payment Models

Over the past several years, provider and hospital reimbursement in the U.S. health care system has begun a shift from a volume-based model toward a value-based model. This movement to value-based reimbursement is accompanied by both revived and new interest in alternate payment mechanisms such as pay-for-performance, shared savings programs, bundled payments, and capitation models. This chapter reviews the current landscape of health care reimbursement, the challenges associated with various payment models, and the practical aspects associated with adapting an organizational model and the clinical practice structure in this evolving payment environment.

The Evidence

Since the 1950s, the U.S. has seen rapid and unabated growth in health care spending. Much of this increase has been attributed to the predominant fee-for-service method of reimbursement. A fee-for-service reimbursement model incentivizes providers to deliver a greater volume of services without respect to the quality of care. Fee-for-service also propagates the delivery of care in silos. It does not reward providers for efforts to better coordinate care or for the maintenance of health as individuals or in populations.

Given the negative consequences of a fee-for-service system, payers in the U.S. health care system are implementing a host of alternate payment methodologies to improve quality and contain costs. These alternate payment methodologies will involve increased risk for organizations, both financially and operationally. Figure 14.1 provides a map of current and potential payment methodologies and the degree of associated risk. Though many of these reimbursement models may sound new, most are simply new versions of a previous iteration that have been tested or

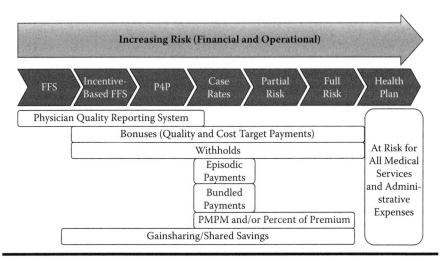

Figure 14.1   Range of value-based arrangements on the risk continuum. (Value-Based Contracting. Health Research & Educational Trust and Kaufman, Hall & Associates, Inc., Chicago: July 2013. Accessed at www.hpoe.org.)

even implemented prior to the current era of health care reform. Additionally, several of the "new" models, though they have different names, are simply a modified version of fee-for-service.

Pay-for-Performance

One of the most basic modifications to the fee-for-service model is pay-for-performance. Pay-for-performance involves the use of a series of explicit financial incentives to deliver predetermined services to achieve a given standard of care. It is an attempt to realign the legacy fee-for-service model to incentivize the delivery of safe, high-quality care. Proponents of pay-for-performance programs acknowledge that in order to achieve greater value in health care, physicians will be required to change practice patterns. Pay-for-performance programs use financial incentives that reward these changes in behavior and practice patterns.

Pay-for-performance programs can be designed along three dimensions: the nature of the quality goal, the form of the financial incentive, and the competitive nature of the program. Quality goals can include benchmarks in health care infrastructure (e.g., electronic health records, patient registries), processes of care (e.g., administration of aspirin following acute myocardial infarction), or medical outcomes (e.g., blood pressure, readmission rates). Financial incentives may take the form of a bonus, penalty, or both, all of which are tied to performance.

Incentives may also vary based on whether the pay-for-performance initiative is structured as a competitive or non-competitive program. In a non-competitive program, providers and delivery systems are rewarded for achieving pre-established, absolute thresholds of quality. All providers in the program may receive bonuses if they all achieve these goals. In a competitive program, providers and hospitals compete against each other for a limited number of rewards. Competitive programs establish clear winners and losers based on relative thresholds of improvement. Pay-for-performance programs can blend these competitive and non-competitive approaches and provide incentives for both absolute performance and incremental improvement.

At the federal level, the Centers for Medicare and Medicaid Services now has an extensive track record of implementing pay-for-performance programs, including initiatives to reduce readmissions and hospital-acquired conditions, programs to increase compliance with clinical processes and projects to improve patient outcomes. Funding for these programs is globally constructed as a percentage withhold of all Medicare diagnosis-related group base payments. For example, the Medicare Readmissions Reduction Program penalizes hospitals with excess readmissions by withholding Medicare payments in the next year.

Many commercial payers also have an extensive track record with pay-for-performance programs. Most fee-for-service reimbursement models now include some elements of pay-for-performance. Legacy fee-for-service agreements without any attachment to quality, safety, or coordination of care are quickly becoming the exception.

Accountable Care Organizations and Shared Savings

Although not initially obvious, another payment methodology with its roots in traditional fee-for-service is the budding ACO shared savings model. An ACO is an entity, either a single organization or a group of health care stakeholders, that accepts collective responsibility for the quality and cost of care delivered to a defined patient population. Medical groups, physician hospital organizations, or integrated delivery systems can form ACOs. In some instances, many organizations will partner to form a new entity that includes additional stakeholders such as retail pharmacy, home care, and skilled nursing facilities.

In an ACO contract, physicians and hospitals continue to operate under the existing reimbursement model, whether that is fee-for-service, inpatient case rates, or Medicare DRGs. At the end of a predefined time period, reconciliation is conducted to determine if the ACO has achieved certain quality and cost control thresholds. If the pre-established thresholds are achieved, the ACO retains a portion of the savings and can distribute the rest of the savings to its stakeholders however it chooses.

ACO shared savings contracts do not change the underlying method of payment, especially in those cases where fee-for-service for physician payments dominates. Instead, these organizations attempt to provide an additional financial incentive to align providers in the pursuit of higher value care across the continuum for an attributed patient population. Because the payment method to providers is not altered and the benefit design for patients may remain unchanged, ACOs continue to face a host of challenges in achieving higher value. Two areas of challenge are patient attribution and risk sharing.

Identifying an Attributed Patient Population

In a shared savings program with an open plan design, such as traditional Medicare or a preferred provider organization, one of the foremost challenges in forming an ACO is to identify the correct population of patients to be attributed to the ACO. The ACO is responsible for cost and quality outcomes within this attributed group of patients, so it is very important that the attribution process be done correctly.

There are many methods for determining attribution. Typically, health plan members are attributed to an ACO based on a historical review of utilization and subsequent identification of those providers or health systems that account for the majority of visits or costs for a given population of patients. Attribution rules are typically created as a hierarchical set of conditions so that if a patient cannot be attributed under one set of logic, he or she may be attributed under a different rule. For example, a woman of childbearing age may be attributed to an obstetrician, even if she has only one visit a year with that physician, if there is no other utilization associated with that member. In contrast, an older patient with multiple comorbidities may be attributed to the provider that has the majority or plurality of associated claims, even if he sees multiple physicians a year.

The attribution process should be recognized and appreciated for its strategic relevance. Attribution fundamentally determines the population for which an ACO is responsible. It is a complex process and should be executed by an ACO analytics team. In an open plan design where members can choose any provider, it is essential that an ACO be attributed a population that has a large proportion of in-network care so that their efforts in managing costs and quality will be effective and accurately reflected in the data. If the attribution process is done incorrectly, the ACO may effectively be "responsible" for patients who do not even seek a majority of their care within the ACO network.

Structure of Risk Sharing

There are two key considerations when establishing an ACO's structure of risk sharing: (1) potential for downside risk and (2) the option for shared savings. If an ACO assumes downside risk, it may be held responsible for member costs that exceed established market benchmarks. ACOs may be incentivized to accept downside risk through the opportunity to participate in a greater proportion of any shared savings. Though this larger potential upside may be tempting for early ACO entrants, new ACOs often lack the degree of infrastructure and operational maturity necessary to ensure that they will not sustain losses in early reporting periods. Based on this, it is recommended that new ACOs do not initially assume downside risk.

An additional negotiating point between an ACO and the payer is the proportion of savings that the ACO is eligible to share. Some shared savings agreements require a certain threshold of savings be achieved before the ACO can earn any savings. Alternatively, the percentage of sharing accrued to the ACO may be tiered and based on the level of savings achieved. For example, an ACO may not be eligible to receive savings until at least $2 million worth of overall savings is realized. After this threshold, all savings may be distributed on a 50–50 basis between the ACO and payer for the first $10 million and if savings are greater than $10 million, the split may be 60% savings to the ACO, 40% to the payer.

Because the underlying reimbursement model is not altered in an ACO arrangement, the shared savings (or losses) are determined at the end of designated reporting periods through a reconciliation process. There is typically some lag in this process, making it difficult to have the kind of timely data and feedback that are necessary to adjust strategies and tactics in response to performance. This lack of real-time monitoring is a common critique of current ACO contracts. Greater investment in data and analytics investment will be required to enable more accurate decision-making by ACOs.

Bundled Payments

Another reimbursement model that may be construed as an "early adopter" model for those working toward population health is bundled payments. In a bundled payment arrangement, providers receive a fixed sum to cover all of the costs associated with the episode of care. This incentivizes care coordination and reduction of redundancies and inefficiencies.

On the surface, bundled payments may appear completely novel. However, almost every hospital and health system has had some experience with bundled payments in the form of Medicare DRG reimbursement. Though it excludes physician billing, Medicare's DRG payment system represents a bundle for all services provided during an inpatient stay.

In a bundled payment system, the episode of care can be defined as inpatient procedure, an outpatient procedure, or a chronic medical condition such as diabetes. The bundled payment includes an established time frame. For instance, in a bundled payment for knee replacement surgery, the episode may start up to one week before the procedure and conclude 90 days following the end of surgery. In this example, the bundled payment would cover all inpatient, ambulatory, post-acute, and physician costs over the nearly 3-month episode of care required for a knee replacement surgery.

Compared to shared savings and ACOs, organizations typically regard bundled payment as a more narrow approach to population health. This model presents opportunities to redesign care, align stakeholders, and redesign incentives, but on a more sharply defined scope. Bundled payment should not be considered an easy route to population health. There are many challenges related to bundle definition, rate setting, and splitting payments appropriately.

Defining the bundle can be a difficult process. It requires defining which services to include, defining the beginning and end of the care episode, and defining criteria for patient inclusion or exclusion. These decisions will dictate whether organizations will accept a flat-rate fee or if the bundles will be risk adjusted.

Establishing bundle definitions not only requires hospital leadership to negotiate with the payer but also to have a detailed understanding of historical costs and patterns of utilization within the facility. Many organizations lack these analytic capabilities. As a result, many delivery systems and providers utilized pre-defined bundles. One popular source is the PROMETHEUS payment model, which includes published specifications and best practices for approximately 20 episodes of care (Health Care Incentives Improvement Institute). Another common reference is Geisinger Health System's Provencare for coronary artery bypass graft surgery. Their method identifies best practices to specify exact occurrences in the care process, tightly coupled with an episode-based payment rate (Paulus, Davis, and Steele 2008).

As in a shared savings model, most bundled payment arrangements do not change the underlying mechanism of payment. Currently, most payers lack the necessary infrastructure to issue a prospective bundled payment for multiple providers. Similarly, most provider organizations lack the capability to accept and process these types of global payments. Additionally, it may not be apparent at the start of an episode of care whether a patient will meet all of the inclusion criteria. As a result, most bundled payments are structured so that existing reimbursement practices are maintained during the episode of care. Physicians bill and are reimbursed on a fee-for-service schedule and the hospital continues its existing method for billing and reimbursement. At the end of some pre-determined period, a budget reconciliation is performed on each episode that was eligible for inclusion. Any savings are then split between the providers participating in the bundle. The percentage split of any savings should be established when parties agree to participate in a bundle.

Capitation

The most aggressive form of risk bearing for providers and delivery organizations is capitation. Capitation involves the advanced payment of a fixed amount to cover the provision of a defined set of health services over a fixed unit of time.

The capitated payment is typically defined as a rate per member, per month. The two basic variations on capitation are global capitation and sub-capitation. Global capitation is used in vertically integrated delivery systems or large, multi-specialty groups that cover the costs of care for all of the health care needs in a population. In contrast, sub-capitation is available for primary care and some specialty care providers who only provide some portion of a patient's care. In primary care, the capitation model emphasizes the role of the primary care provider as a gatekeeper for the utilization of services.

Compared to the other payment models discussed, capitation represents a fundamental departure from fee-for-service reimbursement. Providing an upfront fee provides direct incentives around cost and utilization and provides explicit incentives to align stakeholders. It also provides an early source of revenue to fund the types of personnel and information technology investments that are necessary to ensure effective coordination across the continuum of care. In ACO and bundled payment models, the shared savings, if any, are not available until after some lag in data and the final administrative budget reconciliation. This limits the organization's ability to re-invest those funds quickly and may mute their impact as an incentive. Capitation provides all payment upfront, enabling organizations to plan and invest accordingly.

Capitation does present some unique challenges. It is a form of payment that requires providers to accept risk for all losses from over-utilization or adverse risk selection. In addition, it also involves a trade-off by patients in the choice of providers. These aspects, particularly the latter, contributed to the decline in the prevalence of capitation since the 1990s. The more recent resurgence and interest in capitation is largely due to organizations viewing it as a way to gain more of the first dollar of revenue in an era of declining fee-for-service reimbursements.

Case Study—Advocate Health Care

Advocate Health Care is a Chicago-based health system known for its clinically integrated network, Advocate Physician Partners. Founded in 1995, APP is a joint venture between the health system and its aligned physicians. There are over 4000 physicians in APP, the vast majority of whom are independent and not employed by the health system. APP is considered an umbrella organization, or super-PHO, that represents each of Advocate's individual PHOs. The APP board has a 50–50 split between health system and physician representation. Prior to its launch into ACO contracts, APP had a rich history in clinical integration. This foundation of a shared culture and a tradition of leadership development enabled an early approach into shared savings. APP has ACO shared savings contracts in place for the commercial population, its own employees, and is a participant in the Medicare Shared Savings Program.

The entry into shared shavings contracts has accelerated the redesign of care across the continuum at Advocate. One of the initial tactics Advocate employed was to hire outpatient care managers and embed them in outpatient practices. This "on the ground" team focuses on coordinating care for the most complex, highest risk patients in the attributed population. They act as members of the care team to augment the physician practice in driving patient engagement and compliance and ensuring seamless transitions in care. The physician practices are also augmented by a field operations team that performs population health and clinical integration detailing at the physician practice level. This team provides current, quantitative feedback on performance to the physicians and their practice managers, along with tips for improvement on an ongoing basis.

Two unique resources provided in the post-acute arena are transition coaches and a post-acute network of skilled nursing facilities. This SNF network includes designated facilities in each market within the ACO's geography that have been verified to meet specific standards of care. These sites are also monitored through daily rounds by nurse practitioners and Advocate physicians (called SNF-ists) to minimize unnecessary transfers back to the hospital and safely reduce length of stay. These post-acute care efforts are augmented by a transition coach program. The transition coaches are home health nurses with specific training in the chronic care model. They are designated for discharged patients with the highest risk of readmissions who do not necessarily qualify for or are not appropriate candidates for home health services. Transition coaches educate patients on the signs and symptoms of their condition, encourage and facilitate physician follow-up, and perform at-home medication reconciliation.

The ACO tactics are supported by a clinical integration program that rewards physicians for performance on specific metrics tied to quality, safety, patient satisfaction, utilization, and overall population health. Participating physicians receive monthly feedback on performance at the individual, group, and PHO level through a report card. These report cards are available throughout the organization, demonstrating a commitment to transparency and accountability. Each year, the network establishes clear thresholds for eligibility and a deliberate process for defining measures and thresholds for performance.

The success of APP can be attributed to several factors including: an aligned physician culture, a performance-based system of incentives, care process re-design with the patient at the center, and a focus on metrics and transparency.

Lessons Learned

The implementation of new payment models can involve a dramatic departure from existing reimbursement models. This may require a new set of core competencies, particularly for hospitals and health systems that have built all of their infrastructure and expertise around inpatient care. As a result, significant investment may be required to manage care across the continuum of inpatient, ambulatory, and post-acute settings. These investments include information technology, data and analytics, and care management.

Information Technology

The required IT investments extend beyond electronic medical record capability in the inpatient and ambulatory space. Effective organizations will implement IT solutions that enable data sharing across stakeholders, for example, through an internal health information exchange. Investments in disease registries, patient portals, a longitudinal patient record, and tele-health and remote monitoring solutions are additional helpful technologies. Organizations should take a gradual approach to selecting and implementing each of these solutions. This will help ensure that each is integrated into provider workflow in order to maximize the impact on outcomes and costs of care in the population.

Data and Analytics

To maximize the impact of these IT investments, health care organizations must invest in data and analytics capabilities. This includes the ability to aggregate data from multiple data sources including internal transactional and demographic data, external claims data, and clinical data from EMRs. In order to match data from multiple sources by individual patient, organizations must develop a single master patient index and reconcile the many patient medical record numbers and identifiers across sites of care.

Once the data is aggregated and cleaned, organizations must also have analytic capabilities. This includes the ability to mine information to generate an accurate dashboard of the population along the dimensions of quality, safety, and utilization. Each of these indicators can include clinical integration metrics and measures on emergency department visits, inpatient days, readmissions, and in-network care coordination. In addition to these analytics, ACOs and other organizations must be able to use the data to stratify their populations based on risk. The most basic risk stratification identifies individuals associated with the greatest utilization or cost. This risk stratification enables the organization to perform targeted interventions and to allocate services and resources where they will be most effective and beneficial.

Care Management

Organizations must develop care management capabilities, especially throughout the ambulatory and post-acute care settings. A care management structure can include outpatient care managers, social work, and community-based health coaches. This will likely require augmentation by alternate providers of care including advance practice nurses and pharmacies. All of these personnel must be integrated into team-based care pathways with clearly identified roles and responsibilities to ensure a seamless experience for the patient.

These are significant investments in people, processes, and technology, that may be necessary at the outset of a shared savings or bundled payment agreement. These investments can be challenging given the significant lag in determining any savings or losses in a shared savings contract. There is often no pool of designated funds to pay for any investments in infrastructure or personnel at the beginning of an agreement. In these instances, organizations entering into a new value-based reimbursement scheme may have to invest existing resources. Alternatively, an ACO could request some upfront funds for infrastructure in their payer agreement, separate against any savings accrual. Either way, organizations should be mindful of the significant upfront costs that are required for success.

Value-based reimbursement models, particularly bundled payments, shared savings, and capitation, require sufficient data so physicians and providers can enter with full appreciation of the risks. This requires not only sharing of data with payers, but also developing a true sense of partnership between payers and providers. For some, payer-provider relationships have historically been marked by the routine rituals of difficult negotiations over reimbursement rates. For value-based reimbursement models to succeed, insurance entities and delivery systems must forego past rivalries and enter into truly collaborative arrangements around data sharing, care redesign, and improving the health and well-being of populations.

Much of the discussion has focused on financial incentives for providers and delivery systems. Organizations, however, must also be mindful of the incentives that patients have, particularly in the form of benefit design. Benefit design should be aligned to support care coordination and in-network care. If a patient's plan allows significant out-of-ACO coverage, managing quality and cost is made additionally difficult. Tactics also are required to help activate patients in their own care and enable them to be advocates for their own health. The work in patient engagement is nascent and includes many up-and-coming technologies around self-monitoring. Still, tactics for patient engagement should be considered elements for success in a value-based reimbursement environment.

Action Steps and Strategies to Lead

The transition to value-based reimbursement presents the opportunity to improve population health and possibly offset the decline in traditional fee-for-service revenues. In preparation for a value-based contract, leaders should make a few key determinations:

1. **Understand your threshold of risk.** On the spectrum of lowest to highest assumption of risk, bundled payments have the lowest exposure, followed by shared savings and then capitation. These degrees of risk also correspond to the extent of infrastructure and process redesign that are necessary to be successful in each reimbursement scheme. Leaders must understand their

organization's appetite to sustain potential losses, measured against the degree of existing infrastructure. Once this threshold of risk is established, an organization can next decide the appropriate reimbursement method to begin the population health journey.

2. **Understand your core competencies and the gaps in your capabilities.** Value-based payment is not merely about reimbursement; it is a complete redesign to ensure coordination across the continuum of care. Organizations should take stock of their existing core competencies and identify and understand their gaps in process, people, and technology as they relate to the world of population health. Having this knowledge will provide the roadmap for infrastructure investment and identify key partnerships to establish with other stakeholders in order to be successful.

3. **Involve physicians early and as equal partners in the conversation.** Achieving superior health outcomes in addition to a positive margin in a value-based care environment will require changes in physician behavior and other aspects of clinical practice. Rather than being the lone captain, physicians become one of many important team players on a multidisciplinary care team. As a result, physician engagement is required for any value-based reimbursement program. It is important to have physician leadership as part of the strategy and throughout the process.

Value-based reimbursement is not just about the dollars. It is fundamentally a paradigm shift from a focus on illness to one of health and wellness; from episodic care to coordination; from discharge to transitions; and from production and volume to performance and value. It is important to keep this underlying rationale and motivation in mind when leading any organization on the path toward value-based care.

References

Health Care Incentives Improvement Institute. What is Prometheus payment? http://www. hci3.org/what_is_prometheus (accessed November 4, 2014).

Paulus, R.A., K. Davis, and G.D. Steele. 2008. Continuous innovation in health care: Implications of the Geisinger experience. *Health Affairs* September: 1235–1245.

Chapter 15

The Clinical Leader Role in Emerging Models of Care

The fast-changing health care system is driving the development of new models of care. The traditional face-to-face visit is being replaced by models predicated on new technology, new processes, new providers, and new mindsets. The role of a clinical leader in these rapidly emerging models of care is to leverage not only new technical clinical skills but also new management and leadership skills for future success. To succeed in delivering these innovative care models, clinical leaders must be adept at data analysis, population health, partnership, and change management. Evidence backing new models of care delivery is mounting as retail medicine, population health, and mobile health are drastically altering health care delivery.

Retail Medicine

The concept of "retail medicine" involves health care services delivered in the retail store setting including supermarkets, pharmacies, and drug stores. Providers, most often nurse practitioners or physician assistants, provide care through retail clinics or convenient care clinics. CVS, Walgreens, Target, and Walmart have all invested in retail or convenient care clinics over the past decade.

Retail clinics provide limited yet convenient medical services on a walk-in basis. Common services include vaccinations, flu shots, preventive health services, and treatment for minor ailments such as sore throats, infections, fevers, and sprains.

Retail clinics are particularly appealing to consumers because they provide expanded hours beyond the normal workday, including weekend and evening hours.

The retail medicine model has existed for years, but the number of clinics and number of retailers hosting such clinics has proliferated over the last few years. In 2014, the trade association for convenient care clinics stated that there are over 1500 convenient care clinics in the U.S. (Convenient Care Association 2014). This number is expected to double in the next few years (Insight Driven Health).

Several factors are driving this growth, most notably a generation shift. Individuals in Generation X (between 35 and 49 years old) and Generation Y (34 years and younger) are more likely to visit these clinics, driven by their desire for convenience and easy access. Because these individuals are also generally healthy, the preventive care and treatment for minor ailments provided by retail clinics meet the majority of their medical needs. Beyond the generational pull, however, individuals are also simply beginning to view retail medicine as more responsive to their needs. The traditional health care delivery system imposes significant burdens on consumers regarding scheduling, inconvenience, and rigid structure. Retail clinics offer greater flexibility for individuals looking for new, convenient ways to access health care.

Concerning retail medicine, clinical leaders, even those that are not currently engaged in retail medicine outfits, should consider:

■ How will the evolution of retail medicine impact the health care system in regard to cost, care coordination, patient satisfaction, and clinical outcomes?
■ If and how can existing delivery organizations partner or coordinate with these new "organizations" of care delivery?
■ How can the current health care system evolve to meet the needs and demands that retail medicine is trying to fill (e.g., access, convenience)?

Particularly for leaders within the traditional health care system, there are important questions to consider:

■ Will there be fewer primary care visits because of expanding access through retail clinics?
■ How will this impact utilization levels, the financial viability of medical practices, and existing physician-hospital relationships?
■ How will clinical information be exchanged between retail clinics and other clinicians?
■ Will the health system compete or partner with retail clinics?
■ If not through retail clinics, how will health systems provide convenient access to consumers outside of the usual care models (i.e., physician offices, urgent care, emergency rooms)?

Clinical leaders must guide their organizations to consider and begin discussion around these questions.

Population Health

Population health is defined as "the health outcomes of a group of individuals, including the distribution of such outcomes within the group" (Kindig and Stoddard 2003). Population health has been a key tenet for public health professionals for years but has more recently garnered the attention of leaders, providers, payers, and policymakers in the health care delivery system. Through the Affordable Care Act and other health reform efforts (e.g., patient-centered medical homes, value-based purchasing) the concept of "population health" has been widely touted as key to improving quality and lowering costs. The phrase, however, is defined differently in different circles. When engaging in discussions about population health, clinical leaders must be mindful of which concept and definition they are espousing.

Public health and community health advocates typically refer to "population health" as the health outcomes of all individuals within a geographic area. This more expansive and inclusive definition is referred to as *geographic population health*. As the term "population health" has been adopted by hospitals, health systems, and payers, however, it is more often used to refer to a limited and distinct population—those who seek care within one hospital or health care system. Accountable care organizations and others working to improve population health are not necessarily focused on the health outcomes of the entire geographic community, but rather only on the outcomes of the smaller population of individuals who seek care at their facility. This approach is known as *defined population health*.

It is important for clinical leaders to distinguish between these two types of population health because the strategies to successfully impact health outcomes for each are very different. In a defined population health model, the health care system is clinically and financially responsible for the provision of medical services to a specific group. In this situation, the organization will need proficiency in care management strategies, in risk stratification and prediction capabilities, and in implementing interventions to more efficiently deliver care within the system.

Alternatively, efforts to address geographic population health must extend beyond the facility and traditional health care system to engage community leaders, local government, businesses, and other stakeholders in impacting the socioeconomic, behavioral, and environmental drivers of health outcomes. There is certainly overlap between the skills and interventions needed to impact defined population health and geographic population health but there are also clear differences in strategies and actions in successfully delivering outcomes for these populations (HRET 2013).

To impact defined population health, clinical leaders must possess skills in data analytics and care coordination. Using data analytics, leaders can identify groups and individuals with high utilization and high risk and should target those patients accordingly. Organizations must be able to identify and effectively treat the small groups within their population that have a disproportionate impact on costs. Additionally, coordinating care across multiple settings (i.e., acute, long term, emergency) is essential to manage high-risk, high-cost patients effectively.

To impact the health of a geographically defined population, clinical leaders must be able to do all of the things needed to impact defined population health (data analytics and care coordination) and also be proficient in collaboration, partnership, and public health. Improving the health outcomes of an entire community will require innovative partnerships with many community organizations, social service agencies, local government, and businesses, and will require policy changes with impact beyond clinical care delivery. Examples of policies that support geographic population health include those that address healthy eating in schools, safe neighborhoods with reduced violence, tobacco cessation policies, and the addition of park space, sidewalks, and bike paths to promote exercise. Policies like these that target the behavioral and economic drivers of health have potential to improve health outcomes in the long term.

Currently, very few leaders within the traditional health care system possess this wide range of skills—from data analytics to community partnership. A successful clinical leader will build teams with members who collectively possess and leverage these diverse skill sets. Figure 15.1 summarizes the distinctions between defined and geographic population health.

To successfully lead initiatives to improve population health, clinical leaders must:

- Define which population health level they are managing—defined population health or geographic population health.
- Identify and implement the key interventions needed for the population based on sophisticated data analysis.
- Build skills in data analytics, clinical service coordination, collaboration, and public health so that they can lead population health at different levels.

Mobile Health

The advent and widespread adoption of smartphones and tablets has resulted in a proliferation of mobile applications (apps) focused on medicine and health care that promote the "quantified self," collectively known as "mobile health" or mHealth. Examples of mHealth may include smartphone and tablet applications such as Map My Run, an app that tracks distance, time, calories burned, and more; websites such as WebMD, which provides information related to diagnosis and treatment of disease; and mobile patient monitoring systems such as Fitbit or Nike Fuel Band, which track users' eating, sleeping, and exercise habits.

Mobile health applications allow consumers to easily track health-related data, facilitate self-care, and perform other health and social interactions that previously

Defined Population Health
- Who: Patients who have experienced your health system
- Most Likely to Do: ACOs, health plans, large integrated health systems
- High Leverage Interventions: Managing chronic conditions/ high risk/high utilizers
- Key Players: All health care delivery organizations
- Aligned Payment Mode: Capitated payment or defined population
- Significant Challenge: Defining "attributable" population
- Measures of Success: Cost, utilization, quality of care, patient experience
- Needed Skills: Data analytics and clinical service coordination

Geographic Population Health
- Who: Individuals living in a given geographic area, regardless of whether they have sought care in your health system
- Most Likely to Do: Hospital/health systems that are anchor institutions in their communities
- High Leverage Interventions: Social, economic, health behavior, care management
- Key Players: Community organizations and health care delivery organizations
- Aligned Payment Model: Population-based budget
- Significant Challenge: No readily-available, frequent measure of health
- Measures of Success: Health status, quality of life, mortality, quality of care
- Needed Skills: Community collaboration and public health

Figure 15.1   Geographic vs. defined population health. (Health Research & Educational Trust, 2014.)

could only be completed in the presence of a clinician. Mobile health applications are also moving beyond monitoring eating and exercise habits and now help individuals monitor their heart rate, track their daily sugar levels, and self-diagnose non-life-threatening illnesses. The growth of mobile health has been compounded by an influx of venture capital investments. Financial markets are making big bets on mobile health gaining greater traction and making a significant impact in health care.

Clinicians and clinical leaders may perceive mobile health applications to be a threat. Mobile health has the potential to erode the ability of health care providers to optimally manage their patients' care if patients move increasingly away from traditional settings due to the impression that mobile devices and apps are adequate substitutes for human practitioners. Mobile health applications also present new opportunities, however, for patients to become more actively engaged in their care. This may result in improved outcomes through better compliance with the care plans prescribed by a physician and greater engagement in social and behavioral activities that have a substantive impact on health status, such as healthy eating and exercise habits. Though there are risks associated with mobile health, there is also infinite potential for positive impact. As a clinical leader, there are many opportunities to encourage and embrace consumer use of mobile health applications to maximize the potential of these innovations to improve health. Clinical leaders must align the interests of consumers, mobile health application producers, and the bricks and mortar health care system. For example, leaders should consider initiatives to integrate information from mobile applications with the system electronic health record. Mobile health holds great potential to further engage consumers beyond the medical model, an exciting prospect to change the health behaviors that have such a significant impact on health status. Clinical leaders should embrace the opportunity to leverage mobile health as an enabling factor for consumer engagement.

By the time you read this chapter, there will likely be new innovations in care delivery, consumer engagement, and the ability to impact the health outcomes of populations. As a clinical leader, your role is to examine the benefits and risks of opportunities for innovations to maximize your organization's ability to deliver high quality, low cost, patient-centered care.

Case Study

Anne Arundel Health System is a 350-bed, $600 million health system in Annapolis, Maryland. Chief Medical Officer Dr. Mitchell Schwartz oversees the organization's physician enterprise and accountable care organization initiatives. This interview with Dr. Schwartz describes the ways clinical leaders can respond to new and disruptive models of care.

Q: **What is the impact of retail medicine on the practicing clinician in your health system today?**

A: Retail medicine can be viewed as a threat or an opportunity. Much depends on the particular medical marketplace in which you work. Retail medicine provides a low-cost access point for patients. If there is a true value-based relationship with an insurer, coordination with this type of provider system should lower costs. In fact, patients who would often be seen in the emergency department can be referred to a lower cost retail option. Clinicians should not view this as a threat. On the other hand, if there is not a value-based payment structure, primary care and emergency care may perceive this to be a threat. The clinical leader should be able to understand the potential opportunity retail medicine provides to the health system for preparing for the move to value-based care.

Q: **What is the greatest promise of population health for your organization? What does that mean for the clinical leader?**

A: In the past, the primary focus of a health care organization was the hospital. The hospital was designed to care for acutely ill patients, driven by volume and dependent on substantial capital investments. Quality was determined by process measures. Alternatively, population health holds clinicians responsible for the care of a population, re-orienting their goals toward health and outcomes measures. This alignment creates the opportunity for the health care organization to evolve into a system of care by working with other stakeholders in the community to deliver quality care for low cost. The clinical leader must engage with providers, typically those who are based in the community. One core competency for clinical leaders will be the ability to effectively communicate and educate other clinicians about their changing responsibilities within an evolving health care environment.

Q: **How does your organization respond to mobile health?**

A: Mobile health is one novel way to activate and engage patients. In a population health model of care, patient activation is a critical component for success. Mobile health is just one way to manage a large population of patients without having to see patients for the traditional office visit. A smartphone can be used to remind patients about therapy and maintain a record of weights, activity, or serum glucose levels. As with other shifts in health care, this may be perceived as a threat, particularly if there is no value-based payment system. Mobile health offers the clinician a more efficient form of interacting with patients. This new workflow, managed by a clinical team, may very well lead to success when reimbursements are dependent on patients actually following through on plans for care.

Q: **What skills would you advise other clinical leaders to develop to deal with the challenges and opportunities of retail medicine, population health, and mobile health?**

A: The medical landscape is a rapidly changing environment. Population health, retail medicine, and mobile health are challenges to the status quo. The standard interactions and relationships with patients are quickly evolving and expectations of the care delivery process are rising. This destabilization threatens care providers, especially those who are at a point in their careers when change is not perceived as an option. A clinical leader needs to address these issues. The clinical leader must be able to think broadly, well beyond the scope of a hospital-based clinician. That strategic thinking must then be distilled into simple, straightforward points that can be easily communicated. The burning platform, the rationale for change, should be a part of that communication. Lastly, clinical leaders must be able to build a creative team that is committed to continuous learning. The rapid changes underway require a structured learning process that enables the team to maintain a proactive and decisive approach to the market forces impacting their health system.

Q: **How do you prepare the clinical leader for other new models of care?**

A: The changes taking place in health care will force clinical leaders to be more creative in seeking out novel approaches to the challenges of providing value-based care. The responses will have common themes—accepting some amount of financial risk, required process improvement, and a higher level of accountability. Leadership skills will be necessary to help a health system respond to those changes. Change management, which has been codified by Kotter (2014), requires a series of steps that enables leadership to move large organizations toward a defined set of goals. Moving from a superb clinician, recognized for clinical skill, to a leadership position requires training, coaching, and experience. Those clinicians interested in that role can seek out that training in formal leadership academies as we have had here at Anne Arundel Health System. Connecting to a mentor and using smaller projects as a teaching tool will also help a great deal. Clinical leaders must be willing to experiment and possibly fail, as that is one aspect of the learning process. Additionally, clinicians typically care for a small group of patients each day. Those interested in leadership positions should be oriented toward building systems that enable other clinicians to thrive in a new environment, thereby expanding their impact by helping to care for a multitude of patients within their community.

Lessons Learned

Regardless of the emerging model of care at hand—population health, retail health, mobile health, or other—the clinical leader must develop a number of non-clinical leadership skills that will be essential to these and other models of care that will improve the health of the populations we serve. In 2014, the American Hospital Association asked various leaders from over 400 hospitals what they saw as talent gaps for the next three years in their organization. Over 1000 responses from hospital and health system chief executive officers, chief operating officers, chief medical officers, chief nursing officers, chief financial officers, board chairs, and other senior leaders identified the following as the most pressing talent gaps:

- Community and population health management experience
- Data analytics
- Ability to develop non-traditional health partnerships
- Transformation and change management

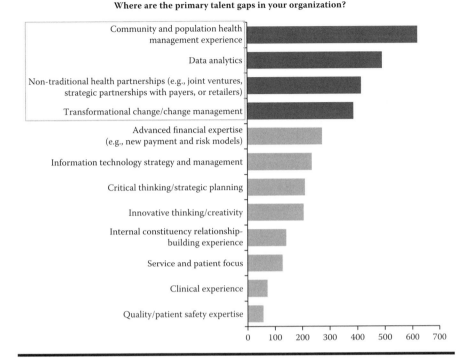

Figure 15.2 Top talent gaps for leadership in hospitals and health systems. (American Hospital Association. Redefining the H Survey, 2014.)

Figure 15.2 shows the results of all identified gaps and specifically highlights the top identified talent gaps that directly align with the clinical leader skills needed to address and cultivate emerging models of care. Community and population health management is self-evident, data analytics is a foundation for all emerging care models, forming nontraditional health partnerships critical for population health, and the ability to lead through change management is critical for the implementation of any new care model.

Action Steps and Strategies to Lead

Considering the most prominent emerging models of care (retail medicine, population health, mobile health) and the most impactful skills that leaders need to develop (data analytics, change management, collaboration within and outside of health care), the clinical leader should accelerate the development of these skills and competencies by:

1. **Challenging current assumptions about health care delivery**

2. **Developing and implementing segmented strategies**
3. **Focusing on care coordination across the continuum**
4. **Seeking out multiple, diverse, and effective partnerships**
5. **Actively engaging consumers and patients in their health and health care**

The first step is to challenge the current operating assumptions in health care. New generations, new technologies, and new processes challenge our current mindsets such as: face-to-face visits are important for clinical decision-making, patients should not self-diagnose constantly, consumers will prefer seeing doctors to other providers, and the most reliable source of information is always the doctor. Both retail medicine and mobile health are changing those assumptions.

The growth of diversity within our population will require strategies to further segment in our analyses. Consumer segments possess distinct characteristics about motivation and preferences related to seeking care, following up, and adhering to treatment regimens. Clinical leaders must have different strategies for different segments to effectively engage patients and track and impact their health.

New care models and reimbursement models are elevating the importance of care coordination. Care coordination is also taking on new meaning. It can mean an emergency department coordinating with a primary care physician, electronic health record integration with consumers' mobile health devices, collaboration between an acute care facility and retail clinic, or coordinating efforts with a county health department. As more players enter health care—and more players will be necessary to effectively impact health status and health outcomes—greater coordination is needed. Handoffs and transitions of information and service are risky and the most successful organizations and enterprises will be those that are able to facilitate smooth, efficient, and effective transitions. Care coordination and transitions will increase; leaders should actively seek out and identify new partners. Clinical leaders should take advantage of the entrance of new organizations into the health care field.

Though there is no turnkey solution to engaging consumers and patients in their health and health care, the number and potential of both emerging and undiscovered opportunities are immense. Clinical leaders that partner with their patients through the use of personal health records, sharing of their data with all members of the health care team, using mobile health devices to improve their health behaviors, and working with other health and social service providers will increase their ability to impact their patients' health.

The current and impending changes in health care can cause anxiety. However, the successful clinical leaders of the future will be inspired and excited at the opportunities to improve health and health care in new ways and with new partners. Clinicians with exceptional clinical technical skills will become exceptional clinical leaders through the development of competencies in data analytics, population health, partnership, and leading change all with a focus on providing high quality, high value, and patient-centered care.

References

Convenient Care Association. www.ccaclinics.org. Accessed on October 24, 2014.

Health Research & Educational Trust. 2014. Leading Improvement Across the Continuum: Skills, Tools and Teams for Success.

Insight Driven Health. Retail clinic counts will double between 2012 and 2015 and save $800 million dollars per year. Accenture. http://www.accenture.com/us-en/Pages/insight-healthcare-reform-retail-medical-clinic-foe-friend-summary.aspx. Accessed on October 25, 2014.

Kindig, D., and G. Stoddart. 2003. What is population health? *American Journal of Public Health* 93(3): 380–383.

Kotter, J. The 8-Step Process for Leading Change. Kotter International. http://www.kotterinternational.com/the-8-step-process-for-leading-change/. Accessed on October 27, 2014.

Steinhubl, S.R., E.D. Muse, and E.J. Topol. 2013. Can mobile health technologies transform health care? *JAMA* 310(22): 2395–2396. doi:10.1001/jama.2013.281078.

Chapter 16

Compendium
of Action Steps

Leading health care transformation will require new skills and competencies. This final chapter summarizes the "action steps to lead" from the previous fifteen chapters.

Chapter 1: The Health Care Landscape

Action Step	*Description*
Communicate the imperative for health care transformation and the steps to achieve it.	• Develop messaging for staff, leadership, governance, patients, and the community. • Effectively describe how national drivers (i.e., reimbursement changes, demographic shifts) have a local impact. • Describe how changes and decisions, often difficult ones, are necessary given the larger context of transformation.
Understand the relationship between cost and quality in practice and how to drive value.	• Develop proficiency in measuring and managing costs and quality. • Identify ways to reduce waste and excess costs to increase value. • Educate your clinicians on the relationship between cost, quality, and value.
Build, deploy, and lead improvement teams across all dimensions of care.	• Teach and empower others in the organization to conduct performance improvement cycles and lead performance improvement teams. • Support a culture of continuous improvement.
Build and lead effective multidisciplinary teams.	• Tear down siloes and work across units, departments, and disciplines. • Enable clinicians to practice at the top of their licenses. • Develop effective communication plans and strategies with internal and external partners.
Leverage data to improve clinical and organizational practice.	• Develop competencies in data collection and analysis. • Use data to drive decisions. • Build a culture of transparency and continuous improvement guided by ongoing data collection.
Realize the role of the patient as consumer.	• Engage patients and families as partners in care. • Optimize opportunities to engage patients as consumers to change health behavior and outcomes.

Chapter 2: Effectively Implementing Quality and Safety Improvement

Action Step	Description
Become proficient in at least one improvement model.	• Become proficient in your organization's model for improvement (e.g., Lean, Six Sigma) and act as a resource for others. • If your organization does not have a designated method, lead your team, unit, department, or organization to adopt a methodology to promote continuous improvement.
Create a culture of safety.	• Promote transparency, accountability, and open communication. • Encourage employees to identify and report mistakes and near-misses.
Become data driven.	• Identify improvement opportunities based on data. • Develop improvement projects with specific, data-driven aims. • Use measurement and reporting to demonstrate value. • Support decisions with data.
Empower frontline staff to lead.	• Engage employees—nurses, pharmacists, physicians, others—in quality improvement initiatives. • Defer to expertise—those who work with the process daily often have best knowledge and insights on how to fix a problem. • Inspire a shared vision, challenge current processes, and enable staff to act.
Provide resources to support improvement work.	• Provide the appropriate financial, human, and time resources that are necessary to achieve an improvement project's aim. • Advocate to senior leadership on behalf of your teams' efforts.
Lead by example.	• Lead an improvement team yourself and model the skills and behaviors that contribute to successful quality improvement efforts. • Teach and empower others in the process to build a cadre of improvement leaders within your organization.

Chapter 3: Spreading Improvement

Action Step	Description
Find opinion leaders and champions to support spread.	• Physicians and nurses are obvious stakeholder groups, but consider recruiting champions who are nurse assistants, pharmacists, or physical therapists if these groups are key stakeholders in the process at hand. • Champions must be willing commit to and advocate for spread efforts.
Consider the implementation/ dissemination model.	• Strategize outreach and education methods based on the target population. • Consider the hospital's structure, infrastructure, standard operational processes, and potential knowledge gaps.
Use data to demonstrate the effectiveness of the implemented practice.	• Track and use data to persuade skeptics. • Data is a powerful catalyst to spread improvement.
Use stories to engage other leaders and explain the "why" for spread.	• Data is important, but the human aspect of the potential intervention is equally compelling. • Put a face on data by emphasizing the intervention's potential to save the life of a relative or friend.
Track spread adoption through data.	• Use two types of measures: those that demonstrate the extent of spread and those that document the impact of the implemented changes. • Measure the rate of spread—how fast is the organization improving?

Chapter 4: Physician Champions

Action Step	Description
Identify stakeholders to constitute a guiding coalition.	• Acknowledge physicians as a key constituency to engage and influence. • Identify other stakeholders, both internal and external, whose voice should be included in planning and implementing the improvement effort.
Seek guidance and counsel from other physicians.	• Ask colleagues to whom they turn for advice and whose opinion is highly regarded. • When assessing potential candidates, ensure they are opinion leaders, have strong communication skills, a passion for patient-centered care, and an inherent willingness and adaptability to grow and develop.
Actively guide and assist physician champions.	• Demonstrate the behaviors that promote change. • Be an active listener, connecting to the "why." • Utilize storytelling and rely on evidence-based, objective data.

Chapter 5: Building a Culture of Safety

Action Step	Description
Assess your organization's culture.	• Utilize a tool such as the AHRQ Hospital Survey of Safety Culture or Safety Attitudes Questionnaire to determine gaps in safety culture and identify opportunities for improvement.

Actively manage workplace culture, including culture of safety.	• Primary mechanisms that leaders can use to change, embed, and transmit culture:
	  • What leaders pay attention to, measure, and control on a regular basis;
	  • How leaders react to crucial incidents and organizational crises;
	  • How leaders allocate resources;
	  • Deliberate role modeling, teaching, and coaching;
	  • How leaders allocate rewards and status;
	  • How leaders recruit, select, promote, and excommunicate.

Encourage and reward reporting of safety events.	• Investigate the causes of all safety events and near misses. • Provide active and ongoing encouragement to staff to report safety events. • Reward employees who report, especially self-report, safety events or near misses.
Utilize a non-punitive policy and decision-making algorithm for assessing individual culpability in safety events.	• Develop and adhere to a non-punitive policy and process for establishing individual culpability in safety events. • Algorithms should acknowledge the organization's role in providing the correct policies, procedure, training, and work environment for staff to succeed. • This process should be a human resources function, not a quality or safety function.

Chapter 6: Principles and Practices of High Reliability Organizations

Action Step	Description
Continuously monitor organizational culture.	• Recognize that a high reliability organization has a unique cultural and leadership mindset. Commit to and own this mindset. • Commit to an ongoing evaluation and reinforcement of culture.
Establish and communicate a compelling "why" for the high reliability journey.	• Include aspirational goals and examples of high reliability organizations. • Relate the "why" back to the mission of the organization.
Educate the organization on the key components of high reliability.	• Sponsor and support organization-wide efforts to educate employees on the key principles of high reliability. • Demonstrate how high reliability will impact employees' daily work.
Generate and celebrate quick wins.	• Once the organization understands the "why" and "what" of high reliability, begin to roll out discrete tactics (e.g., the daily huddle) to create a powerful initial and visible example of a new organizational way and rhythm of operating.

Chapter 7: Key Quality and Safety Measures

Action Step	Description
Integrate measurement for improvement into organizational culture.	• Allocate non-patient care staff time to focus on performance improvement projects. • Provide adequate resources to support improvement efforts. • Promote a culture that is data-driven and focused on performance improvement. • Lead by example.
Choose a few "big dot" measures to track at the organizational level.	• Guide and define organizational priorities by choosing to focus on a set of key measures. These choices will help staff understand leadership priorities. • Minimize data fatigue and confusion by focusing on a few essential measures. • Promote transparency and accountability through creating clear lines of sight between the outcome and process and identify who owns the process.
Engage front-line staff in data collection and analysis.	• Those who engage with the process on a daily basis often have the best insight into how to fix the process. • Empowering front-line staff to lead builds organizational capacity, promotes a culture of performance improvement, and enables staff to have greater say in how they do their work.

Chapter 8: Using Data for Feedback and Improvement

Action Step	*Description*
Support teams in developing plans for data collection, reporting, and analysis.	• Data collection and analysis requires commitment and resources. • Clinical leaders should support teams in developing feasible plans for data collection that are efficient and effective.
Provide ongoing feedback through dialogue and draw clear connections between data and recommendations (i.e., clinical guidelines) or what actions are necessary to improve the process.	• Data is not useful if it is not reviewed on an ongoing basis. • If clinicians do not understand the data or do not see it as valuable, discontent, skepticism, and rebellion can result. • Promote transparency, allow dialogue and discussion of the data, including strengths and caveats, and guide colleagues to engage with the data in a way that is productive.
Use graphical methods to display data.	• Find simple, concise ways to display data. Emphasize the relationship between action and results. • Make the data accessible for all engaged in the improvement initiative.
Explain change and variation in terms of special cause vs. common cause.	• The distinction between special and common cause variation is a core element of using data for improvement. • Leaders should speak in terms of common vs. special cause variation.

Chapter 9: Leading Effective Teams: For Clinical Care and for Performance Improvement

Action Step	Description
Define the aims and objectives of the team first, then build the team accordingly.	• Teams should be built according to the purpose or aim. • Promote collaboration through recruiting multidisciplinary team members. • For all teams, engage a patient or family member representative.
Prioritize training and support for teamwork.	• Provide initial training in specific teamwork skills and ongoing coaching to promote a culture that supports teamwork. • Designate non-patient care time for team meetings, reimburse individuals for team activities, develop communication plans and decision protocols that reinforce teamwork.
Engage patients and their families in both care teams and improvement teams.	• Patient and family advisors provide important insights related to quality, safety, and efficiency. • Teams should be built around and focus on the needs of the patient.

Chapter 10: Engaging Patients and Families

Action Step	Description

Determine the current state of patient and family engagement using an assessment tool.	• All improvement initiatives should begin with an assessment of the problem.
	• Examples:
	  • Strategies for Leadership: Patient- and Family-Centered Care – A hospital self-assessment inventory
	  • Patient- and Family-Centered Care– Organizational Self-Assessment Tool
	  • Checklist for Attitudes about Patients and Families as Advisors

Develop a clear vision of how your organization will engage patients and families.	• Communicate and role model this vision. • Integrate patient and family engagement throughout the organization's culture and work systems.
Demonstrate commitment through providing resources and infrastructure to support patient- and family-centered care.	• Many barriers relate to limited time and resources. • Leaders must communicate the evidence that supports patient and family engagement initiatives and publicly commit to supporting those initiatives. • Provide resources (financial, time, infrastructure) to support patient and family engagement efforts.

Chapter 11: Improving Care Coordination and Reducing Readmissions

Action Step	Description
Start with the data.	• Look for patterns, drivers, and root causes. • Stratify data by condition, practitioner, readmission source, and time frame. • Target interventions based on what the data shows to be high need.
Assess and prioritize your improvement opportunities.	• Leaders should vocalize organizational priorities and devote resources accordingly. • Prioritize based on patient population, stages in the care process, or leverage other ongoing improvement efforts.
Engage key stakeholders.	• Work with partners inside and outside the hospital. • Engage partners in the development and execution of initiatives. • Move beyond the hospital—community partners are often better equipped to address non-medical factors that impact readmissions.
Monitor progress.	• Monitor data to identify successful strategies. • Keep the team engaged through showing and celebrating progress.

Chapter 12: Addressing Variation in Utilization

Action Step	Description
Engage clinicians with data-driven feedback.	• Engage physicians and clinical stakeholders early and often. • Convene a group of physicians to review data and hypothesize drivers of unwarranted variation. • Base decisions on evidence and data.
Standardize operational processes using quality improvement interventions.	• Quality improvement methodologies such as Lean, Six Sigma and Plan–Do–Study–Act can lead to improvements in quality, patient satisfaction, and efficiency.
Implement evidence-based clinical guidelines and appropriateness criteria.	• Target areas where there is not consistent adherence to evidence-based guidelines.
Initiate and sustain culture change.	• Promote a culture of safety, transparency, improvement, and excellence. • Benchmark performance to top performers.

Chapter 13: Physician Alignment and Clinical Integration

Action Step	Description
Understand why you are forming the clinical network.	• Physicians and health system leaders should agree that health care is definitely moving away from volume-based reimbursement. • Commit to a transition to pay-for-value.
Identify key physician opinion leaders and organization champions.	• Care coordination requires physician partnership at every level in the network. • Identify champions early in the planning process and involve them in all aspects of the design and implementation of the program. • Engage independent physicians.
Set up the correct governance structure.	• Composition of the board should be half physicians and half hospital representatives. • Consider recruiting a majority of independent physicians. • Educate physicians on their role as a board member and the committee structure.
Set the right metrics for your stage of development.	• Metrics for physician performance should be appropriate for the stage in the journey. • Initially, use well-established quality metrics. • Next, use metrics that reflect and promote aligned goals. • Finally, mature organizations should use metrics that example progress toward the Triple Aim: better patient experience and improved population health at a lower cost.

Chapter 14: New Payment Models

Action Step	Description
Understand your threshold of risk.	• Bundled payments involve the least assumption of risk, followed by shared savings. Capitation has the most risk. • The degree of risk corresponds to the extent of infrastructure and process redesign necessary to be successful. • First, establish a risk threshold. Adopt payment models based on the risk threshold.
Understand your core competencies and the gaps in your capabilities.	• To be successful under value-based payment, organizations may need to redesign care processes to promote coordination across the continuum of care. • Analyze existing core competencies and identify gaps in processes, people, and technology as they relate to population health.
Involve physicians early and as equal partners in the conversation.	• Physicians must become partners in care teams. • Engage physicians in leadership roles throughout the process.

Chapter 15: The Clinical Leader Role in Emerging Models of Care

Action Step	Description
Challenge current assumptions and mindsets of health care delivery.	• Care delivery is moving beyond traditional settings through retail medicine, mobile health, and population health strategies. • Shift the paradigm to innovate in ways to partner with and supplement these services instead of resisting or competing. • Focus on the needs of the patient—how will changing needs affect how health care should be delivered to optimize outcomes?
Develop and implement segmented strategies.	• There is no one size fits all solution. • More data and greater analytic capability enable stratification and targeted intervention to maximize success.
Focus on care coordination across the continuum.	• Ensure seamless transitions. • Create new communication methods. • Engage patients, family members, and caregivers to ensure smooth transitions.
Seek out multiple, diverse, and effective partnerships.	• Move beyond the hospital walls. • Leverage the skills of community-based organizations. • Form partnerships inside and outside the health care system. • Rally around the common goal of providing safe, high quality, patient-centered care.
Actively engage consumers and patients in their health and health care.	• There is endless potential to improve patients' health and experience of health care. • Leverage new technologies (i.e., mHealth, apps, telehealth). • Engage patients before they are sick; provide ways to stay healthy and maintain treatment regimens to avoid hospital visits.

Index